his book is a critical evaluation of
e European Enlightenment in the
ht of contemporary experience,
rspective and needs. The ques-
n which the author sets out to
swer is whether or not, in the light
the events of the first half of the
th century, the belief in human
ogress is still tenable.

The author begins with the scien-
c revolution of the 17th century.
shows how men's basic assump-
ns about the growth of modern
ence, and especially about the
piricist approach to knowledge
plicit therein, contributed to the
a of progress. The ideas of such
nkers as Bacon, Descartes and
scal are closely analysed.

Mr. Sampson then proceeds to a
tical analysis of 18th-century ideas
human perfectibility, "natural
tory," universal history, utopia, as
wn in the works of writers like
rtley and Helvetius, D'Alembert,
usseau, Bossuet and Voltaire,
rcier, Condorcet, Godwin and
lney. Having surveyed the
development of the separate constituents of the belief in progress, he
goes on to examine the impact of
these developments upon the basic
premises of our contemporary
value judgments. He suggests that
the hiatus left by the decline of the
belief in Natural Law was filled by a
philosophy of history which found
expression in two major forms:
Hegelianism and Marxism; and he
attempts to relate the growth of
these systems to the general stream of
the Enlightenment.

The author concludes by
considering the moral implications
of the subject in terms of the thought
and experience of our time. The
history of ideas is here used to
illuminate the background of
sociology, the problems of social
philosophy, and the fears and hopes
of man in the 20th century.

R. V. Sampson is Lecturer in
Government at the University of
Bristol.

PROGRESS IN
THE AGE OF REASON

R. V. SAMPSON

PROGRESS IN
THE AGE OF REASON

THE SEVENTEENTH CENTURY TO
THE PRESENT DAY

HARVARD UNIVERSITY PRESS

CAMBRIDGE, MASSACHUSETTS

1956

FIRST PUBLISHED 1956

9 0 1
Sa 48 P

PRINTED IN GREAT BRITAIN

Contents

Acknowledgements

I AM deeply grateful to the following for their help and encouragement: the Warden and Fellows of Keble College, Oxford; the Warden and Fellows of Nuffield College, Oxford; the University of Bristol, and in particular, the Vice-Chancellor of the University and the Professors of Economics.

My warmest thanks are also due to the following, who read the MS. and made helpful suggestions: Dr. E. J. Bloustein, Professor G. D. H. Cole, Professor H. D. Dickinson, Professor Morris Ginsberg, Professor S. Körner, Mr. J. D. Mabbott, Professor Bertram Morris, Professor M. J. Oakeshott, Dr. H. G. V. Schenk, Mr. W. H. Walsh and Mr. P. M. Williams.

Acknowledgements for the use of copyright material appear on page 254.

R. V. S.

October 1956

CHAPTER I

Introduction

PROFESSOR CARL BECKER once announced that he " would not willingly charge a reputable historian with harbouring a Philosophy of History." [1] In the Anglo-Saxon historical tradition, the term philosophy in relation to history is suggestive of a dangerous predisposition to erect systems of ideas on inadequate empirical evidence.[2] To confess to a philosophy of history is to stand self-convicted of historical *hubris*, if not of actual incompetence. If few among contemporary historians would still subscribe to von Ranke's view that the historian's task is confined to establishing the facts as they really were, many would be found to sympathize with H. A. L. Fisher's now equally famous dictum that he was not among those to whom the study of the past had vouchsafed a knowledge of any pattern in history. Nevertheless, if philosophy of history has in the past suffered at the hands of English scholarship that neglect which sometimes accompanies ill-repute, the subject has in our own day been the object of a vigorous revival of interest.

Since few terms are more susceptible of ambiguity and, indeed, widely differing interpretations than " philosophy of history," it would be as well to begin with an examination of possible definitions. Philosophy, as traditionally pursued, has been a twofold activity. It has been a logical study of the status or validity of knowledge and belief; and, in addition to this

---

[1] C. L. Becker, *Everyman His Own Historian: Essays on History and Politics*, New York, 1935, p. 207.

[2] Cf., for example, Mr. G. M. Young, " Philosophies of History are many, and all of them are wrecked on the truth that in the career of mankind the illuminated passages are so brief, so infrequent, and still for the most part so imperfectly known, that we have not the materials for a valid induction." (*Victorian England: Portrait of An Age*, 1944 ed., p. 184.)

critical function it has not hesitated to undertake speculation in an attempt to add to our " knowledge " in fields where sense data were lacking. The fact that this last form of activity is generally disowned by contemporary philosophers as a pursuit falling outside the scope of the professional philosopher, has not yet meant that those philosophers of the past who engaged primarily in speculative activity have ceased to be called such. Similarly, in the field of history, the term " philosopher of history " is as yet not confined exclusively to denote such figures as Dilthey, Croce, Collingwood, who were primarily interested in the critical activity of investigating the nature and status of historical knowledge. The term is also held to embrace those like Comte, Marx, Spengler and Toynbee, who were primarily interested in formulating hypotheses concerning the general direction of the historical process. The speculative function of philosophy of history may not properly be divorced from the critical function, since any hypothesis concerning the direction of " laws " of history must presuppose certain epistemological assumptions concerning what kind of know- ledge it is possible to have about the past. Nevertheless, it is possible to formulate such hypotheses without making explicit the epistemological assumptions; it is possible, in short, to engage in speculative philosophy of history without contribut- ing to critical philosophy of history. The term, as used by Becker in the above quoted remark, refers to the speculative activity ; and it is in this sense that the term is used in the present context.

The term " philosophy of history," however, even when thus delimited, still embraces methods of historical interpretation differing radically from one another. Philosophies of history will generally be found to fall within four different categories, and it is the more important to make some such division in view of the widespread prejudice concerning philosophy of history as such. For while we may be suspicious of some modes of interpreting history, it does not follow that all such modes which may be subsumed under the general heading " philo- sophy of history " are equally suspect. Since labels have their convenience, I propose to discuss my four classes under the following heads: (i) Theories of theological or metaphysical monism, (ii) Theories of secular monism, (iii) Sociological Theories, and (iv) Relativistic Theories.

(i) The first group would include any theory which held that the historical process as a whole has its course shaped by extra-human agencies, Divine Providence for example in Bossuet or the Absolute Idea in Hegel. On this view history represents the fulfilment of a plan, which gives unity to all historical events. And, moreover, since the willing agency behind the historical drama is by definition not susceptible of human investigation, there can on this view be no question of our apprehending that unity empirically until after the events in which we ourselves are engaged have been played out.

(ii) Secular monistic theories share with the first group the belief that the historical process forms a single coherent whole with a unity of its own. Beneath the apparent chaos of the welter of historical events will be found an underlying uniformity; and this order will be found to be inherent in the events themselves. In contrast to group (i) theories, however, it is held that the key to this understanding lies not in any extra-sensory " Mind " but in the evidence provided solely by the historical events themselves. Although under no logical compulsion to do so, theories of this kind tend to embrace materialism in the theory of knowledge they rest upon, as in the case of Marx and Engels, much the most important example in this category. Common to this group of theories is the view that on the basis of the historical plan, direction or laws revealed by a study of the evidence, some degree of prevision of the future is possible to the actors at present engaged in the historical sequence.

(iii) Theories of this class do not make so bold as to claim that they have discerned a single unity within the entire historical process, but do assume that it is possible and fruitful to make comparative studies of societies, cultures and civiliza-tions in history, and on the basis of the findings to attempt to formulate hypotheses concerning uniformities appearing to have general validity. Durkheim is one of the most distin-guished examples of this school. Noteworthy, too, as a rare example of this approach among professional historians is the

American, Professor Edward P. Cheyney,[1] who attempted to establish such " laws " as the law of the mutability of civilizations, of the interdependence of mankind, the law of democracy or free consent, guaranteeing the eventual failure of those attempting to establish non-democratic systems.

(iv) Theories of this category are still more modest in their pretensions. They do not make the assumption that there is necessarily any repetition in history, but that the historical process is a continuous procession of events. " Such is the unity of all history," wrote Maitland, " that any one who endeavours to tell a piece of it, must feel that his first sentence tears a seamless webb." [2] This being so, it is not only possible but eminently desirable that actors in the most recent historical phase, namely the present, should assess the limits of practicable choice open to them in the light of the trend of events. Only in the changing kaleidoscope of the historical perspective can men determine the wisdom of their policies and projects in the present. For example, we today need to assess the relative stabilities of democratic capitalism and totalitarian communism; the judgment we make on such issues should be quite independent of any value judgment; it should be made in the light of our historical perspective. And such judgments, it is submitted, constitute a function of philosophy of history. It is in this sense that the term was used by John Stuart Mill in his *Autobiography*, where he maintained:

> " . . . that all questions of political institutions are relative, not absolute, and that different stages of human progress not only *will* have, but *ought* to have, different institutions: . . . that any general theory or philosophy of politics supposes a previous theory of human progress, and that this is the same thing with a philosophy of history." [3]

[1] *Vide* the discussion of Cheyney's work in H. Ausubel, *Historians and Their Craft*, Columbia University Press, 1950, pp. 230–36. More typical, however, of the professional American historian's viewpoint is the remark of Frederick Jackson Turner at the annual convention of the American Historical Association in 1910. After a thinly veiled reference to Henry Adams' remarkable hypotheses, he continued, " It is not given to all to bend the bow of Ulysses. I shall attempt a lesser task." (Quoted by W. H. Jordy in *Henry Adams: Scientific Historian*, Yale University Press, 1952, p. 245.)

[2] F. Pollock and F. W. Maitland, *History of English Law*, 1898 ed., Vol. I, p. 1.

[3] *Autobiography of John Stuart Mill*, World's Classics, 1944 reprint, p. 137.

The supreme difficulty which is inseparable from judgments of this kind is that we are so close to our immediate past, to the nineteenth century, for example, that our perspective of history is noticeably weakened in objectivity and reliability the closer we get to the present. For this reason the pattern we impose upon recent events, as we select from the vast mass of available data to make a coherent picture, is only too apt to be determined not so much by the logic of the events themselves as by the projection of our own values into the past with consequent distortion of the selecting mirrors. This is seen in the extraordinary facility with which our examination of the historical record leads us to conclude that " history is on our side." Nevertheless, the difficulties of the task are irrelevant to the legitimacy of the enterprise.

It is important to keep the fourth group well in mind, since it may well be that through lack of sympathy with the claims to validity of a theory falling within any one of the first three groups we may forget that a given writer may yet have much of value to contribute to philosophy of history in the more restricted sense of type (iv).

This brief analysis has been concerned to make distinctions founded upon differences of method. Needless to say, there is no relation between such a classification and one organized according to differences of content. For example, he who espouses a theory of inevitable progress, or degeneration or cyclical repetition, might claim to hold this view of the whole of human history on metaphysical grounds (i), or similarly on empirical grounds (ii), or only for certain historical phenomena under specified conditions (iii). I do not propose to attempt any sort of classification of philosophies of histories according to their content for the good reason that I shall in this study confine myself to the development during the European Enlightenment of the " progressive " philosophy of history. By its nature the belief in progress is a belief about the historical process, and as such concerns philosophy of history. It should be noted, however, that it is not exclusively so; since it is possible to hold to a belief in progress on strictly *a priori* grounds arising out of psychological theories concerning the nature of man. And in a study of the development of the belief in historical progress, some account must be taken of the development of the psychologically grounded belief in perfectibility.

II

It is a commonplace that every generation must write its own history afresh, since there can obviously be no finality in historical writing. Criteria of relevance must depend at least in part on the direction of present interests; the focus of the historical picture must again depend upon perspective, the essence of which in history is the factor of time. Objectivity is and can only be guaranteed by the traditions of scholarship in handling evidence, in believing what the evidence obliges us to believe; but no objective criteria exist which will inexorably determine which particular facts of the mass of available competing facts should be selected as worthy of a place in the collective memory of a people, which we call history. This element of subjectivity is assuredly inseparable from any historical undertaking. Without it, there would emerge not a coherent, intelligent narrative or analysis, but a shapeless, patternless amalgam of isolated facts. It was a very distinguished French historian (and soldier), Marc Bloch, who wrote, " This faculty of understanding the living is, in very truth, the master quality of the historian." [1] In view of the continuity of history and the difficulty of ever making a break with the past, it would indeed be surprising if the historian were to be successful in proportion to the extent in which he succeeded in isolating himself from the interests and influences of his contemporaries.

Among the contemporary ways of looking at the world in competition with one another, two are more especially the children of the Age of Enlightenment. I refer, of course, to revolutionary Marxism and, for want of a better phrase, to liberal progressivism. If the latter school are the direct descendants of the *philosophes*, the Marxists are no less the children of the eighteenth century. Marx attempted to achieve for the nineteenth century proletariat what the Voltaireans had accomplished for the eighteenth-century bourgeoisie. There can

[1] Marc Bloch, *The Historian's Craft*, English Translation of *Apologie pour l'Histoire*, 1954, p. 43.

be no doubt that Marx himself viewed his own role in this light. In an obituary letter on Proudhon in January, 1865, he wrote to J. B. Schweitzer, " Perhaps posterity will epitomize the latest phase of French development by saying that Louis Bonaparte was its Napoleon and Proudhon its Rousseau-Voltaire."[1] But contemporary Voltaireans in the content of their beliefs were for Marx examples of historical anachronism, men who had failed to appreciate that history had in the meantime synthesized afresh and thus rendered out of date the old bourgeois categories. But for all the virulence with which he pursued contemporary Voltaireans, there were sufficient affinities between them in their basic assumptions to reveal a common parentage. Neither John Stuart Mill nor Morley, for example, would have found anything to quarrel with in Marx's belief that the historical process was a progressive one, that social progress was in large measure dependent upon the fruits of scientific method. They would likewise have agreed that it was necessary to adopt as a working hypothesis the assumption that all human problems are in principle soluble provided only reason is permitted to dispel the accretion of emotion and prejudice in the interests of objective investigation. They would even have found mutually intelligible such terms as " progress " and " reaction," however they might have differed in their detailed interpretation of the content of those terms.

It is, above all, these basic assumptions common to both schools which have been assailed in our own time. Partly, of course, the current trend is to be explained by the fears aroused by Marxism as an armed doctrine, backed by the authority of a major world power, with whom friendly relations have not yet been realized. The mere fact that something is believed to be true by a Marxist *ipso facto* puts that belief at a serious disadvantage in the competition of ideas circulating in Western intellectual markets. But this fact would not in itself account for the strength of the reaction among thoughtful, educated people against the Enlightenment tradition when contrasted with the comparatively widespread acceptance of this tradition among the educated of two generations or even one generation

[1] Karl Marx and Frederick Engels, *Selected Works*, Moscow, 1950, Vol. I, p. 360.

ago. It may be objected that this is to neglect or at least underestimate the continuity of the tradition of protest among the intellectuals themselves against the spirit of Enlightenment. After all, were not the views of critics like Taine, Brunetière, Faguet in the ascendant at the turn of the century? And for them the eighteenth century was an age which contributed nothing of permanent value to philosophy; a classical age which cared nothing for the idiosyncrasies of the individual; an age blinded by the fury of its polemics; an age illustrative of the shallowness that accompanies an incapacity to understand and reconcile opposing views. And if we move forward to the twenties of the present century we find Julien Benda in his *Treason of the Intellectuals* indicting his contemporaries precisely for their neglect of, or rather their revolt against, the eighteenth century.

> " I will, however, observe that these *adoucissements* [the growth of humanitarianism] ought not to be credited to the account of the age we live in; they are the effects of the teaching of the eighteenth century, against which precisely the ' masters of modern thought ' are in revolt. . . ." [1]

We need, it is true, to keep present intellectual fashions carefully in perspective; nevertheless, this perspective should not blind us to the fact that the present attack upon the Enlightenment tradition is conceived at a profounder level than that of the intellectuals of a generation or two ago. For they accepted the conventional categories shaped out of the insistence of the Encyclopædists upon the value of tolerance, faith in reason and science, and on the secular sufficiency of progress. The critics accepted these postulates of their opponents, and unequivocally announced their own hostility to égalité and fraternité, and also to a liberté which in their eyes was destructive of the true liberty of the human spirit. They boldly took their stand upon a metaphysics or special Revelation which postulated knowledge other than the dogmatically empirical and values which considered secular inequity and inequality to be of subsidiary importance when measured against the eternal obligations of the individual to God. Today, the descendants

---

[1] J. Benda, *La Trahison des Clercs*, Paris, 1927, p. 244.

of this intellectual tradition have passed over to the offensive
in a denial of significance to the conceptual categories of
" progress " and " reaction " themselves. Distinctions resting
on such outmoded criteria are, it is suggested, not merely
invalid; they are in the contemporary intellectual climate
strictly nonsensical. This view, enunciated in innumerable
books and periodicals, is closely paralleled by a revival of
emotional faith and mass evangelism at a more popular level.
For an admirably succinct statement of it, it would be hard to
better the following statement, taken from the writings of the
well-known Russian emigré philosopher, Nicolas Berdyaev:

> " . . . we still go on with our endless tedious discussions
> about progress and reaction, just as though everything in the
> world had not been turned upside down and as though our
> old criteria had not lost every shred of significance. Just try
> to judge world-history with reference to reaction or revolution,
> try to place your ' right ' and your ' left ' . . . The absurdity
> of this sort of thing will strike you immediately. . . ." [1]

We are in fact invited to attend the funeral obsequies of an
age that is no more, whose categories no longer even make
sense. An entire epoch of protest from *Candide* to *The Devil's
Disciple*, from *The Social Contract* to *A Dream of John Ball* and
Germinal, spoke a language whose basic concepts, we are now
assured, are no longer, if they were ever, intelligible. The very
language of protest smacks of *hubris*, if not of impiety. The role
of the philosopher is simply to understand the world, to
recognize its necessity. His perennial criterion must be, " If my
explanation is correct, would the world be exactly as it is, and
not otherwise." The first part of wisdom is to recognize that
philosophical activity can make no difference one way or the
other to the world which men inhabit. And if this is an un-
palatable lesson to those whose maladjustment is manifest in
the illusion that the world may be shaped nearer to their
heart's desire, they may console themselves that in view of
modern therapeutic psychic techniques, their condition is not
incurable.

In short, the age in which we live is an age of disillusion.

[1] N. Berdyaev, *The End of Our Time*, 1933, pp. 76–77.

The high hopes of the nineteenth century, the expectations implicit in the exuberant optimism of the early Wells and James Harvey Robinson have not been fulfilled. The agencies of improvement, the fruits of reason and science have proved to be threatening instruments of destruction beyond even Wells' imagining. In the matter of human behaviour itself, we have witnessed in Nazi Germany a reversion to barbarism by the side of which the deeds of Attila and Torquemada assume a vastly diminished perspective. In these circumstances it is hardly to be wondered at if the prophets of the Age of Reason no longer find favour. At the same time, there is perhaps something a little unseemly in the haste with which a three-centuries-old tradition is proclaimed to be at an end. "Since the end of the eighteenth century," writes Arthur Koestler in his autobiography, " the place of God has been vacant in our civilization; . . . Now, however, after the shattering catastrophes which have brought the Age of Reason and Progress to a close, the void has made itself felt." [1] Assertions of this kind, which constitute the small change of much contemporary discussion, are rarely accompanied by supporting argument. Indeed, the dogmatic insistence suggests rather the authors' own need for reassurance, a will to believe that a scapegoat for disaster has been found and that the scapegoat can finally be exorcized by insistence that it is no more. The Age of Reason is dead, and the Age of Faith is opening before us. Professor Arnold Toynbee, after his monumental investigations into the morphology of civilizations, concludes that the only way in which we may hope to evade the disintegration of our own culture is by returning to the " God incarnate in a Man." Either, it is implied, we shall embrace the truths of revealed religion or we shall infallibly fall victims to the power which reason has wrested from Nature but which reason has not learnt to control.

III

Whatever the truth of this may be, it would suggest that the time is perhaps not inappropriate for students to turn once again to an examination of the traditions of the eighteenth century in

---

[1] A. Koestler, *Arrow in the Blue*, 1952, pp. 52–53.

Europe. But before doing so, it may be permissible in an
Introduction to enter one *caveat*. A general observation on the
conditions of eighteenth-century France must be emphasized,
not as a plea in mitigation of the deficiencies of the *philosophes*,
but in explanation of the harshness of their style. Few writers
are more vulnerable to criticism not so much for the content of
their beliefs as for the way in which they held them. The
philosophes, it must be remembered, lived in an age of arbitrary
monarchical rule, when the traditions of the public service
more often than not rested upon the outcome of the competition
between the most ancient families of France to place their
daughters as strumpets to the throne. Excluded from the
responsibilities of power and influence as they were, the
philosophes in their writings only too frequently reflect their
frustration; and the resultant note of acrid sourness provides
an easy target for later and more urbane ages. Mademoiselle
de Lespinasse, in whose salon so many of the most distinguished
intellects of the time found a congenial atmosphere for discussion, once wrote to a friend, " In this country, a man with any
energy, high standards, or genius, is like the caged lion in a
menagerie. He feels his power as a torture: he is like a
Patagonian compelled to walk on his knees!" [1] It was,
moreover, an age when the forces of the Counter-Reformation
displayed all the virulence of a movement still powerful but
conscious that it was a spent force. It was an age of religious
intolerance symbolized at the beginning of the period by the
Revocation of the Edict of Nântes and towards the end by the
judicial torture and execution of Calas and La Barre. It was
an age when Voltaire, Diderot, and even Marmontel all saw
the inside of the Bastille or Vincennes; when the Editor-in-
Chief of the *Encylopædia* discovered that a major portion of his
life work had been irretrievably bowdlerized by his own printer
out of fear of the Censorship. [2]

In the circumstances of the Ancien Régime, it is hardly to be
wondered at if the Encyclopædists, writing as they did in the

---

[1] Marquis de Ségur, *Julie de Lespinasse*, London, 1907. Letter quoted on p. 211.
[2] An authoritative examination of Le Breton's excisions of Diderot's original
page proofs is to be found in D. H. Gordon and N. L. Torrey, *The Censoring of
Diderot's Encyclopedie and the Re-Established Text*, Columbia University Press, 1947.

heat of the struggle, and only too conscious of the contrast between the immediate powers of Church and State and the power of their own pens, were often guilty of work that can fairly be termed arid and shallow. We need not be surprised if they have a century and more later been judged, in the phrase of Émile Faguet, " plutôt des polémistes que des philosophes." [1] And it is the rare polemic that contrives to be other than ephemeral. Yet the remarkable thing about the writings of the *philosophes* is precisely that they have not lost their freshness and savour with the passing of the generations. Simple and unsophisticated, uncritically or even crudely stated, their views may oftentime be, but beyond question they are still alive. It is easy enough to caricature for the purposes of ridicule beliefs that all too often degenerated into the canons of a coterie. To take the trouble to understand what they were about is a more difficult but also a more legitimate enterprise.

[1] E. Faguet, *Dix-Huitième Siècle* (*Éditions Contemporaines*), p. xvii.

CHAPTER II

The New Method: Science and Progress

FAITH in the methods of science, and the exploitation of its fruits is so all pervasive in the life of modern European and American society as to distinguish it in a unique way both from societies like the Hindu and the Chinese, where until recently life has been entirely governed by ancient custom, and from the past societies of Europe which preceded the birth of modern science. When that crucial change came about is still something of a vexed question. Revolutions of such magnitude in our attitudes of mind are necessarily long in the making, and it is always difficult to pin-point the period of decisive change. In accordance with the eighteenth-century tradition which viewed the mediæval epoch as a dark age brought to a sudden close by the Renaissance, it was for a long time held that there had been no interest in investigation of the world of experience before the period of Leonardo da Vinci and Vesalius. Subsequent researches have not substantiated this view. The tradition of experimentation as a means of verifying hypotheses, although not consciously worked out as a system, nor practised with very much success, nevertheless does appear to be an unbroken one going back as far as the thirteenth century. Experience as a criterion of truth, discovery by experimentation that certain natural phenomena took place regardless of incantations, for example, were common to thinkers like Roger Grosseteste (who wrote on optics), Peter of Maricourt (who wrote an important treatise on magnetism), Albertus Magnus, and Roger Bacon. In the next century, the nominalism of Ockham and his school provided a restricted intellectual climate not unfavourable to empirical investigation. Theories of gravity as well as the theory of the diurnal rotation of the earth upon its axis were discussed at length by John Buridan,

Albert of Saxony, and Nicholas Oresme. While Nicholas did not foreshadow Copernicus to the extent of advancing the heliocentric hypothesis in place of the geocentric hypothesis of the Ptolemaic system, he considered the diurnal rotation of the earth on its axis a theory which offered a more economical explanation of the known facts than the alternative hypothesis, although still adhering to the old view in the absence of conclusive proof.

When the credit has been paid to the forerunners of the Renaissance investigators, we should nevertheless be on our guard against the opposite error of underestimating the revolutionary nature of the advances in science associated with the Renaissance. Few among contemporary students would be prepared to go so far as Professor Lynn Thorndike, when he wrote in 1914, " It should equally be realized that the rise of modern science can no more be associated with the so-called Renaissance than with the so-called Middle Ages." [1] As Professor Thorndike has himself shown, there was no clear distinction in the mediæval period, certainly not in the thirteenth century between science and magic. The credulity of Roger Bacon when confronted with such phenomena as elixirs of life, dragons and fabulous beasts is well known. How difficult it was for the mediæval mind to emancipate itself from legend and superstition is shown by the curious intermixture of the fantastic in the work of so distinguished a writer as Bodin at the end of the sixteenth century. Moreover, there was none but the most superficial analysis of the nature of scientific method in the mediæval period. When research itself was so little advanced, it would have been surprising had contemporary interest done other than concentrate on speculation at the expense of developing a critique of underlying theory.

It must also be remembered that whatever the achievements of a tiny handful of vigorous intellects, their character was far from stamping itself upon the cultural ethos of their time. For signs of a decisive change in the mental outlook of a vastly

---

[1] L. Thorndike, *Roger Bacon and Experimental Method in the Middle Ages*. Reprinted from *The Philosophical Review*, XXIII (1914) in *The Making of English History*, edited by R. L. Schuyler and H. Ausubel, New York, 1952. *Vide* p. 98.

enlarged public, we have to wait until the sixteenth century. The tempo of change then reached such a climax that we rightly perceive in the Renaissance the dawn of a cultural climate with recognizable affinities with our own. The inventions of the printing press and the ship's compass, the enlargement of the known globe by Columbus and Vasco da Gama, the Copernican confirmation of the ancient Alexandrian hypothesis that the earth was no more than one of innumerable planets revolving round the sun, the disruption of the unity of Catholic Christendom at the hands of the Reformers, the revival of classical learning and scholarship, the expansion of the Universities, the increase in wealth and leisure, the expansion of world commerce with an attendant shift in its main axis from the Mediterranean to the Atlantic, together constituted a physical and mental upheaval of unprecedented proportions. The world whose mental preconceptions were shaped by Montaigne, Bacon, Descartes and Pascal was a world qualitatively different from the mediæval world. It was a world characterised by confidence, optimism, insatiable curiosity and scepticism. It was a world determined to vindicate the right to untrammelled inquiry, to equip itself to resist that organized hostility which at its most fanatical was capable of burning Giordano Bruno and forcing the recantation of Galileo.

It is necessary to insist on this since some contemporary writers still urge that, notwithstanding a certain amount of deplorable intolerance, Christian theology was in no wise inimical to the development of scientific inquiry. Father Copleston, the distinguished Jesuit philosopher, for instance, urges that " the development of empirical science is in no way alien in principle to the Christian theology which formed the mental background in the Middle Ages. For if the world is the work of God it is obviously a legitimate and worth-while object of study." [1] Yet it is against precisely this view that Francis Bacon (to whom Father Copleston pays generous tribute as " the herald of the scientific age ") found it necessary to direct some of his sharpest polemic. On purely a priori grounds it would seem odd that Bacon should have

[1] F. Copleston, S.J., *A History of Philosophy*, Vol. III, 1953, p. 167.

wasted so much powder and shot on a purely illusory threat.
The mental attitude that Bacon at least deemed to be widely
held as a heritage from the earlier period was defined by him
in his *Of the Advancement of Learning*. He there attacked the
attitude based on the view " that the aspiring to over-much
knowledge was the original temptation and sin, whereupon
ensued the fall of man; that knowledge hath in it somewhat
of the serpent, and therefore where it entereth into a man it
makes him swell—*Scientia inflat*, [knowledge puffeth up;]
. . ."[1] He returns to this same charge in the *Filum Labyrinthi*:

> " He thought also, how great opposition and prejudice
> natural philosophy had received by superstition, and the
> immoderate and blind zeal of religion; for he found that some
> of the Grecians which first gave the reason for thunder, had
> been condemned of impiety; and that the cosmographers
> which first discovered and described the roundness of the
> earth, and the consequences thereof touching the Antipodes,
> were not much otherwise censured by the ancient fathers of
> the Christian Church; and that the case is now much worse,
> in regard of the boldness of the schoolmen and their depend-
> ancies in the monasteries, who having made divinity into an
> art, have almost incorporated the contentious philosophy of
> Aristotle into the body of Christian religion. And generally
> he perceived in men of devout simplicity, this opinion, that the
> secrets of nature were the secrets of God and part of that glory
> whereinto the mind of man if it seek to press shall be oppressed;
> and that the desire in men to attain to so great and hidden
> knowledge, hath a resemblance with that temptation which
> caused the original fall: . . ."[2]

Certainly there was widespread suspicion in the Middle
Ages of those who trafficked in natural mysteries, and no very
sharp distinction was drawn between astrologers and al-
chemysts on the one hand and witches and sorcerers who were
believed to have established relations with the satanic powers,
on the other. For many the spirit of inquiry represented the

[1] Bacon, *Of the Advancement of Learning*, *Works*, edited by Spedding, Ellis and
Heath, 1859, Vol. III, p. 264.
[2] Bacon, *Filum Labyrinthi*, *Works*, Vol. III, pp. 499–500.

real *hubris* of man. The fate that had overtaken Adam
for his daring to taste of the tree of knowledge suggested
that the attempt to pry into Nature's secrets was liable to
forfeit the protection of the Deity. Since the divine
curse, the depravity of Nature was contrasted with the state
of Grace made manifest in the spirit. That this attitude
died hard is clear from the intensity of Bacon's attack
upon it.

Again, in the matter of explanation of natural phenomena,
mediæval science was handicapped by its general acceptance
of the teleological form into which the Greeks cast their
questions concerning causality. Why, Aristotle asked, does
the acorn grow into the oak; why do fire and air move up-
wards, earth and water downwards; why does man live in
the political society of the *polis*? Why are some men born to
be slaves, others to be citizens? And the hypothesis found to
be most satisfying by its apparent irreducibility was one which
posited an unmoved Mover, who had given to everything at
its creation an imminent Form or Essence, the striving to
realize which constituted the essential or real nature of the
entity in question. Thus all motion, all development was
explicable on the assumption of a final cause which all entities
were compelled to reach towards in the attempt to escape the
state of imperfect potentiality in the present. Explanation
rested upon a providential and intervening Deity, whose
power of attraction towards union with itself was required to
sustain the world in being. This hypothesis presented no
difficulties to a Christian theology, which posited the existence
of an omniscient and all loving Father, whose divine will had
created human beings in his own image. The mediæval
synthesis defining the causal principles inherent in the nature
of things was thus smoothly achieved. In the majestic language of Dante,

> " In the order I speak of, all natures incline
>   Either more near or less near to their source
>   According as their diverse lots assign.
> To diverse harbours thus they move perforce
>   O'er the great ocean of being, and each one
>   With instinct given it to maintain its course.

> This bears the fiery element to the moon;
> This makes the heart of mortal things to move;
> This knits the earth together into one.[1]

On these assumptions, the essential function of reason came often to be regarded as a means of demonstrating the truth of things already known through faith rather than as an instrument of inquiry into the unknown on the basis of observation and induction. The world of experience was, of course, explored, but within the limits prescribed by the prevailing cosmic faith. The business of the intelligence was that of reconciling our qualitative experience of the world with the rational categories imposed by faith. Scholastic logic was, as Bacon insisted, better suited to demonstration and argument than to the purposes of discovery. In its concern to defend the certainty of our knowledge of final causes, interest was diverted from the more rewarding, if more mundane task of unravelling the secondary causes. "The human understanding is unquiet," wrote Bacon,

> "it cannot stop or rest, and still presses onward, but in vain. Therefore it is that we cannot conceive of any end or limit to the world; but always as of necessity it occurs to us that there is something beyond. . . . But this inability interferes more mischievously in the discovery of causes: for although the most general principles in nature ought to be held merely positive, as they are discovered, and cannot with truth be referred to a cause; nevertheless the human understanding being unable to rest still seeks something prior in the order of nature. And then it is that in struggling towards that which is further off it falls back upon that which is more nigh at hand; namely, on final causes: which have relation clearly to the nature of man rather than to the nature of the universe; and from this source have strangely defiled philosophy." [2]

If we turn to examine the mediæval conception of history or rather their view of the relation of man's purposes to those of past and future generations, we find similar reliance on reason as a means of finding teleological explanations compatible

[1] Dante, *Paradiso*, translated by Laurence Binyon, London, 1943, Canto I, 109–117.

[2] Bacon, *Novum Organum*, *Works*, Vol. IV, p. 57.

with a theology of history prescribed by faith. The cyclical theory of historical development, current among the Greeks, has given way to the Augustinian conception of history as a kind of drama whose central plot had been conceived prior to its enactment by human beings. The main outline of the plot coincided in all essentials with the account of man's past given in the Scriptures. The six-day creation about 4000 B.C., the original sin in the Garden, the condign punishment of the Flood, were followed by a rendering of all subsequent history as the working out of the conflict between the City of God and the City of Satan, between those predestined to salvation and those whose sinfulness had forfeited the divine love. And finally, came the awful climax, which although not yet realized was yet believed to be not incalculably distant, when the temporal conflict would be brought to a close by the Day of Judgment, when at the Second Coming the trumpets would sound, the dead would rise from the grave, the blessed finally joining the saints in heaven and the wicked reaping their rich deserts in that inferno which Dante had immortalized.

If a belief in final causes often resulted in an impatience with detailed empirical research into physical phenomena, the acceptance of this theology of history was no less responsible for a diminished interest in historical research. Monastic chroniclers there were, of course, but the function of the chronicler is scarcely that of the historian. Since the main outline of the past was prescribed by faith, the potential historian lacked incentive to pursue exhaustive inquiries into historical records in the hope of filling in the details of a plot already known. And since knowledge of the plot extended into the future no less than the past, the human perspective was enlarged to include the goal of an eternal life contrasting sharply with the ephemeral life of earth. Measured against the claims of eternal blessedness, the transient sufferings of the temporal world assumed a reduced significance. The fact, too, that this world was doomed to perish in a proximate future rendered superfluous any conception of the progressive satisfaction and enlargement of human wants as a central criterion of moral values in this life.

In short, the fact that modern research has shown that some

empirical investigation was undertaken in the Middle Ages has not robbed of its truth the traditional conception of the characteristic features of Scholasticism. In the excessive rationalism of its traditions it stood in need of the chastening discipline of factual experiment. Bacon's own diagnosis of the position could hardly be bettered,

> " For the wit and mind of man, if it work upon matter, which is the contemplation of the creatures of God, worketh according to the stuff, and is limited thereby; but if it work upon itself, as the spider worketh his web, then it is endless, and brings forth indeed cobwebs of learning, admirable for the fineness of thread and work, but of no substance or profit." [1]

In a world where the primary function of reason lay in the reconciliation of the facts with causal explanations already given by metaphysics, the notion of progress could have no meaning. In a society where the merely mundane was considered of subsidiary importance by virtue of its transience, the progressive advancement of human well-being was scarcely likely to constitute a central incentive to action.

Professor Bury in his *The Idea of Progress* has listed three necessary conditions before the conception of progress could be developed. First, it was necessary to undermine the intellectual subservience of the age to the thought of the classical philosophers, to get rid of the " too great a reverence and a kind of adoration of the mind and understanding " (Bacon) of the Ancients in general and of Aristotle, " the Philosopher " in particular. Secondly, it was necessary that the opportunity of this life should be valued for its own sake, so that knowledge could be harnessed to the task of satisfying human needs more fully by enabling man to understand and therefore to control the forces of nature. And thirdly, it was necessary that there should grow up in the educated mind a conviction that the laws of Nature were constant, since " There can be no certainty that knowledge will continually progress until science has been placed on sure foundations." [2] From the social standpoint, it might be added that it was also necessary to

---

[1] Bacon, *Of the Advancement of Learning, Works*, Vol. III, pp. 285–86.
[2] J. B. Bury, *The Idea of Progress*, 1928 ed., p. 66.

break through what Bagehot called " the cake of custom " in the shape of the all-powerful authority of fixed institutions, both ecclesiastical and political, and the rigid social divisions based on status, inseparable from the feudal structure of society. For only under the relaxation of the grip of these conditions on the individual, could the latter hope to acquire the necessary confidence and experience in guiding his life by observation and reflection in place of the inherently static method of appealing to authority.

By the beginning of the sixteenth century, there is ample evidence to show not only that the humanistic values of the Renaissance were beginning to gain a widespread acceptance, but that the awe of classical authority which, if anything, had been strengthened by the Renaissance discovery of ancient manuscripts, was beginning to loosen its hold over men's minds. The revolt against ecclesiastical authority symbolized in the Reformation was not long in bearing fruit in new individualism which fired the spirit of research as well as strengthening the appeal to the private conscience in spiritual matters. Indications that the first two of Bury's conditions for the dawn of the idea of progress were close to realization are to be found in two of Bacon's best known aphorisms, viz. " *Antiquitas sæculi iuventas mundi* " and " Knowledge is power." The second of these was the slogan under which Bacon fought his campaign to make the satisfaction of human needs a principal criterion of the legitimacy of human endeavour particularly in the field of knowledge.[1] The first summarized the growing awareness that knowledge was cumulative, and that sixteenth-century investigators, so far from being unable to rival the achievements of ancient Greece and Rome, had the immeasurable advantage of being able to start at the point where they left off. Much has been made in this respect of the famous battle of the Ancients and Moderns, fought out in such books as Perrault's *Parallel of the Ancients and Moderns*, and Fontenelle's *Dialogues of the Dead*, and *Digression on the Ancients and Moderns* published in the last twenty years of the seventeenth century. But important though these were, their con-

[1] Cf. the discussion in John Dewey, *Reconstruction in Philosophy*, New York, 1920, Ch. II.

tribution was essentially that of the publicist in giving a wider currency to thought already developed and familiar to contemporary intellectuals. As far back as 1580, Montaigne had published the following remarkable passage in the famous essay entitled *Apology for Raimond Sebond*.

> " The heavens and the stars have been swinging round for three thousand years, as all the world had believed, until Cleanthes of Samos, or according to Theophrastus, Nicetas of Syracuse, presumed to proclaim that it was the earth that moved revolving about its axis, through the oblique circle of the zodiac. And, in our days, Copernicus has so well grounded this theory, that he very lawfully uses it for all astronomical conclusions. What can we make of that, except that we need not bother our heads about which of the two theories is right? And who knows but that a third opinion, a thousand years hence, will overthrow the two former? . . . Thus when we are offered some new theory, we have great reason to distrust it, and to remember that before it was introduced the contrary was in vogue; and as that was overthrown by this, a third discovery may start up, in time to come, which may knock the second on the head. Before the principles which Aristotle introduced were in repute, other principles satisfied human reason, as his satisfy us at this moment. What letters-patent, what special privilege have these, that the course of our discoveries should stop at them, and that they should for all time to come possess our belief? They are no more exempt from being thrust out of doors than their forerunners." [1]

Here the relative and progressive aspects of knowledge are frankly recognized, and this striking passage is the more important to note for the subsequent influence, which, we shall see, Montaigne exercised upon Pascal.

The third of Bury's conditions for the growth of the idea of progress, namely, the establishing of a widespread belief in the immutability and invariability of the laws of Nature, calls for comment, in that Bury asserts that this was largely the special achievement of Descartes, thus raising the issue of historical continuity. Descartes himself believed that if a true theory of knowledge which would take into account the methods actually

---

[1] *The Essays of Montaigne*, translated by E. J. Trechmann, O.U.P., Vol. II, p. 15.

being applied by contemporary mathematicians and physicists, was to be founded, it was necessary to cut loose from the leading strings of all previous thinkers on the subject, and recommence *ab initio*. Contemptuous of Scholastic method and profoundly impressed by the " certainty " accruing from the methods of deductive geometry, Descartes had little historical sense and made no effort to conceal his disparagement of the study of history as an inferior branch of knowledge that could not expect to yield more than doubtful hypotheses.

> " . . . when one is too curious about things which were practised in past centuries, one is usually very ignorant about those which are practised in our own time. Besides, fables make one imagine many events possible which in reality are not so, and even the most accurate of histories, if they do not exactly misrepresent or exaggerate the value of things in order to render them more worthy of being read, at least omit in them all the circumstances which are basest and least notable; and from this fact it follows that what is retained is not portrayed as it really is, and that those who regulate their conduct by examples which they derive from such a source, are liable to fall into the extravagances of the knights-errant of Romance, and form projects beyond their power of performance." [1]

Apart from the interesting side light here thrown on the possibility that Cervantes' masterpiece may have played its part in diminishing both respect for human knowledge of the past and the professional status of the historian, the above passage reveals Descartes' own conviction that, by virtue of the nature of the materials with which the historian worked, there was and could be but little of value to be learnt from a study of the past. It is not surprising then, that Descartes failed to appreciate the nature of his own indebtedness to the intellectual tradition that had nurtured him.

This emphasis of the Cartesians on the revolutionary aspect of the new method combined with their denigration of the past resulted in the establishment in France of a historical tradition which consisted of contrasting the follies, cruelty and tyranny of the past with the enlightenment of the present—a tradition

[1] Descartes, *Discourse on the Method*, *Works*, edited by Haldane and Ross, Vol. I, pp. 84–85.

which reached its apotheosis in the world of thought in the historical writings of Voltaire, and in the world of action in the night of August 4th, 1789, when in a spasmodic orgy of revolutionary fervour representatives of all classes of the population joined in the symbolic destruction of the title deeds of the *ancien régime* in France.

Now although Bury is plainly aware of Descartes' own attitude towards the past, and indeed makes the pertinent point that this it was in particular which prevented him from formulating a theory of the progress of knowledge, for which it is essential to grasp the idea of sustained historical continuity; yet he is inclined to accept uncritically the Cartesians' own assessment of the completeness of the break with the past, in attributing to Descartes almost sole responsibility for inculcating the belief in the fixed immutability of the laws of Nature. Descartes' mechanistic universe certainly made superfluous intervening Providence, but this Cartesian emphasis on the rigidly rational order of Nature, this belief that every event can be related to its predecessors in such a way as to illustrate a general principle, has its roots in the old Stoic conception of the laws of Nature which govern the universe according to principles intelligible to the powers of human reason. And this conception played an extremely important part in shaping the tradition of European thought, through the specific medium of the Roman law.

Descartes' own lack of understanding of the significance of historical knowledge, his contempt for tradition arose directly from his theory of knowledge. Believing it possible on the basis of certain indisputably self-evident premises to proceed by a process of deductive reasoning to discover the final truth concerning the causal mechanisms of the actual world, Descartes started out from a position which denied in principle than an individual's knowledge was in any way dependent on his knowledge of the historical past. ". . . Those who have learnt least about all that which has hitherto been named philosophy, are the most capable of apprehending the truth," [1] he wrote. And here again, he betrayed his kinship

---

[1] Descartes' Letter to the Translator of the *Principles of Philosophy*, *Works*, Vol. I, p. 208.

with the scholastic tradition he believed himself to be so drastically repudiating. Like his predecessors he believed that certainty was an attainable ideal in the field of knowledge; he differed from them in that he claimed that whereas all previous attempts had been wrongly based and had accordingly been self-defeating to an extent that the ideal of certainty itself was being threatened (Cf. Montaigne *passim*), he had himself succeeded where all others had failed.

" But although all the truths which I place in my Principles have been known from all time and by all men, nevertheless there has never yet been anyone, as far as I know, who has recognized them as the principles of philosophy, that is to say, as principles from which may be derived a knowledge of all things that are in the world." [1]

Thus, while Descartes attacks the scholastics' methods of procedure in the search after knowledge as resting ultimately on an appeal to absolute authority in the shape of revelation, tradition or simply the *ex cathedra* statement of the Philosopher, he failed to perceive that he too was in effect setting up Reason as a new kind of absolute authority. The philosophy of the Schools was inherently unprogressive, in Descartes' view, simply because it made no single principle the basis of an original indisputable proposition and could thus never hope to construct a body of certain knowledge. And progress for Descartes was essentially the capacity to move further along the road towards the ideal of certainty. And this it was which constituted the merit of the new method. By starting out from a first principle the complete truth of which no one could possibly dispute, it enabled the student to discover ultimate truths about the nature of reality itself. If it did not reveal knowledge of this kind, then it was not knowledge. The merely probable Descartes was not prepared to accept as knowledge. Thus, his interpretation of the new scientific method was fundamentally scholastic in spirit. Providing criteria of absolute certainty, it would enable man to eliminate all that had mistakenly passed for knowledge in the past and then proceed bit by bit to fill in the gaps which remained on

[1] Descartes' Letter to the Translator of the *Principles of Philosophy*, *op. cit.*, p. 209.

the map of knowledge until the fixed goal of certain knowledge of the whole of the real world had been reached or at any rate approached. The gradual forward movement of our species along this road towards the fixed and final goal was what Descartes understood by progress. Scientific method was, in his eyes, not an instrument, providing its own self-correctives as it proceeded, whose goal was not ultimate truth but the preservation of its own necessary conditions of functioning in the task of advancing the inquiry. Rather was it a method, itself possessed of final, ontological status, which represented the triumph of the ancient philosophic quest for certain truth.

The real world for the scholastics was substantially the commonsense world of everyday experience, a world of immediately intelligible qualities. Able to take the existence of this world of Being for granted, they deduced from it the existence of God. In Descartes' case, the position was exactly reversed. Living as he did in the post-Copernican world, when the deceptiveness of the senses had received their classic illustration, and when physicists were substituting quantitative for qualitative criteria for interpreting the stuff of reality, Descartes wished to vindicate the status of the new mathematical-empirical sciences as instruments for the provision of knowledge of the real world. The only means to this end was proof of the existence of a God, whose perfection would preclude the possibility of his deceiving us. In contrast to the scholastics, then, Descartes based his physics on his metaphysics, and not vice versa. Hence his assertion that true knowledge was necessarily beyond the reach of the atheist. With the arguments with which he proceeded in the *Meditations* to demonstrate the existence of such a God, we are not here concerned. It is sufficient to establish that scientific method, as conceived by Descartes, could not hope to establish the legitimacy of its procedure without a supporting metaphysic; that the method by itself could provide no guarantee that there was any necessary connexion between the way in which our thought represented the order and causal relations of nature and the way in which nature itself was actually constructed. Consequently, since progress consists in movement towards the goal of final certainty in human knowledge, scientific method as an instrument of that progress could only be justified on absolute grounds. Then the new method, metaphysically authenticated, with a status of validity worthy of Scholastic recognition, could be appealed to as an instrument of knowledge of impregnable authority. Scholastic subservience to authority had been maintained; but the nature of that authority had been transformed to meet the new methods and findings of a world more empirically minded than that to which the traditional scholastics were accustomed.

So far we have been discussing Descartes' view of progress in knowledge arising out of the new method as he conceived it. But for him, no more than for Bacon, progress in the pursuit of knowledge was not an end in itself. Rather was it necessary to attain that " good understanding or universal Wisdom," to which he so often refers as the ultimate goal and final cause of all human endeavour. Again we find that in his theory of the progress of humanity at large, as in his theory of the progress of knowledge, the criterion is not to be cherished for its own sake, but because its pursuit will ultimately lead us to a knowledge of the moral law, that " law which obliges us to procure as much as in us lies, the general good of all mankind." [1] " Certainly it appears to me strange," he writes in the *Regulæ*,

> " that so many people should investigate human customs with such care, the virtues of plants, the motions of the stars, the transmutations of metals, and the objects of similar sciences, while at the same time practically none bethink themselves about good understanding, or universal Wisdom, though nevertheless *all other studies are to be esteemed not so much for their own value as because they contribute something to this.*" [2] (My italics.)

All the sciences are integrated in a fundamental unity, but it is the science of morality which is at the apex of the pyramid, that science which enables me " to learn to distinguish the true from the false, in order to see clearly in my actions and to walk with confidence in this life," [3] the science which is served by the others as handmaidens of her supremacy.

[1] Descartes, *Discourse on the Method, Works,* Vol. I, p. 119.
[2] Descartes, *Rules for the Direction of the Mind, Works,* Vol. I, p. 2.
[3] Descartes, *Discourse, op. cit.,* p. 87.

" Thus philosophy as a whole is like a tree whose roots are metaphysics, whose trunk is physics, and whose branches, which issue from this trunk, are all the other sciences. These reduce themselves to three principal ones, viz., medicine, mechanics and morals—I mean the highest and most perfect moral science which, presupposing a complete knowledge of the other sciences, is the last degree of wisdom." [1]

Such was the completeness of Descartes' faith in reason as the supreme court of appeal in all matters, excepting only that sphere in which truths are given by revelation, that he looked with confidence to the day when reason would be able to solve even the value problems of men in a " most perfect moral science." But in the meantime, since the physical sciences themselves were still only in their infancy, and since the action of living cannot wait upon the culmination of scientific knowledge, Descartes decided to conform to the traditional modes of conduct accepting their dicta as a " provisional ethic." Now the *philosophes* in the eighteenth century, living after the appearance of Newton's *Principia* (1686) which seemed to them to have established the final truth concerning the fundamental principles of the universe, were no longer content to emulate Descartes' patience in the matter of morals, and accept those prescribed by authority, pending the triumph of scientific method in this sphere also. What was for Descartes more or less in cold storage became in the following century a matter of urgent concern, and the central problem of interest awaiting a solution by the new methods, which had triumphed so unreservedly in the physical world. But so far from saluting Descartes as the one who had eagerly looked forward to the day when a science of morals might be accomplished, the *philosophes* made him a target of many attacks as the man responsible for the rigid separation of mind from matter. Dividing the world of existent things by two distinct, irreducible quantitative attributes—thinking and extension—*res cogitans* and *res extensa*—he could be accused of setting up a barrier prohibitive of the application of scientific method to phenomena of the mental world. Did his dualism not guarantee to the problems of morals, politics and religion immunity

[1] Descartes' Letter to the Translator of the *Principles of Philosophy, op. cit.*, p. 211.

from the application of the analytic instrument of methodological doubt, of the principle *de omnibus dubitandum*? To an age that considered it its historic mission to overthrow the claims of supernaturalism and authority in both Church and State, using as its sole weapon the pure light of reason, the suggestion that there might be a sphere in which reason was not competent to arrive at the truth, seemed akin to apostasy to the reactionary adherents of superstition and supernaturalism. In the eighteenth century, both conservatives and radicals saw in Cartesian dualism a theoretic reinforcement of the conservative in morals, politics and religion. Yet, at the same time, by establishing a habit of mind attached to the principle of holding nothing to be true until there is positive evidence in its favour, Descartes was the spiritual father of the *philosophes* who insisted on ignoring all merely historical claims to validity, unless they could be vindicated at the bar of right Reason. In a very real sense, the war on privilege, on inequality, on all institutions and beliefs whose sole title deeds were prescription, culminating in the giant upheaval of the Revolution of '89, may be said to have had a Cartesian lineage.

The Cartesian theory of progress suffered fatally from its failure to grasp the significance of historical continuity. The method was something akin to a miracle, vouchsafed to its founder by a divine revelation,[1] which enabling men in the future to arrive at certain knowledge in a way that was denied to men in the past, not merely guaranteed future progress, but divided human history cataclysmically into two epochs—the pre-Cartesian and thus unprogressive epoch and the post-Cartesian epoch of progress, opened up by the Athena-like birth of the Method. But although Descartes' view tended to dominate the thought of the eighteenth century, we would not, on that account, be justified in overlooking an alternative view of the nature of scientific method, of the knowledge it can give, and of the kind of progress to be expected from it—a view advanced by an intellect of quite extraordinary acumen,

---

[1] The decisive event in Descartes' life, as he himself recorded (in the lost *Olympica*, summarized by his biographer), was the vision which came to him on the eve of St. Martin's Day, 1619, " the Spirit of Truth descending to take possession of him," and vouchsafing to him the faith, which he never lost, that a universal mathematics was possible.

namely Blaise Pascal. It is true that prior to Descartes, and in contrast to him, Montaigne had emphasized the relativity of knowledge (Cf. p. 22 above) and the influence he exercised on Pascal has been decisively demonstrated.[1] It is also true that Bacon had in his *Novum Organum* (" the scaffolding with which the new philosophy has been built "—Voltaire) insisted that his method should be understood as a flexible and developing one.

> " Nor again do I mean to say that no improvement can be made upon these. On the contrary, I that regard the mind not only in its own faculties but in its connexion with things, must needs hold that the art of discovery may advance as discoveries advance." [2]

But no one before Pascal realized so clearly as he both the relative and the social aspects of inquiry. For he clearly stated the thesis that knowledge (other than revealed knowledge) was the fruit of a co-operative, social enterprise extending continuously through successive generations, and further, that it was always relative to the nature of the method of inquiry itself. The combination of these twin insights resulted in a theory of progress in the sphere of human knowledge, which, in sharp contrast to that held by Descartes, was based not on an antecedent metaphysical guarantee, but on the continuously unfolding and developing methods whereby knowledge was acquired. Or, as Brunschvicg puts it:

> " Instead of establishing *a priori* the fixed limits (cadres) in which scientific knowledge, whatever the future progress of investigations, would remain infallibly entrenched, Pascal shows us physics in search of its principles, which consist in nothing other than the experiments themselves." [3]

Pascal, accepting the Cartesian dichotomy of mind and matter, spirit and flesh, made it the foundation of a clear-cut distinction between the kinds of knowledge that we may have

---

[1] *Vide* Léon Brunschvicg, *Descartes et Pascal, Lecteurs de Montaigne*, New York, 1944.

[2] Quoted by Leon Roth in *Descartes' Discourse on Method*, 1937, p. 58, from the *Preface* to the *Novum Organum*, *op. cit.*, Vol. i, p. 130.

[3] Brunschvicg, *op. cit.*, p. 162.

of the two spheres. It is true that Descartes himself frequently went out of his way to assure the reader that his criteria of validity were not to be taken to be applicable to those truths revealed to us from on high. But, even if we do not share the suspicions of those who believe these remarks should be taken as asides to placate contemporary misgivings, this rigid dualism of two separate spheres of knowledge is at most implicit in Descartes, and not in consonance with the essential temper of his method of procedure, *de omnibus dubitandum*. For Pascal, on the other hand, the distinction is fundamental and systematically worked out in a remarkable piece of writing which has survived in fragmentary form, entitled *De L'Autorité en Matière de Philosophie*.[1] He was led to this epistemological analysis as a result of the necessity he found himself under to defend against contemporary Aristotelians in general, and the Jesuit, Father Noel in particular, the possibility of the existence of a vacuum. To the contemporary mind, the Aristotelian principle that Nature abhors a vacuum, was an unquestioned axiom, and even Descartes was scathing in his comments on the presumption of the young experimental physicist who thus dared to question so fundamental a truth. But Pascal had seen a repetition of the experiment conducted by the Italian scientist, Torricelli, in 1644, whereby a vacuum was created in an inverted tube of mercury, the existence of which was proved by the fact that water rushed into the tube when it was overturned. He proceeded therefore to carry out a number of experiments under differing conditions, which demonstrated the existence of the vacuum beyond all doubt; and then went on to establish, as Torricelli himself had suspected, that the cause of this phenomenon was atmospheric pressure.[2] After making short work of such technical objections as were raised by the Jesuit, Father Noel, Pascal was led to attack in the fragment cited above, the psychological roots of such obduracy in the face of experimental findings, by demonstrating the con-

[1] This work first became known when published in the 1787 edition of Pascal's works. It was subsequently reprinted under the title, *Préface sur le Traité du Vide. Vide Pensées, Fragments et Lettres de Blaise Pascal*, edited by M. P. Faugère, Paris, 1897, Vol. I, p. 103.

[2] *Vide The Physical Treatise of Pascal*, translated by I. H. B. and A. G. H. Spiers with a Preface by F. Barry, New York, 1937.

fusion that existed in the minds of men like Noel. They failed to appreciate (a) the peculiar nature of the " authority " of scientific method as contrasted with the Authority of the Ancients, and (b) the complete and distinct autonomy of the two spheres of knowledge, in one of which scientific method was the appropriate tool, and in the other of which appeal to Authority was the only legitimate method.

In his opening sentence, he goes directly to the heart of the matter. Respect for authority, he says, has now reached such a pitch that any innovation can only be advanced at the author's own peril, while the citation of a text of antiquity suffices to silence the most powerful reasons that may be advanced. Now the correction of this attitude lies not in denying the function of authority in these matters, but in recognizing where and where not it is valid to introduce such an appeal. The distinction he makes is that between research into matters of historical fact such as is comprised under the disciplines of history, geography, languages and theology, on the one hand, and subjects " which fall under the senses or under the reason," such as geometry, arithmetic, music, physics, medicine and architecture, on the other. In the case of the former category, the method of appeal to authority is not only appropriate but necessary and final, since from the original sources " it is evident that one can acquire a complete knowledge of the subject, and that it is impossible to add anything thereto." [1] But in the second category, the task is one of " seeking to discover hidden truths "; and for this purpose authority as a method is useless, reason only serving as the appropriate and adequate instrument of inquiry. The two methods have their separate spheres and their separate rights. " Now the one had all the advantage; here the other reigns in its turn." [2]

The method of authority is applicable most unreservedly in the sphere of theology,

> " in such wise, that, to give complete certainty to matters the most unintelligible to the reason, it suffices to show that they are

[1] Pascal, Préface sur le Traité du Vide, Œuvres de Blaise Pascal, edited by Leon Brunschvicg and Pierre Boutroux, Paris, 1908, Vol. II, p. 131.
[2] Ibid., p. 132.

contained in the sacred books; just as in order to show the
uncertainty of things most probable, it is only necessary to
show that they are not contained therein." [1]

The reason for this is that the human reason is not equipped
to arrive at theological truths by its own unaided efforts, since
theological principle is above both reason and nature, and is
accessible to us only through supernatural power.   In this
sphere we cannot legitimately speak of progress; as Pascal is
plainly aware the method of authority is inherently unprogressive. But the case is the reverse with the other sphere of
knowledge. If we are " to abash the insolence of those who
dare to innovate in theology," we are, on the other hand, " to
strengthen the courage of those who are too afraid to make
discoveries in physics." [2]   For the advancement of knowledge
in this sphere requires the expenditure of both time and
trouble; knowledge here is cumulative, when it is conducted
as a joint enterprise between living scientists and their predecessors.

> " The secrets of nature are hidden; although she is always
> active, her effects are not always discovered. . . . The experi-
> ments (expériences) which give us our knowledge of nature
> are continually multiplied; and as they are the only principles
> of physics, the effects are multiplied in proportion." [3]

For this reason, we can with the slightest effort, taking advantage of the results of the ancients, surpass them in knowledge.
To revere the ancients as though they had exhausted the
possibilities of human knowledge, is tantamount to identifying
human reason with animal instinct, since the crucial difference
between animal and human faculties is the progressive character of " the effects of human reasoning powers." Man, " who
is born only for infinity," starting out from a position of
complete ignorance, progresses in his education not only
through his own experience, but also, thanks to his powers of
memory, through the experience of his predecessors, as it has
been handed down to him. Moreover, the experience of the
individual is paralleled by that of the species, in such wise

[1] Pascal, *Préface sur le Traité du Vide, op. cit.*, p. 131.
[2] *Ibid.*, p. 133.   [3] *Ibid.*, p. 136.

that men are in the same condition to-day as would have been the ancient philosophers, had they been able to go on working continuously down to our own day.

> " Thus it comes about that, by a special prerogative, not only does each individual advance daily in the sciences, but that all men together make a continual progress therein, in proportion as the universe grows older, because the same thing happens in the succession of men as in the different ages of an individual." [1]

In view, then, of this essentially social and public character of scientific method, we may regard the succession of men through the ages as a single individual who is learning and progressing continuously.   When considered in this light, it becomes apparent, as Bacon had observed, that the ancients were in fact in the stage of childhood, while we ourselves in the present constitute relatively to them the true ancients.

There emerges from this analysis evidence of a new awareness of the peculiar status of scientific method or authority in contrast to the absolute, received authority of revelation.   The latter method gives us knowledge which is certain, absolute and final, and is accordingly unprogressive.   But its application is rigorously confined.   Now in the sphere where scientific method is legitimate, Descartes was quite wrong to insist on a metaphysical guarantee to ensure the certainty of our findings, for the simple reason that certainty is not to be looked for, where the sole tool of enquiry is the very fallible human reason.   Descartes' mistake lay in his failure to see the implications of his dualism, in his failure to see that it was impossible to demand any more than probable knowledge (not on that account to be despised) of subjects which " fall under the senses or the reason."   Herein lies the peculiar status of conclusions drawn from the application of scientific method, a peculiarity which distinguishes it fundamentally from the other kind of authority, namely the absolute.   Scientific conclusions are in the nature of hypotheses, true not in any absolute sense as are theological conclusions, but only relative to the peculiar method employed.   Thus scientific knowledge, as

[1] Pascal, *Préface sur le Traité du Vide, op. cit.*, p. 139.

interpreted by Pascal, was truly progressive, in that it implied no absolute certainty, and was both cumulative and self-corrective.

Descartes, impressed by the certainty which he considered to be an attribute of our mathematical knowledge, was content to accept the first principles on which the structure of deductive knowledge was raised, on the grounds that their truth was self evident. Yet the fact remains that we have even in the case of geometry to take those first principles for granted. What is the source, what the authority of these first premises which we cannot demonstrate? Is their certificate of validity provided by experience or by the independent activity of our minds? Perhaps reason is not their source at all. " The heart has its reasons, which reason does not know." [1] " We know truth, not only by the reason, but also by the heart, and it is in this last way that we know first principles; and reason, which has no part in it, tries in vain to impugn them." [2] The sceptics are right in perceiving the weakness and limitations of reason; but they are not justified on that account in impugning the certainty of all our knowledge. " This inability ought, then, to serve only to humble reason, which would judge all, but not to impugn our certainty, as if only reason were capable of instructing us." [3] That Pascal is not here subscribing to the Cartesian ontological view of the status of knowledge, in his use of the word " certainty," will shortly appear.

> " For the knowledge of first principles, as space, time, motion, number, is as sure as any of those which we get from reasoning. And reason must trust these intuitions of the heart, and must base them on every argument. . . . And it is as useless and absurd for reason to demand from the heart proofs of her first principles, before admitting them, as it would be for the heart to demand from reason an intuition of all demonstrated propositions before accepting them." [4]

In other words, we have pragmatic but not ontological justification for proceeding on the basis of these premises to build

---

[1] Pascal, *Pensées*, Everyman translation, 1954 reprint, § 277, p. 78.
[2] *Ibid.*, § 282, p. 79.   [3] *Ibid.*   [4] *Ibid.*

the structure of our knowledge about the world of nature.
But lest there be any doubt about the completeness of Pascal's
understanding of the relative nature of our knowledge of these
matters—relative, that is, to the methods of human enquiry—
let me quote the following remarkable passages from the
Pensées, which, taken together, contain more than a hint of
Hume's famous analysis of causal necessity.

> "When we see the same effect always recur, we infer a
> natural necessity in it, as that there will be a tomorrow, etc.
> But nature often deceives us, and does not subject herself to
> her own rules." [1]

And again,

> "Our soul is cast into a body, where it finds number, time,
> dimension. Thereupon it reasons, and calls this nature,
> necessity, and can believe nothing else." [2]

In other words, there is no guarantee that what we take to be
the necessary laws of nature may only represent the reflection
of the necessary laws of our own thinking, which we have no
choice but to accept, since they are the indispensable conditions of our thinking at all. Whereas Descartes, who conceded
the relative nature of our knowledge of sensible qualities,
thought that he had demonstrated in contrast the absolute
nature of the knowledge we acquire through the understanding, Pascal, on the other hand, maintained that all our
knowledge (other than that through revelation or authority
in its legitimate sphere) was necessarily relative to the knowing agent and his methods of inquiry.

Pascal's relativism is important, because it made possible not
merely an alternative interpretation of the nature of the new
method, but contained implicit within it an alternative theory
of the nature of progress. For the Cartesians progress becomes
possible with the miracle of the new method which, by its
capacity to provide us with knowledge of ontological status,
separates by an unbridgeable gulf the new era from the past
when men sought to attain truth by methods foredoomed to
failure. Thus launched, progress consists of a continuous,
onward march to the attainment of an already prescribed

---

[1] Pascal, *Pensées, op. cit.*, § 91, p. 29.   [2] *Ibid.*, § 233, p. 65.

goal, which is static and unchanging, the moral goal of universal wisdom. In other words, man still has a final cause, the conception of which he has in outline, but the details of which require filling in, in which process consists the nature of progress. This conception of progress is on the whole the dominant one of the eighteenth century, but we cannot on that account afford to ignore the alternative view contained in Pascal, particularly in his earlier work. On this view, the fixed goals disappeared, and progress consisted in following the method (which was essentially that of Bacon, Descartes, Galileo, etc.), but in insisting on its flexibility, and recognizing that its results could be given no metaphysical guarantee of certainty, but were true only in relation to the method whereby they had been acquired. The great step forward which this view represented consisted in its recognition of the continuity of progress. Scientific method, thus conceived was cumulative, self-corrective, a joint enterprise between the generations building on their predecessors' work. Of course, it is only fair to add that we have been isolating and throwing into relief one highly significant aspect of Pascal's thought, which was mixed with a great deal else which to the modern mind may seem out of harmony with the view of method here outlined. Although, for example, we have just emphasized Pascal's grasp of the idea of historical continuity, it must be noted that he classified history, as a discipline, within the category of those subjects whose sole criterion of truth was the appeal to authority; that again, he was unduly impressed with the power of the contingent in determining historical development. "This *je ne sais quoi*, so small an object that we cannot recognize it, agitates a whole country, princes, armies, the entire world. Cleopatra's nose; had it been shorter, the whole aspect of the world would have been altered." [1] Again, in the field of morals, so far was he from championing the rights of reason, that he went out of his way expressly to defend moral doctrines which were admittedly repugnant to reason.

"For it is beyond doubt that there is nothing which more shocks our reason than to say that the sin of the first man has rendered guilty those, who, being so removed from this source,

[1] Pascal, *Pensées, op. cit.*, § 162, p. 48.

seem incapable of participation in it. This transmission does not only seem to us impossible, it seems also very unjust. For what is more contrary to the rules of our miserable justice than to damn eternally an infant incapable of will, for a sin wherein he seems to have so little a share, that it was committed six thousand years before he was in existence? Certainly nothing offends us more rudely than this doctrine; and yet, without this mystery, the most incomprehensible of all, we are incomprehensible to ourselves." [1]

Tempting though the subject is, we cannot here pursue the question of Pascal's mysticism, or the grounds on which he based his moral beliefs. But it is important to note that he specifically excluded morals from the sphere in which the new method, as he conceived it, could be legitimately applied. In this respect he went far beyond Descartes, who whatever his own moral conservatism, looked forward in principle to the eventual attainment of a science of morals. Yet it was in precisely this field that the " progressive " forces in the eighteenth century looked for the main advance in the social betterment of the human lot. The new method proved so successful in the field of natural science, that men sought to achieve a similar mastery over human nature itself by the application of similar methods in the humanistic disciplines. Consequently the next stage in the development of the idea of progress calls for an examination of the attempts to found a science of human nature or a science of psychology.

[1] Pascal, *Pensées, op. cit.,* § 434, p. 121.

CHAPTER III

Of Human Perfectibility

" Progress, man's distinctive mark alone,
    Not God's, and not the beasts': God is, they are,
    Man partly is and wholly hopes to be."

THE ABOVE lines are from Browning's *A Death in the Desert*, but they might well be taken to summarize that element of the idea of progress that gained ground in the seventeenth century. In the writings of Bacon and Pascal, as we have seen, in Fontenelle and others, the idea was developed that a capacity for progress was a peculiar property of human nature. Man, alone of all forms of life, was endowed with sufficient powers both of memory and communication, to enable him to inherit a living body of knowledge from his predecessors, and by beginning at the point where they left off, to proceed in each generation to add to the store that had been amassed through the ages. The notion received its most vivid illustration at the hands of Pascal in his famous analogy of the life of the species to the life of the individual human being. And since knowledge was power—power above all, over physical nature, as it seemed to those who lived to see the birth of modern physical science—man was a creature able to exert increasing control over and independence of his environment. Although the argument was by no means unhistorical, as the innumerable comparisons with the achievements of the Ancients testify, the main emphasis, none the less, in enunciating the grounds for this theory of progress, was not on the empirical historical record of the species, but on the nature of man himself. This type of argument in support of the belief in progress—that which, historically, first launched the belief and gave it its certificate of credibility—may, then, be termed the essentially non-historical argument from the facts of human nature, as they were then understood.

Human problems have never been confined to the intractability of their physical surroundings, nor human aspirations to the task of overcoming that intractability. A large proportion of human frustration and suffering has always been attributed to the obdurate perversity of human nature itself. Man's notorious " inhumanity to man " has exercised the minds and consciences of men at least as much, if not more, than the problem of his dependence on the blind forces of nature. Consequently, it is not surprising that the eighteenth century, fresh from the triumphs of its predecessors in the quest to control the forces of physical nature, should have sought by similar methods to extend that control to the hitherto blind forces of human nature. The belief gained ground that social wellbeing depended upon knowledge of social processes and, above all, of the psychological processes of the individual. Knowledge could be power not only over nature, but, it was hoped, over man himself. Although human nature might remain intractable, universal, and unchanging, it did not follow that human behaviour was likewise beyond the power of man to control. By an increased knowledge of human nature, might it not be possible to use that knowledge to re-direct anti-social behaviour into socially fruitful channels? In a word, if the seventeenth century elaborated the belief in man's capacity to progress indefinitely in the acquisition of knowledge, the eighteenth century, with more confidence than the facts of the case warranted, extended the belief to include man's capacity to achieve moral and social progress. We should note, however, that this argument for progress was in principle essentially an extension of the first argument, namely the argument from human nature. But, since it played such an important role in the eighteenth century in giving wider currency to and heightened powers of emotional satisfaction to the belief in progress, it is necessary to examine its development in some detail, before passing on in subsequent chapters to the historical types of argument in support of the idea of progress.

Optimism, sometimes not easily distinguished from sluggish

contentment, was in the air in the eighteenth century. It is true that Leibnizian metaphysics, with its emphasis on the beneficence of Providence in ensuring that we live in the best of all possible worlds, provoked one of Voltaire's most piquant ironies, " Si c'est ici le meilleur des mondes possibles, que sont donc les autres? " [1] But in England, in particular, the disarming simplicity of this solution of the problem of evil was peculiarly welcome to an age which prided itself that its most representative maxim was " Quieta non movere," and this philosophy, with its ready appeal to emotional contentment, exercised a considerable influence.

> " All discord, harmony not understood;
> All partial evil, universal good;
> And, spite of pride, in erring reason's spite,
> One truth is clear, Whatever is, is right."

When parodied in this fashion by Pope, the attitude is clearly exposed as one that is fundamentally hostile to the belief in progress. If Providence has in its own inscrutable purposes arranged everything for the best, it ill becomes the reasonable man to seek to effect transformations in the order of things as they are. And yet, paradoxical though it may seem, this was not the conclusion drawn by some of the best minds in the eighteenth century, who none the less were powerfully influenced by the doctrine. The thought of reformists like Hartley and Priestley, was, as we shall see, highly coloured by this type of Providential optimism, but its effect was only to spur them on to greater efforts in the cause of remedying present ills. The fact that existing evil might be a necessary concomitant of all that was good in the world did not prevent them from seeking to eliminate as far as possible their current afflictions; and their confidence to attain that end was based on their belief in the malleability of human behaviour, to the neglect of which in the past the avoidable suffering of humanity was mainly attributable.

In this belief, we have their own testimony for it, that they were very largely influenced by the writings of Locke, who stands at once at the end of the seventeenth century and at the

---

[1] Voltaire, *Candide*, Ch. VI.

beginning of the eighteenth.   That Locke acted as a kind of
intellectual watershed for the main streams of thought in logic
and epistemology, in education and politics in the eighteenth
century, is natural enough in view of the extent and originality
of his work in those fields.   " I do not know," writes a modern
French writer, " if there has ever been a dealer in ideas who,
more unmistakably than he, has shaped his century.   He went
forth from the schools, the universities, the learned circles, the
academies, to reach the profane; he became one of the indispensable accessories of the intellectual mode." [1]   But it is less
easy to understand why he should have exerted the influence
he did in the field of morals, as this discipline was then understood.   Locke never wrote on morals, as such, and his observations thereon are scattered piecemeal throughout the *Essay
Concerning Human Understanding*.   It is true that on at least
three occasions in the *Essay* he asserts that morals should be
capable of reduction to an exact science.

> " Upon this ground it is that I am bold to think that morality
> is capable of demonstration, as well as mathematics: since the
> precise real essence of the things moral words stand for may be
> perfectly known, and so the congruity and incongruity of the
> things themselves be certainly discovered; in which consists
> perfect knowledge." [2]

This would appear to imply that moral statements are analytic
statements in the same way that mathematical statements are,
and hence capable of demonstrative certainty, since, unlike
our " sensitive " knowledge or synthetic statements, they are
not dependent upon things outside ourselves.   In other words,
when we say that something is good, we define goodness in
such a way as to exclude certain activities, such as homicide
for example, and hence can deduce with certainty that homicide is not good.   The certainty that moral statements are thus
endowed with is that which accrues to a purely verbal proposition.   The original definition or first principle is presumably

[1] Paul Hazard, *La Pensée Européenne au XVIII ème Siècle*, Paris, 1946, Vol. I, pp.
54-55.
[2] Locke, *An Essay Concerning Human Understanding*, edited by A. C. Fraser, 1894,
Book III, Ch. XI, § 16 (Vol. II, p. 156). Cf. also Book IV, Ch. IV, § 7 (Vol. II,
p. 232) and Book IV, Ch. XII, § 8 (Vol. II, p. 347).

certain, on the analogy with mathematics, on the grounds of the clearness and distinctness of the ideas with which they are concerned.

Elsewhere, however, in the same work, he advances a utilitarian theory of morals which anticipates the associationist psychology of Hartley.

> " Things then are good or evil," he writes, " only in reference to pleasure or pain. That we call *good*, which is apt to cause or increase pleasure, or diminish pain in us; . . . And, on the contrary, we name that *evil* which is apt to produce or increase any pain, or diminish any pleasure in us. . . ." [1]

If then the consequences of an action have to be measured in order to evaluate the moral quality of the action, it is clear that objective factors are necessarily involved in our arriving at any moral statement with regard to that action. In other words, a moral statement, on the utilitarian view is a synthetic statement, and not an analytic one; and on Locke's own view of the status of our knowledge of the external world, any science of morals will be capable not of certainty, but of probability only.

Whatever we may make of this evident inconsistency in Locke's thought on morals, it is important to note that he believed a science of morals possible; for it was the attempt to implement this hope that constituted the main objective of Locke's successors in the field of morals in the eighteenth century. More generally pervasive, however, in its influence in encouraging the eighteenth century *philosophes* to believe that man could take a positive role in shaping his own destiny by making the human mind the creature of a planned environment, was Locke's attack on innate ideas. The doctrine which he was concerned to overthrow was that which proclaimed that there are " some primary notions . . . characters, as it were, stamped upon the mind of man, which the soul receives in its very first being; and brings into the world with it." [2] In contradistinction to this, Locke had no difficulty in demonstrating that such principles, so far from being

---

[1] Locke, *An Essay Concerning Human Understanding, op. cit.*, Book II, Ch. XX, § 2 (Vol. I, p. 303). Cf. also Book II, Ch. XXI, *passim.*
[2] *Ibid.*, Book I, Ch. II, § 1, 28th ed., 1838, p. 8.

innate, are the result of long environmental training and experience; that even if they commanded universal assent— and they do not—this would not prove them to be innate. This is equally true of the most deeply cherished moral sentiments, which, so far from being enshrouded in the mystery that attaches to that which is engraven on the soul of man by his Maker, are purely conventional and subject to human observation. This is borne out by experience, for we readily perceive that moral standards differ according to the changing environments of different times and places. It is the power to endure and the ease with which they pervade a given culture so thoroughly that gives moral sentiments the peculiar dignity which has misled some men into believing them to be innate.

> " . . . doctrines, that have been derived from no better original than the superstition of a nurse, and the authority of an old woman, may, by length of time, and consent of neighbours, grow up to the dignity of principles in religion or morality." [1]

But from this, it does not necessarily follow, as Sir Charles Morris points out, that the mind is a purely passive instrument, the " *tabula rasa* " of Locke's supposition, since there is nothing incompatible in the above theory with the assumption that " the mind is gifted, as part of its essential nature, with capacities to do something to or make something of any impressions which it receives . . ." [2]   It was, none the less, the vivid conception of the *tabula rasa*, the picture of the mind as a virginal sheet of " white paper," on which by planning the environmental influences to suit the ends which we wish to achieve, we may write what we will, that caught the imagination of eighteenth century reformers, and inspired them to attempt to transform human society to something more nearly approaching their heart's desire. So far from man, being born into the world with the curse of original sin to weigh him down, as Bossuet believed, or being born naturally good, as Rousseau believed, the raw material of man, as supplied by nature, was neutral. And we could have only ourselves to blame if men grew up to be the socially dangerous

[1] Locke, *An Essay Concerning Human Understanding, op. cit.*, Book I, Ch. III, § 22, 28th ed., 1838, p. 33.
[2] C. R. Morris, *Locke, Berkeley, Hume*, 1931, p. 26.

creatures they often were, and on the reverse side, the remedy for these ills which we had permitted to develop, lay entirely within ourselves.

It was one thing, however, to assert that the moral sense in man was not innate,[1] and that human behaviour was the creature of its environment; and quite another to be able so to regulate that environment as to produce specific, desired results. To achieve this, something more was required than Locke's hint that a deductive moral science was possible; it was necessary that a science of morals, not merely deductive but synthetic also, should be attempted. If we are to influence the operations of nature, physical or human, it is necessary that we should first discover that the relations between the given phenomena are uniform, or at least discover causal trends if not actual constancy of relations; so that by securing a first event, we may have good grounds for believing that a second event which we wish to realize will in fact be likely to ensue. The ideal, of course, at which to aim, which will ensure our ability to effect the maximum control over pheno-mena, is the reduction of many observed uniformities of relations to the statement of a single law, capable of explaining all the existing known relations of the phenomena concerned. It was the discovery of such a law, namely the principle of gravity or universal attraction in the physical world, that had constituted the supreme achievement of Newton's genius. To emulate Newton in the field of psychology and morals was the challenge which met and was taken up by Locke's successors in this sphere in the eighteenth century. Newton himself had hinted at this possibility, when he wrote, " if natural Philo-sophy in all its Parts, by pursuing this Method, shall at length be perfected, the Bounds of Moral Philosophy will also be enlarged." [2] The idea of a " moral Newtonianism " was thus widely canvassed in the first half of the eighteenth century, and it was as a contribution to the fulfilment of this conception

[1] It should, however, be noted that in expounding his political theory in *The Second Treatise of Civil Government*, Locke's view of the moral nature of man seems to assume as self-evident an innate capacity to intuit certain truths of natural law.

[2] Quoted by Basil Willey, *The Eighteenth Century Background*, 1949 ed., p. 138, from Newton's *Opticks*, 1704 (1931 reprint), Book iii, pt. i, qu. 31.

that David Hartley published in 1749 his influential *Observations on Man*, in which the principles of utility and the association of ideas played a consciously analogous role to the principle of gravity in physics.

Hartley, although he denied that he believed in the materiality of the soul, none the less advanced a theory of psychology and physiology, which rendered the hypothesis of a soul completely redundant; and may, accordingly, be ranked as a materialist in the tradition of Hobbes. Developing the sensationalism of Locke so as to deny that the latter's "ideas of reflection" were anything more than ideas ultimately derivative from the senses, and wishing in Newton's words to "derive the rest of the phenomena of Nature by the same kind of reasoning from mechanical principles," he provided a physiological theory in terms of which the will, the emotions and all thought were resoluble into "vibratiuncles" (tiny vibrations) set up by external phenomena in the "medullary substance of the brain." Fortunately, however, Hartley's psychology did not stand or fall on the truth of his physiology, and it was, in fact, the edition of Hartley, brought out by Priestley in 1775 (*Hartley's Theory of the Human Mind*), from which the physiological sections were omitted, that gave Hartley his unrivalled influence as a psychologist in the eighteenth century.

> "It is of the utmost Consequence to Morality and Religion," he wrote, "that the Affections and Passions should be analysed into their simple compounding Parts, by reversing the Steps of the Associations which concur to form them. For thus we may learn how to cherish and improve good ones, check and root out such as are mischievous and immoral, and how to suit our Manner of Life, in some tolerable Measure, to our intellectual and religious Wants." [1]

The purpose herein expressed is carried out by showing how all human passions are derived from the ultimate and unanalysable sensations of pleasure and pain. These primary sensations are, however, by the principle of association, capable of being compounded through various complex combinations

[1] Hartley, *Observations on Man. His Frame, His Duty, and His Expectations*, 1749, Vol. I, p. 81.

into pleasures and pains of seven different types, which Hartley lists and treats separately as sensation, imagination, ambition, self-interest (subdivided into gross, refined, and rational), sympathy, theopathy, and the moral sense. Beginning at the animal stage, endowed only with the pleasures and pains of sensation, we are capable through our power of association of graduation through the higher stages, until we arrive at a fully developed moral sense, which alone is worthy of man. But note that the moral sense is defined not as a unique faculty but as the resultant of a combination of all the others, and like them, is resoluble ultimately into the primary sensations. The problem thus opened up for the moralist is how best to secure that men will seek to realize the higher types of pleasures in preference to the lower. That they will seek pleasure and try to avoid pain is a primary axiom; but given this, it is within our power to control the type of thing with which pleasure and pain will be associated.

> " Some Degree of Spirituality," he declares, " is the necessary Consequence of passing through Life. The sensible Pleasures and Pains must be transferred by Association more and more every day, upon things that afford neither sensible Pleasure nor sensible Pain in themselves, and so beget the intellectual Pleasures and Pains." [1]

This he believes to be perfectly feasible, since our observation tells us that on balance there are far more pleasures than pains, so that

> " when the several Parts of these complex Pleasures are sufficiently united by Association, the Pains which enter their Composition will no longer be distinguished separately." . . . " Or, in other Words, Association, under the Supposition of this Corollary, has a Tendency to reduce the State of those who have eaten of the Tree of the Knowledge of Good and Evil, back again to a paradisiacal one." [2]

As the child learns to associate its parents with the pleasures that it derives from them, forgetting the original motive it comes to experience the emotion of love for them; similarly

---

[1] Hartley, *Observations on Man, op. cit.,* p. 82.   [2] *Ibid.,* p. 83.

the miser, associating money with the pleasure to be derived from the things it will buy, forgetting the original association comes to experience the emotion of greed. Thus the task of the moralist is so to organize the environmental influences as to secure the association of pleasure with objects which are socially desirable. If man is incapable of altruism, he is not incapacitated from benevolence.

" It [benevolence] has also a high Degree of Honour and Esteem annexed to it, procures us many Advantages, and Returns of Kindness, both from the Person obliged and others; and is most closely connected with the Hope of Reward in a future State, and with the Pleasures of Religion, and of Self-approbation, or the Moral Sense. And the same Things hold with respect to Generosity in a much higher Degree. It is easy therefore to see, how such Associations may be formed in us, as to engage us to forego great Pleasure, or endure great Pain, for the sake of others; how these Associations may be attended with so great a Degree of Pleasure as to over-rule the positive Pain endured, or the negative one from the fore-going of a Pleasure; and yet how there may be no direct, explicit Expectation of Reward, either from God or Man, by natural Consequence, or express Appointment, not even of the concomitant Pleasure which engages the Agent to undertake the benevolent or generous Action. And this I take to be a Proof from the Doctrine of Association, that there is, and must be, such a Thing as pure disinterested Benevolence; also a just Account of the Origin and Nature of it." [1]

Such in brief outline was the doctrine of the perfectibility of man, as expounded by Hartley. Man is so constituted that he is impelled by a universal law to pursue his own happiness, but so far from this meaning that the life of man, left to follow his own passions, will be solitary, nasty, brutish and short, as Hobbes had concluded from a similar premise, man is destined to attain to an increasing capacity for benevolence and social good will. The reason why Hobbes had not perceived this lay in the fact that not until Hartley (though he generously acknowledged his debt to Locke and Gay) had men been cognisant of the operation of the other fundamental universal law, the law of association, which the all-wise Creator had

---

[1] Hartley, *Observations on Man, op. cit.,* pp. 473–74.

provided to offset the anarchic consequences of an unqualified hedonism. Like Adam Smith and Priestley, Hartley had an unshakable conviction in the existence of a perfect Being, who, in his wisdom, is determined to maximize happiness throughout the universe. This it was which furnished the real source of his belief that the principle of association was the secret of man's perfectibility. Both Newton and Hartley believed that the law they had discovered, the principles of gravity and association respectively, were merely the efficient causes, the final cause of which being the will of God. This could lead sometimes, with Hartley, to an acceptance of a passive *laissez-faire* attitude, as when, for instance, we find him writing that

> " . . . even Avarice and Ambition are, in their respective ways, carrying on the benevolent Designs of Him who is *All in All*. And the same thing may be hoped of every other Passion and Pursuit. One may hope, that they all agree and unite in leading to ultimate Happiness and Perfection." [1]

There was, he believed, or at any rate was desperately anxious to believe, a divine guarantee that the law of progress was Nature's law, and that good would ultimately triumph over evil, in spite of the vividness of his predictions of the forthcoming storms which " threaten Ruin and Dissolution to the present States of *Christendom*." [2] Running counter to his spirit of *laissez-faire* was an activist spirit of reform, which could be illustrated from much of his writing. In the following passage, we see the two conflicting attitudes appear in one and the same breath.

> " . . . we have a Power of suiting our Frame of Mind to our Circumstances, of correcting what is amiss, and improving what is right. . . . That Association tends to make us all ultimately similar; so that if one be happy, all must. . . ." [3]

God was in His heaven, and according to His benevolent intentions, His will revealed in the operation of the law of association ought to secure the best of all possible worlds; but at the same time, Hartley, like many another perfectibilist, was not so naïve as to lose all sense of realism, and could not

[1] Hartley, *Observations on Man, op cit.*, p. 463.   [2] *Ibid.*, Vol. II, p. 441
[3] *Ibid.*, Vol. I, p. 84.

always resist a backward glance at the past follies of mankind, which still showed little sign of having exhausted themselves. But on the whole, Hartley emphasized the passive rather than the activist attitude towards the perfectibility of man, in which he firmly believed and which he himself did all he could to advance. The curious contradiction lay in his ability to maintain side by side with a thorough-going humanistic materialism a devout piety, which finally led him to qualify even his faith in the complete perfectibility of man.

> " We ought therefore, whenever false flattering Hopes, with relation to our future Condition in this Life, rise up to View in our Imaginations, and tempt us, instantly to reject them; and in the Language of the Scriptures, *to rejoice as though we rejoiced not;* to remember that we *are Strangers and Pilgrims here,* that we only *dwell in Tabernacles, have no continuing City,* but *expect one to come, the New Jerusalem,* of which we are Denizens, *where our Treasure and Hearts ought to be.*" [1]

If Hartley was chiefly concerned to emphasize the principle of natural harmony which of itself tended to protect man against the consequences of his natural egoism, his French contemporary, Helvetius, was not long in drawing more activist conclusions from the hedonistic, associationist psychology. Inheriting the sensationalism of Locke, in the radicalized version developed in France by Condillac,[2] Helvetius sought to build a science of morals, which by stressing the exclusive nature of the role played by environmental influences in shaping human behaviour, left the door open to illimitable improvement of that behaviour in a future enlightened by the insights of the new moral science. Locke, wrote D'Alembert, " reduced metaphysics to what it ought to be in fact, the experimental physics of the soul." [3] Helvetius, writing in the same tradition, similarly and erroneously convinced that Locke's main contributions had been in the field of psychology, wrote in his Preface to *De L'Esprit,* " I have

[1] Hartley, *Observations on Man, op. cit.,* Vol. II, p. 362.
[2] Condillac's *Essai sur l'Origine des Connaissances Humaines* appeared in 1746.
[3] D'Alembert, *Preliminary Discourse to the Encyclopædia, Œuvres,* 1805, Vol. I, p. 276.

believed that one could treat morals like all the other sciences, and make a morality like an experimental physics."

The psychology which he proceeds to develop is essentially that of Hartley's, the only difference being that Helvetius sometimes writes as though human behaviour was in every instance the outcome of a deliberate calculation of the probabilities of the balance of pleasure over pain attendant upon alternatives of action. Crude though his hedonism is, however, it does give him increased confidence in the comparative certainty with which the moralist and the legislator can predict the direction of human behaviour under given circumstances. Hitherto, he complains, moralists have been content to lay down moral maxims and indulge in exhortation, regardless of the comparative futility of trying to argue against laws of human nature. Instead of first seeking to understand those laws and discovering that behaviour is moulded by the dominant institutions of society, they go on proclaiming those things that men ought not to do, irrespective of the fact that all their institutions are designed to incite them to do those very things. True, he admits, they may by their " beautiful moral maxims "

> " have corrected some individuals of faults with which, perhaps, they reproached themselves; but otherwise they have effected no change in the customs of nations. And why is this the case? It is that the vices of a people are, if I may venture to say so, always hidden at the bottom of its legislation: it is there that you must rummage, to pull up the roots productive of its vices." [1]

Of what use, he asks impatiently, to declaim against the fact that men are self-seeking; that nature is what it is. We might as well complain that the mountain that blocks our view should continue to do so, impervious to our desires. The fundamentals of human nature are beyond our power to change; we have no choice but to accept them; but what we can do, if only we will take the trouble to understand how they operate, is to transform the nature of the social consequences which they have hitherto, in our ignorance, been allowed to produce.

[1] Helvetius, *De l'Esprit*, Paris, 1758, Vol. I, p. 152.

"The continual declamations of moralists against the wickedness of men, merely demonstrate the poverty of their knowledge of the issue. Men are not wicked, but subject to their interests. The cries of moralists will certainly not change this spring of the moral universe. It is not of the wickedness of men that one ought to complain, but of the ignorance of legislators, who have always put the interest of the individual in opposition to the general interest." [1]

Helvetius is, above all, a thorough going environmentalist, who asserts as strongly as any modern psychologist of the school of Adler or Wexberg that the psychic structure of the individual is explicable solely in terms of the myriad complexities of the post-natal conditioning influences, which, of course, vary enormously with every single individual. The only difference between a man of genius and more ordinary mortals, on this view, is that the former has been subjected to quite exceptionally favourable environmental determinants. Helvetius does, in fact, spend some time in demonstrating why it is, this being the case, that so few men of the genius category are thrown up by our society.[2] But it was, of course, in the implications that the doctrine had for morals that Helvetius and his contemporaries were mainly interested. The consequences here are most vividly and briefly stated in a deservedly little known novel attributed to Helvetius, which was posthumously published and "translated" into English in 1774 under the significant title *The Child of Nature, Improved by Chance*. The theme of the novel, if such it can be called, is briefly the story of how through many stirring vicissitudes of fortune, environmental influences, against heavy odds, not only preserved the chastity of a Leicestershire barmaid, but elevated her to membership of the aristocracy. On one occasion, Fanny, the heroine, piqued by the obliviousness of a clergyman to her charms, is driven to simulate a philosophic interest, a stratagem which proves completely successful.

"Are there any other vices," asks Fanny in the ensuing dialogue, "than those we hold from Nature?" which elicits the response, "The worst, and more dangerous, Miss, come from education, and the inequality among mankind. Nature

[1] Helvetius, *De l'Esprit, op. cit.*, p. 73 n.
[2] *Ibid.*, Vol. II, Discours III, Ch. XXVII, *passim*.

never made a murderer, a thief, a perjurer, and all the villains
we hear of, or meet with. To society only, they owe their
existence. Want, pride, ambition, avarice, are the causes
productive of the crimes that are daily committed; charge
not Nature with them." [1]

Elsewhere, Fanny's mother, who is possessed of a penchant for
speculation, which must have been unusual for a publican
even in the eighteenth century, forcefully affirms the same
principle.

> " Like our affections, our judgments, true or false, are not
> free; they are the necessary effect of the ideas we have re-
> ceived. For this reason, it is both absurd and inhuman to
> persecute a man for his religious opinions, since he could not
> chuse the parents who gave him life, nor be at liberty to adopt
> or reject their opinions. Born in Turkey, or upon the banks
> of the Ganges—educated in a family, the votaries either of
> *Brama* or *Mahomet*, would it have lain in my power to be a
> Christian ? " [2]

But if Nature could not be held responsible for the many
undesirable aspects of human behaviour, and if the educative
influences of the social environment had the exclusive power
here attributed to it, the question as to the cause of the distortion of the social influences is forced upon us. Since Nature
gives us a fair start, since the scales are not weighted against us
in the shape of evil tendencies innate in man, how did man
contrive so to mismanage his affairs as to produce the deplorable state of affairs prevailing in mid-eighteenth century
France? And, granted a satisfactory explanation of this
phenomenon, what guarantee was there that the same dis-
turbing cause or causes would not continue to operate in the
future as in the past? On what grounds, in other words, did
Helvetius base his confidence in the perfectibility of man?
Helvetius, it must be admitted, is inclined to vacillate on this
issue, and his different answers to the problem tend to conflict.
At times he seems to suggest that the world's ills are almost
entirely attributable to ignorance, which will inevitably tend
to diminish with the passage of time, as a result of the scientific

---

[1] *The Child of Nature*, London, 1774, Vol. II, pp. 35–36.
[2] *Ibid.*, Vol. II, p. 151.

enlightenment of morals by a process in which such works as his own will play a leading part.

> " Who doubts," he asks rhetorically, " that, more assiduous in this study, moralists could not then bring this science to that high degree of perfection that good minds can now only glimpse, and perhaps to that which they do not imagine it can ever attain ? " [1]

Until now, governments, institutions, legislation have been incoherent and mutually inconsistent, have appeared to reflect nothing more than the random hand of chance or fate. Failure to appreciate the intimate connexion between the morals of a people and its institutions and legislation has resulted in a total absence of planning. The case is an exact parallel with that of peasants, who wishing to empty their fields of garbage and waste products, throw into the stream these un-wanted objects, which carried away by the currents, then piled up in the reeds, gradually form an island, which no one fore-saw and no one wanted. The remedy for this is evidently increased knowledge and enlightenment. And at times Helvetius' enthusiasm for the efficacy of this solvent touches heights, which must seem to a later and still more " enlight-ened " age, rather pathetic.

> " These principles once received," he wrote, " with what facility would the legislator extinguish the torches of fanaticism and of superstition, would he suppress abuses, would he reform barbaric customs, which perhaps useful at the time of their establishment, have since become so disastrous to the universe ? " [2]

And again,

> " . . . in the matter of ideas, ignorance is always compelled to give way before the immense power of the imperceptible progress of enlightenment, that I compare to those slender roots which, worming their way into the clefts of rocks, grow there and break their way through." [3]

---

[1] *De l'Esprit*, Vol. I, pp. 170–71.
[2] *Ibid.*, Vol. I, p. 165.
[3] *Ibid.*, Vol. II, p. 206.

Elsewhere, however, he recognizes that there are powerful moral forces pitted against social amelioration, and about the elimination of these he is less confident. The " sinister influences " play almost as large a role in Helvetius as they were afterwards to do in his great disciple, Jeremy Bentham.

> " The errors of men, Fanny," to quote again from the above-mentioned " philosophical novel," " are the necessary effects of their ignorance, which would soon vanish before experience, reflection and philosophy, were not a few men interested to keep truth and reason chained at the feet of superstition and folly." [1]

This powerful group he divides into two main types, the fanatics or intolerants and the " demi-politiques," by which he means those who, for one reason or another, have a vested interest in received opinions. The only course open to their victims, if they are not to stand passively by while these men prevent them from reaping the benefits of the new applied moral science, is to expose them once and for all as " the cruellest enemies of humanity; to tear from them the sceptre that they hold from ignorance, and of which they make use to rule over stupid peoples." [2] But this, he regretfully admits, is a task beset with difficulties, which, although not insuperable, it would be rash to minimize. The reason for this is interesting, since, in advancing it, Helvetius is driven into the error which it is the main burden of his work to castigate, the error of complaining that human nature is what it is. The sinister interests are so powerful that enlightenment alone cannot be counted upon to overthrow them. Courage is also required, the courage of men prepared to sacrifice their own interests for the common good. And Helvetius' common honesty compels him to admit that such men are extremely rare. Indeed, it would almost seem that such types were almost excluded by definition on the extreme hedonism of Helvetian moral science. However, in recognizing that in the present condition of men, there can be no panaceas which do not include the virtue of self-sacrifice among their specifics, Helvetius is brought up against the dilemma which racked so

---

[1] *The Child of Nature*, Vol. II, p. 152.   [2] *De l'Esprit* ,Vol. I, 235.

painfully the intellectual conscience of the younger Mill in the crisis of his utilitarianism some seventy years later.

> "There are men," writes Helvetius, "who, persuaded that a citizen without courage is a citizen without virtue, feel that the property and even the life of an individual are, so to speak, only in his hands as a deposit that he ought always to be ready to restore, when the public safety requires it: but men such as these are always in too small numbers to enlighten the public. . . ."[1]

While Helvetius was too superficial a thinker to recognize the chasm that this admission opened under his feet, he recognized clearly enough that it necessitated a certain qualifying of the exuberance with which he had previously hailed the perfectibility of man. "Thus," he concludes, "morals and legislation, that I regard as one and the same science, will only bring about imperceptible progress,"[2] the perception of which will take a long time.

Deliberately provocative in its manner, lavishly illustrated with stories and anecdotes, often of an amusing character, Helvetius' *De L'Esprit* was assured of a wide circulation, which its public burning did nothing to diminish. Its influence in its own day was enormous. Together Hartley and Helvetius constituted the twin sources of the utilitarian, perfectibilist tradition which Bentham was to establish as one of the most influential currents of thought in the nineteenth century. But while it is true that the essentials of the doctrine of perfectibility are contained in Hartley and Helvetius, something should be said of two English writers, who if they added little of importance, did much by the fervour with which they embraced the creed and by the eloquence with which they wrote, to propagate the doctrine. In Bentham perfectibility is for the most part implicit rather than explicit, whereas in the pages of Joseph Priestley and Godwin, the perfectibility of man is extolled with all the passion that is normally evoked only by a religious creed. The ideas of Priestley, we shall have occasion to discuss elsewhere,[3] since his multifarious intellectual interests included a curious insight into the significance of

---

[1] *De l'Esprit, op. cit.*, Vol. I, p. 236.   [2] *Ibid.*   [3] Cf. Ch. VIII.

historical knowledge, on which he mainly drew to substantiate his belief in progress. It should be noticed, however, that he does also use the argument from human nature in a somewhat similar though more developed vein to that used by Bacon and Pascal.

At the very outset of his *Essay on the First Principles of Government*, he regards as axiomatic that any " tolerably well educated " man of his own day, who has emerged from " an improved Christian country," will necessarily be much happier both in himself and in his capacity to share that happiness with others, than his opposite number in any country of any previous age could possibly have been. And on these grounds it seems to him reasonable to assume that a similar relationship will inevitably hold good between the hypothetical citizen of the present and his opposite number in any future age. For Priestley as for Hartley the ultimate source which guarantees his confidence that this progressive process is continuous and in the nature of things is Divine Providence. The proximate cause of the process, however, or the instrument in the hands of Providence in furthering this end of the " progress of the species towards perfection " is the fabric of society in general and of government in particular. For man in the allegedly pre-social state of nature, specialization of function is as a method out of the question. And specialization is the *sine qua non* of all progress, for without it, the generations are bound by the practices of their predecessors, and no improvements are possible. Once man succeeds, however, in launching himself upon the social stage of his development, he no longer remains in a static condition, for then, " the powers of all have their full effect; and hence arise improvements in all the conveniences of life, and in every branch of knowledge." [1] Given the social faculty of specialization and the human memory, all the acquired knowledge of the past can rapidly be mastered; where a subject exceeds the range of any single individual, the remedy is the simple one of further specialization. The upshot of this, on the Baconian maxim that knowledge is power, is that

---

[1] Priestley, *An Essay on the First Principles of Government, and on the Nature of Political, Civil, and Religious Liberty*, 2nd ed., 1771, p. 4.

" the human powers will, in fact, be enlarged; nature, including both its materials, and its laws, will be more at our command; men will make their situation in this world abundantly
more easy and comfortable; they will probably prolong their
existence in it, and will grow daily more happy, each in himself, and more able (and, I believe, more disposed) to com-
municate happiness to others. Thus, whatever was the
beginning of this world, the end will be glorious and para-
disaical, beyond what our imaginations can now conceive." [1]

This view, he acknowledges, may be considered rather extra-
vagant, but he feels that it follows from a proper understanding
of the realities of our nature, which open up a vista, the very
" contemplation of which always makes me happy."

Godwin, writing in the same tradition, differs from his
predecessors in the revolutionary fervour which pervades his
writing. Publishing his massive *Enquiry Concerning Political
Justice* in 1793, Godwin shared to the full the sentiment of most
of his radical contemporaries that " Bliss was it in that dawn
to be alive." For him the revolution offered the most convincing testimony that the perfectibilist dream would soon be
realized. In the pages of Godwin we see the faith in the perfectibility of man shining at its brightest and pushed to its
utmost limits. He himself leaves us in no doubt as to the
sources of his ideas, since he acknowledges his debts to Locke,
Hartley, Holbach, Rousseau and Helvetius. Confessing his
hope that the day may not be far distant when men will come
to feel that freedom and equity are as necessary to the human
organism as food and air, he proceeds to explain why such a
hope is no mere pious aspiration, but based on the nature of
things. First, the moral characters of men are the sole result
of their perceptions. " We bring neither virtue nor vice with
us at our entrance into the world." [2] Secondly, the most
effective means at our disposal of operating on the human
mind, of inscribing what characters we will on the original
white sheet, is the institution of government, an engine of
great power, hitherto largely misused. And thirdly, " perfectibility is one of the most unequivocal characteristics of the

---

[1] Priestley, *An Essay on the First Principles of Government, op. cit.*, pp. 4–5.

[2] Godwin, *An Enquiry concerning Political Justice, and its Influence on General
Virtue and Happiness*, 1793, Vol. I, p. 16.

human species," [1] as a result of the three great instruments of
advancement, literature for the diffusion of knowledge, education for the impression of the right principles on the young,
and political justice whereby social practice is informed by
moral principle.

If anyone should be disposed to question that perfectibility
is a law of man's nature, let him consider for a moment the
contrast between ' man in his original state, a being capable of
impressions and knowledge to an unbounded extent, but not
having as yet received the one or cultivated the other," [2] and
man, who progressing through the stages of acquiring language,
the alphabet, and that power of induction implicit in the
nature of thought, has at last succeeded in covering the earth
with " houses, inclosures, harvests, manufactures, instruments,
machines, together with all the wonders of painting, poetry,
eloquence and philosophy." [3] If we thus contemplate the
staggering achievements that have marked the career of man
so far, is it possible to doubt that the future is equally pregnant
with opportunity or to believe that the " wisdom of our
ancestors was such as to leave no room for future improvement." [4] The fact that until now there has been no advancement in the fields of morals and social institutions comparable
to that made in the other sciences, should serve as a challenge
to renewed endeavour and more energetic application rather
than to depress us. But perhaps it will be objected that
nations, like individuals, must be subject to the processes of
growth and decay; that the period of advancement corre-
sponds to the period of youth, to be remorselessly followed by
the period of old age, when as a result of the luxury and
depravation made possible by the power of a nation in its hey-
day, a process of disintegration, beyond the power of any
legislation to remedy, will set in. The objection is refuted by
repudiating the analogy on the grounds that in the case of
nations, fresh generations of men are constantly replacing those
who are leaving the stage, and youth is accordingly perpetually renewed. Moreover, " the power of social institutions
changing the character of nations is very different from and
infinitely greater than any power which can ordinarily be

---

[1] Godwin, *op. cit.*, p. 11.   [2] *Ibid.*, p. 43.   [3] *Ibid.*, p. 49.   [4] *Ibid.*, p. 50.

E

brought to bear upon a solitary individual." [1]   The social forces of the urge to emulation and the fear of shame interact upon large bodies of men, who thus acquire new impulses and the power to break through old restrictive habits.   Through their mutual exertions they infuse one another with their spirit of zeal, so that the power of the whole social unit far exceeds the strength of the sum of the individuals who compose it.

But no more than Helvetius could Godwin overlook the objection to his theory that the present state of the world, even a world in revolution, was one which included a vast amount of human suffering, only a small proportion of which was explicable in terms of such " natural " phenomena as the Lisbon earthquake, for example.   His answer to this difficulty does not differ in essentials from that provided by Helvetius. Like Helvetius, Godwin was a strict moral necessitarian, but was more successful than his French predecessor in adhering to the language of necessity, which he advocated.

> " It would be of infinite importance to the cause of science and virtue to express ourselves upon all occasions in the language of necessity.   The contrary language is perpetually intruding, and it is difficult to speak two sentences upon any topic connected with human action without it." [2]

Consequently all vice is reduced by Godwin to error, and although error ought on the face of it to be far from self-perpetuating, since it can be relied upon to bring its own retribution rapidly in its wake, nevertheless our errors tend to be perpetuated by the sustaining and corrupting force of government, above all of monarchical government.   Politically Godwin was a republican with strong anarchist leanings, and in his eyes the principle cause of all the mischief was the institution of government.

> " It reverses the genuine propensities of mind, and, instead of suffering us to look forward, teaches us to look backward for perfection.   It prompts us to seek the public welfare, not in innovation and improvement, but in a timid reverence for the decisions of our ancestors, as if it were the nature of mind always to degenerate, and never to advance." [3]

[1] Godwin, op. cit., p. 73.   [2] Ibid., p. 317.   [3] Ibid., pp. 31–32.

But this source of our present woes, Godwin treats simply as a passing encumbrance; for how is it possible to believe that once the eyes of reasonable men have been opened to this iniquity and its pernicious but easily remediable consequences, those same men will be so unreasonable as to continue to suffer needlessly? Godwin easily assumes the reasonableness of men.

" Is there a nation upon the face of the earth," he asks rhetorically, " that would submit to the impositions of its administration, the wars it occasions, and the lavish revenues by which it is maintained, if they knew it to be merely an excrescence and a disease in the order of society ? " [1]

None of the eighteenth century *philosophes* had a more bountiful or naïve faith in the power of unaided reason to strike off the chains which held men back from perfect freedom and equity than Godwin. It was no mere faith in the power of truth to let light into the dark places of the mind, to give to the despairing the strength and hope to face the seemingly intractable. It was not merely the conviction that " In reality the chains fall off of themselves, when the magic of opinion is dissolved." [2] Godwin believed over and above this that there was in the universe a given quantity of truth; that, with the passage of time, human reason by the law of its nature continued ceaselessly to subtract from the total of truth by acquiring parts of it for itself. We had already gained large quantities, but, in order to eliminate the evil of monarchy, a further quantity was still required.

" The discovery of truth is a pursuit of such vast extent, that it is scarcely possible to prescribe bounds to it. Those great lines, which seem at present to mark the limits of human understanding, will, like the mists that rise from a lake, retire farther and farther the more closely we approach them. A certain quantity of truth will be sufficient for the subversion of tyranny and usurpation; and this subversion, by a reflected force, will assist our understandings in the discovery of truth." [3]

On the basis of this assumption, Godwin is able to develop a theory of historical progression, in which the *a tergo* propulsion is provided solely by the capacity of the human mind to

[1] Godwin, *op. cit.*, pp. 74–75.   [2] *Ibid.*, p. 64.   [3] *Ibid.*, p. 23.

acquire enlightenment and to propagate its liberating ideas. In our time, we have become so familiar with the thesis that the French Revolution would have taken place whether or not the *philosophes* had lived and written, that a French historian[1] has been urged to amass a weight of evidence in support of the opposite view that the *philosophes* played a decisive role in shaping the events that led to the Revolution. Godwin, however, went much further than this in the immodesty of his claim for the influence of the intellectuals in shaping the course of history. Why, he asks, were the American and French revolutions carried through with the virtual unanimity of opinion in both countries, whereas in the case of England tyranny could only be resisted at the cost of civil war? The answer is extremely simple. The Americans resisted George III and the French decapitated Louis XVI nearly a century and a half after the English had executed Charles I; the difference in the conditions governing the contrasted revolutions is entirely explicable in the lapse of time that had occurred. For in that century and a half, the great political truths enunciated by such men as Sydney and Locke, Montesquieu and Rousseau, had been given wide circulation, and had thus had time to exert their inevitable influence. Even in the American and French revolutions there was still a hard core of minority opinion, which required yet more time to enlighten it; and consequently the resistance of this minority had occasioned some bloodshed. If only, therefore, Godwin concludes, these revolutions had occurred a little later, there would have been no violence, no bloodshed whatever; for by that time, reason would have had time to accomplish its work, all would have been enlightened, and unanimity would have prevailed.[2] In other words, the only philosophy of history that is required is the knowledge that time is always on the side of the enlightened, and that since the enlightened, by definition, are striving to eliminate all the sources and fruits of error, the historical process is an indefinitely progressive one. Thus Godwin derives what is implicitly a historical theory of pro-

---

[1] *Vide* M. Roustan, *The Pioneers of the French Revolution*, English Translation, 1925.
[2] Cf. Godwin, *op. cit.*, Vol. I, pp. 203–204.

gress from his original arguments in favour of progress from the nature of the human mental structure, with its capacity to generalize, to recognize its own powers and its consequent " restless desire after further progress."

It would be easy to multiply quotations both from the writers treated here and from others among their contemporaries to illustrate the confidence of the eighteenth century that mankind was continually growing happier and happier, and that the process could be expected to continue indefinitely. We have in this chapter been concerned with this belief and its development in so far as it was based on the argument from human nature, but, before proceeding to examine the historical arguments, a brief critique of the central tenets of this belief is called for.

On the positive side, we must recognize the validity of the belief that man is peculiar among the animals in that he is possessed of faculties which enable him to build on the work of his predecessors so that each generation does not have to start over again from scratch. But it does not follow from this that because man has this capacity he will always continue to avail himself of it. That presupposes both the will to use the capacity and the ability to maintain it intact. It so happened that in the post-Renaissance period of European man, the will to use the capacity received remarkable stimulation, and, since the vision of man is notoriously bounded by limiting temporal and spatial factors, it is not surprising that the *philosophes* should have made the fairly common error of mistaking the actual for the normal. Although overstated, the point is well made by Julien Benda, " If we except two or three epochs of light and of very short duration, but whose light, like that of certain stars, still illumines the world long after their extinction, in general humanity lives in the night. . . ." [1] As for the ability of man to maintain his capacity for storing and adding to the knowledge of his forebears, this was assumed in the eighteenth century since it did not occur to any serious thinker to suppose that man might be capable of such powers of self-destruction.

---

[1] J. Benda, *La Trahison des Clercs*, Paris, 1927, pp. 241–42.

But there is still another conclusion which may be fallaciously supposed to follow directly from the above premise concerning the definitive qualities of human as opposed to animal nature. The deduction from this fact that man is therefore an inherently progressive animal, is elliptical in that it rests upon some such suppressed premise as the acquisition of knowledge or at any rate the things it makes possible is the *summum bonum* of human existence. Even if increase in human knowledge leads inevitably to the amelioration of human conditions; even if increase in human power increases human happiness (and neither of these assumptions would any longer command the universal assent that they were apt to be accorded in the eighteenth century) it still does not follow that because man's nature is such as to enable him constantly to increase his knowledge, he is on that account an inherently progressive creature, unless we accept uncritically the belief that human happiness is the supreme value of life on earth.

All the writers whom we have discussed in this chapter, identified morals with psychology, or rather made morals a branch of psychology. They assumed that since psychology is the discipline which gives us knowledge of human desires and wants, it is by this feature also distinguished by its capacity to solve all value problems. Reason, on this view, could not only determine the means to be pursued in order to attain a given end, but could also determine the legitimacy of the end itself. Writing either before Hume or before the implications of Hume's analysis of the role of reason had had time to be absorbed by contemporary thought, there was as yet no clear apprehension of the distinction between fact and value. Nor is this a matter for surprise, when we consider how common this error still is some two centuries after Hume. Witness, for example, the following statement by a leading psychologist of our day: " Values happen to be facts of *mental* life, and psychology, since its task is the study of mental life, is also concerned with the examination of values as parts or aspects of this mental life." [1] This was precisely the error that was so widespread in the eighteenth century. Because *desires* happen to be facts of mental life, they concluded that *values* were like-

---

[1] J. C. Flugel, *Man, Morals and Society*, 1945, p. 11.

wise facts of mental life, and accordingly that the solution of moral problems was a task with which the science of psychology was by itself competent to deal.

Since they believed further that human nature was a given constant; that the elemental, constituent desires and wants as opposed to the channels of expression into which those wants happened to run, were permanent characteristics of human nature, they concluded that there was a rationally determinable system of values of enduring validity. Consequently, progress was for them the term used to signify a process whereby man approached ever more closely to the realization of a system of values, whose eternal validity was taken for granted. The theory of progress, implicit in all their thinking, was a teleological one. The end was given; it remained constant, and the criterion of progress was the evidence of upward movement towards this given, fixed goal, which represented the satisfaction of all existing human wants. Hence the popularity of utopias, in which the details of the final goal were filled in with all the qualities of emotional vividness in the writings of the eighteenth century. This upward movement was guaranteed for Christian thinkers like Hartley and Priestley by the omnipotence and benevolence of Divine Providence. For secularists like Helvetius and Godwin, it was guaranteed by the combined belief that man was bound by the law of his nature to go on acquiring knowledge, and that this knowledge, as it was acquired, gave man increasing power to realize for all men fundamental values, which were given in the nature of things. "There is in the nature of things," wrote Godwin, "a gradation in discovery and a progress in improvement, which do not need to be assisted by the stratagems of their votaries." [1]

It would, however, be unfair to dismiss the writers here discussed on this critical note. Above all they must be credited with the realization that the application of human intelligence offered better prospects of solving the many problems that beset them than the traditional reliance on the dogmas of authority in the shape of the ancient institutions of Church and State. In their determination to rid themselves of social

[1] Godwin, *op. cit.*, Vol. I, p. 251.

evils, foremost among which was social irresponsibility and intolerance on the part of those on whom the obligation to govern rested, it is scarcely a matter for surprise that in the first flush of their enthusiasm and new found vigour, they should have exaggerated the legitimate functions and the efficacy of the method on which they relied. The faith in reason, rightly applied, and critically held, is a worthy faith. Their mistake lay both in the uncritical way in which they held that faith, and in the way in which they minimized the strength and power to resist of deep-seated and often unconscious emotional needs and prejudices, when subjected even to the solvent of the voice of reason.

CHAPTER IV

" Natural History "

NATURE, a modern writer has well said,[1] is for all the *philosophes* " the guest of honour." However much they might disagree as to what constituted the natural, the French *philosophes* at least were generally of one accord that the contemporary state of France could not be included within that category. The appeal to Nature in the eighteenth century, as so frequently in previous ages of discontent and unrest, was an instrument of reformist criticism, which sought in its hatred of what *was*, some sanction higher than that of custom and established usage as a normative principle. The great advantage of the appeal to Nature is its capacity for evoking a powerful emotional response; its great weakness is its susceptibility to extraordinarily divergent interpretations. This ambiguity may be illustrated by distinguishing three distinct senses in which the term is commonly applied in current usage, although often susceptible of more than one rendering in the same context. Of the three meanings here ascribed to the word, the first involves a statement of value, while the other two constitute statements of fact.

(i) " The consumption of a cannibal by a fellow cannibal is unnatural "—in the sense that the consumption of a cannibal by a man-eating tiger would not be unnatural. The contention here is that cannibalism is a practice which is *unworthy* of fundamental human nature. While, that is, there is no sense in saying that the consumption of humans by a tiger is unworthy of the beast, it *is* meaningful to say that a similar practice on the part of a man is unworthy of him. There is here a strong sense that man is destined for better things or is

---

[1] *Vide* Carl L. Becker, *The Heavenly City of the Eighteenth-Century Philosophers,* 1932, p. 51.

" meant " to manifest conduct of a higher standard. The term " natural " is then understood in the teleological sense that that which is the best a creature can do is the best for it. Implicit in this usage of the term is the notion of development. (Note, however, that if the word " natural " were substituted for the word " unnatural " in this example,[1] the adjective would change its meaning in general usage to that of " normal," thus making the sentence a tautology.)

(ii) " The inhabitants of Bali lead a more natural life than those of Chicago." Nature here is identified with the primitive or original as contrasted with the civilized, the simple as contrasted with the complex. As in example (i) the notion of development is implicit in this usage. (Note that while the statement in this example is a factual one, in the sense in which it is here interpreted, the word " natural " in the above statement is frequently value-charged by people who wish to imply that the primitive is more desirable than the civilized way of life.)

(iii) " ' Things that go bump in the night ' are not natural." It may be urged that in the current jargon, " natural " is here being used in contrast to the " supernatural." But whether or not the hypothetical author of the above statement believes in the supernatural, he is here using the term " natural " to indicate conformity to observed causal sequences, in contrast to the abnormal or extraordinary or that which does not accord with the previous experience of most people.

All these meanings of the word " natural " were in common usage in the eighteenth century, although they were rarely, if ever, clearly distinguished from each other.[1] The conception of nature with which we are here concerned, however, is compounded of the meanings illustrated in the above examples. For, taken together, they formed the basis of a belief in the in-

---

[1] Note, however, the following attempt at clarification of the usage of the term " natural " on the part of Adam Ferguson. " Of all the terms that we employ in treating of human affairs, those of *natural* and *unnatural* are the least determinate in their meaning. Opposed to affectation, frowardness, or any other defect of the temper or character, the natural is an epithet of praise; but employed to specify a conduct which proceeds from the nature of man, can serve to distinguish nothing: for all the actions of men are equally the result of their nature." (*An Essay on the History of Civil Society*, 6th ed., 1793, p. 15.) For a much abler and more detailed analysis of the term " natural " in the eighteenth century, cf. Hume, *A Treatise of Human Nature*, Everyman Ed., Vol. II, pp. 181–82.

evitability of progressive development, which exerted a profound influence in eighteenth-century thought. First, experience tells us that both in the human and the non-human world
there are regularities of the sequence of events of so uniform a
type as to merit the description of law (Example (iii)).
Secondly, man is not a static animal, but one in process of
development at various stages from the simplicity of his
original state (Example (ii)). And thirdly, this development
is directed towards some end, the discovery and definition of
which alone will enable us to understand Nature's purpose.
In terms of the end, we shall be in a position to understand the
necessity of the sequence of stages of development, and thus
explain the ideal law of development. Further it will provide
us with a compelling criterion of value (Example (i)).

There is, of course, nothing new in this. The student, whose
knowledge of political thought was confined to Aristotle's
Politics, would find above no idea that was not contained
therein. The stages of man's development from the individual
via the family, master and slave, " first of all a house and a
wife and an ox to plough " (Hesiod), the village, to the *polis*
or city state, are all here reconstructed. Further, the life of
virtue in the *polis* is declared to be " natural " to man, in the
sense that it represents the highest of which he is capable, and
that immanent within his very nature it represents his final
cause, even as the oak is the *telos* of the acorn. And finally,
in contrast to the " natural " is recognized the contingent, the
accidental or the arrival of results which are not essential,
corruptions of the norm, so to speak. What was new in the
eighteenth century was the extent to which the conception
was applied and worked out in detail, and this development
will now be examined.

One of the fullest and most lucid analyses of this deductive,
historical method as applied in the eighteenth century occurs
in the writings of Dugald Stewart, the Scottish philosopher
and friend of Adam Smith, at the end of the century. When,
he writes,[1] we, from the vantage point of our present culture,

---

[1] *Vide* Dugald Stewart, *Account of the Life and Writings of Adam Smith*, 1793, in
the *Collected Works of Dugald Stewart*, edited by Sir William Hamilton, 1858,
Vol. X.

look back upon primitive cultures, and contrast our own manifold accomplishments with their rude ones, we can scarcely
avoid asking ourselves the questions by what stages man has
passed from the simplicity of his primitive state to his present
complex and highly artificial one.   Whence have arisen all
the different arts and sciences which mark the civilized man?

> " On most of these subjects very little information is to be
> expected from history, for long before that stage of society
> when men begin to think of recording their transactions, many
> of the most important steps of their progress have been made.
> A few insulated facts may perhaps be collected from the
> casual observations of travellers, who have viewed the arrange-
> ments of rude nations; but nothing, it is evident, can be
> obtained in this way, which approaches to a regular and
> connected detail of human improvement." [1]

In this dearth of empirical evidence, are we then under the
necessity of giving up an enquiry of such vital import to us, as
one in which our curiosity has got the better of our powers of
satisfying it?   Stewart denies that this is the case, for while
there may be no evidence of the fact of what happened on
specific occasions, we are none the less in a position to " conjecture " what is likely to have happened, from our knowledge
of human nature, and of " the circumstances of their external
situation."   Moreover, our speculations are not purely *a
priori*, since travellers do provide us with a certain amount of
anthropological evidence, the credibility of which in its turn
often requires *a priori* speculation to supplement it.

> " In examining the history of mankind, as well as in examin-
> ing the phenomena of the material world, when we cannot
> trace the process by which an event *has been* produced, it is
> often of importance to be able to show how it *may have been*
> produced by natural causes." [2]

This is important if only to forestall those credulous minds ever
ready to ascribe to miraculous agency those phenomena of
which no evident rational explanation is easily available.

> " To this species of philosophical investigation, which has
> no appropriated name in our language, I shall take the liberty

---

[1] Dugald Stewart, *op. cit.*, p. 33.   [2] *Ibid.*, p. 34.

of giving the title of *Theoretical* or *Conjectural History*, an expression which coincides pretty nearly in its meaning with that of *Natural History*, as employed by Mr. Hume, and with what some French writers have called *Histoire Raisonnée*." [1]

The next question to arise concerns the kind of field to which this method of enquiry is most appropriate. Following D'Alembert, Stewart recommends the mathematical sciences as " very favourable subjects for theoretical history," and cites Montucla's *History of Mathematics* [2] as an attempt to " exhibit the gradual progress of philosophical speculation, from the first conclusions suggested by a general survey of the heavens, to the doctrines of Copernicus." [3] Again, one of Adam Smith's own earliest works was devoted to a theoretical history of this subject, and was one of the few manuscripts that the author did not see fit to destroy before his death. But the nature of the method is not such as to confine its use to the history of thought or knowledge. It is, above all, capable of fruitful application in the field of government and institutions. And we are fortunate to be able to avail ourselves of Montesquieu's pioneering efforts in applying the method in this field. Before him, most " politicians " had contented themselves with an enumeration of the facts or perhaps an explanation of laws in terms of the wisdom of specific legislators, or even of chance. Montesquieu, on the other hand, grasped the necessary relationship between laws and institutions on the one side and the general conditions of society on the other, and accordingly sought to relate progress in the one with progress in the others. Thus in the field of Roman jurisprudence, for example, instead of the erudition of the antiquary, we are treated to " a philosophical commentary on the history of law and of manners," based on comparative anthropology (travellers' tales), supplemented by the *a priori* method in history.

So far it is probable that modern anthropologists could endorse in broad outline Stewart's observations on method. But when he proceeds to counter the anticipated objection

---

[1] Dugald Stewart, *op. cit.*

[2] Montucla, 1725–99, French author of the first serious history of mathematics, Part I, 1758.

[3] Dugald Stewart, *op. cit.*, Vol. X, p. 35.

based on the possibility of different, or even contradictory theoretical histories, he reveals himself as peculiarly the child of his time. He first answers, reasonably enough, that if the progress outlined in the different theories be plausible, they need not be mutually exclusive, since we should have learnt not to expect a complete uniformity in any two instances of human affairs. He then makes the following damaging admission,

> "But whether they have been realized or no, is often a question of little consequence. In most cases it is of more importance to ascertain the progress that is most simple, than the progress that is most agreeable to fact; for, paradoxical as the proposition may appear, it is certainly true, that the real progress is not always the most natural. It may have been determined by particular accidents, which are not likely again to occur, and which cannot be considered as forming any part of that general provision which nature has made for the improvement of the race." [1]

Implicit in this argument is the Cartesian assumption that there is in the universe a body of fixed, general laws, which operate uniformly, and which are capable of apprehension by human reason, as a result of their fundamentally teleological nature. Nature, that is to say, operates according to purposes, which are rationally intelligible; and, provided we read the book of Nature aright, her secrets will be revealed to us. In this instance, the belief is asserted that one of those laws is a law of progressive development. Nature has so appointed the universe that the fixed order of things is one of progressive change towards the final goal of human happiness and prosperity, the attainment of which is Nature's own supreme purpose. The principal object of all Adam Smith's speculations, for example, says Stewart, particularly in his *The Wealth of Nations*, was

> "to illustrate the provision made by nature in the principles of the human mind, and in the circumstances of man's external situation, for a gradual and progressive augmentation in the means of national wealth; and to demonstrate, that the most effectual plan for advancing a people to greatness, is to maintain that order of things which nature has pointed out. . . ." [2]

[1] Dugald Stewart, *op. cit.*, p. 37.   [2] *Ibid.*, p. 60.

A similar belief he further imputes to Hume, from whose *Essay on Commerce* he quotes the following sentence, " the policy of ancient times was *violent*, and contrary to the *natural* course of things." By which Stewart understands Hume to have meant

> " that it aimed too much at modifying, by the force of positive institutions, the order of society, according to some pre-conceived idea of expediency, without trusting sufficiently to those principles of the human constitution, which, wherever they are allowed free scope, not only conduct mankind to happiness, but lay the foundation of a progressive improvement in their condition and in their character." [1]

But although Nature does operate according to this law, and although it is not beyond the power of human reason to discover, it has to be admitted that the natural order of things is not immediately apparent to him who consults the available evidence to be found in this case in the book of history. In fact, the evidence provided by the past history of our species is often of such a grim and disheartening nature that the undiscerning student might even be led to suppose that progress so far from being natural might be no more than a myth of the human imagination. Stewart himself does not argue in this fashion, but it is implicit in the sentence quoted above (p. 72), " the real progress is not always the most natural." In other words, it is easy to be misled by a study of the empirical facts of history, since one is so liable to interpret what is, in fact, merely episodic or contingent as the uniform, recurrent and characteristic. If scientific enquiry is to proceed aright, and arrive at the goal of divining Nature's true or " real " purpose, we must distinguish these events which Nature meant to happen as part of her great plan from those which were merely thrown up by hazard and unintentionally. The facts of human experience are extraordinarily rich, complex and diverse, and if through this confusing welter, the natural order is to be clearly grasped, it is necessary to prevent the merely historical from looming too large in our vision; it may even be advisable to dispense with such knowledge altogether,

---

[1] Dugald Stewart, *op. cit.*, p. 59.

if we are not to lose sight of the natural or normal course of
progressive change, which is the fundamental law.   It is,
after all, more important " to ascertain the progress that is
most simple, than the progress that is most agreeable to fact
. . ."   It must now be apparent that nineteenth-century
opinion was not without justification in regarding, as it did,
the eighteenth century as the fundamentally anti-historical
century, even if it did produce historians of the stature of Voltaire, Gibbon, Hume and Robertson.

Already in the seventeenth century, there were indications
of a conscious realization of the possibilities of the deductive
method in the field of history.   Nor is this at all surprising
when we recall Descartes' conviction that the methods of
mathematics furnished the only correct model for the discovery of certain knowledge, and his consequent contempt for
so-called historical knowledge.   Despite the virulence of the
attacks of the empiricists on the Cartesians, the *philosophes* had
absorbed more than they realized or cared to acknowledge
from the Cartesian tradition.   This influence is apparent in
Fontenelle's observations on the nature and methods of historical knowledge in his Essay *On History*.   Anyone, possessed
of reasonable intellectual powers, he wrote, should be in a
position to divine " all past history and all the history to
come," without ever having heard of a single historical
event, merely by considering the constant facts of our human
nature.

" Human nature," he would reason, " is made up of ignorance, of credulity, of vanity, of ambition, of wickedness, of a
little good sense and upright dealing over and above all that,
but of which the latter proportion is very small in comparison
with the other ingredients.   Therefore these people will be
responsible for an infinite number of ridiculous things, and a
very small number of sensible ones;   they will often fight
amongst themselves, and then they will make peace treaties,
nearly always in bad faith;   the more powerful will oppress
the weaker, and will try to give to their oppression the appearance of justice, etc.   After which, if this man wished to examine
all the varieties which can produce these general principles,
and make them function, so to speak, in every possible manner,
he would imagine in detail an infinite number of facts, either

things that have in fact happened, or quite similar to those things that have happened." [1]

This theme of a rationalistic history as opposed to the *merely* empirical one recurs again and again in the eighteenth century; and, as in the case of Fontenelle, it is derived from a faith in the existence of a common, unchanging, unhistorical human nature, always and everywhere the same. On the analogy that scientific inquiry in the field of biology is concerned not with the merely episodic or pathological, but with the normal, ideal physiological model of nature, so in the scientific inquiry into psychology, the quest was for the natural or normal man, man in general. " We should distinguish," wrote Rousseau in *La Nouvelle Heloise*, " between the variety in human nature and that which is essential to it." [2] Voltaire strikes a similar note,

> " Man in general has always been what he is. That does not mean that he has always had fine cities and so on: but he has always had the same instinct which leads him to feel affection for himself, for the companion of his toils, for his children, and so forth. That is what never changes, from one end of the world to the other. As the basis of society is always in existence, there always is some society. . . . We all have two instincts which are the basis of society, pity and justice." [3]

Again in Hume, a similar belief is expressed, with the conclusion concerning history boldly drawn.

> " Mankind are so much the same, in all times and places, that history informs us of nothing new or strange in this particular. Its chief use is only to discover the constant and universal principles of human nature." [4]

[1] Fontenelle, *Œuvres*, 1818 ed., Vol. II, p. 430.

[2] Quoted by Becker, *op. cit.*, p. 87, from *Eloise* (1810), I, 4.

[3] Quoted by J. L. Myres, *The Influence of Anthropology on the Course of Political Science*, Berkeley, 1916, p. 46, from Voltaire *Œuvres*, XI, 19, 21.

[4] Quoted by Becker, *op. cit.*, p. 95, from *Essays*, II, 94. Cf. also Bolingbroke, " There are certain general principles, and rules of life and conduct, which always must be true, because they are conformable to the invariable nature of things. He who studies history as he would study philosophy, will soon distinguish and collect them; and by doing so, will soon form to himself a general system of ethics and politics on the surest foundations, on the trial of these principles and rules in all ages, and on the confirmation of them by universal experience." (Letter iii, *On the study and use of History*, 1752, p. 53; quoted by Priestley, *Lectures on History*, 1826 ed., pp. 31–32.) Cf. also D'Alembert, *Œuvres*, 1805, Vol. I, pp. 191–92.

" Man in general," the natural man, or the essential in human nature were all of course generalizations which attempted to express an ideal, normative conception of man, not to describe the nature of any specific historical man, located in time and space. On the contrary, " man in general " was intended to furnish a value criterion in the light of which the shortcomings of contemporary eighteenth-century Frenchmen and their institutions could be measured and found wanting. And of course the history of this ideal conceptual man, the " natural " man, was an ideal, " natural " history, which consisted of distinguishing amid the morass of a myriad empirical events those which were essential (intended by Nature) to the development of the qualities of " natural " man. And in the writing of such a " history," there should be no difficulty in reconstructing on logical grounds what of significance must have happened in any particular phase, where empirical evidence is lacking. The latter on account of its very richness is apt to confuse the interpretation of the essential with the inessential, whereas our knowledge of Nature's ultimate purpose enables us to deduct with accuracy the essential, ideal history of the essential, ideal man.

> " O man," writes Rousseau, " of whatever country you are, and whatever your opinions may be, behold your history, such as I have thought to read it, not in books written by your fellow-creatures, who are liars, but in nature, which never lies. All that comes from her will be true; nor will you meet with anything false, unless I have involuntarily put in something of my own." [1]

The difficulty was that the two histories, the ideal and the actual, were rarely kept apart from one another, since the ideal was contained in the actual, and could not be divorced from it. The ideal became distinct only through the synthesis of the human reason, able to distinguish the essential and purposeful among historical events, as a result of its knowledge of Nature's own final goal. This confusion of the two histories is clearly seen in the various reconstructions attempted by political theorists and others in the seventeenth and eighteenth

[1] Rousseau, *A Dissertation on the Origin and Foundation of the Inequality of Mankind*, Everyman Translation (1947 reprint), p. 162.

centuries of the state of nature, the actual historicity of which was nearly always in doubt. Or rather, I should say, writers were apt to vary in their idea of its function between a purely conceptual, hypothetical, ideal notion, and a descriptive historical account of what actually happened, based partly on current anthropological evidence as well as on deduction. The result was that when the actual historicity of the state of nature was uppermost in the mind of a writer, the conclusion emphasized was that of the natural law of development from a natural state in the primitive sense to the present advanced state of civilization. And where the conceptual, ideal role of the state of nature loomed largest, its function was to lend support to the writers own normative conceptions of what the essential, universal and unchanging (unhistorical) nature of man was. In the first case, the conclusion drawn was one of a natural law of progress; in the second case, it was one of a natural law of universal human rights. Frequently the two ideas exist side by side in the same writer, who fails to distinguish the implicit contradiction between the two conclusions.

This confusion is admirably illustrated in the above quoted *Discourse* of Rousseau. At first, he seems to be quite clear that he is denying the historicity of the state of nature, and using it as a purely ideal figment wherewith to establish his norms.

> " It has not even entered into the heads of most of our writers to doubt whether the state of nature ever existed; but it is clear from the Holy Scriptures that the first man, having received his understanding and commandments immediately from God, was not himself in such a state; . . . we must deny that, even before the deluge, men were ever in the pure state of nature; . . ."[1]

But this need not deter us, since we are in no wise interested in the empirical facts of what happened, of whether or not there ever was an historical state of nature.

> " Let us begin then by laying facts aside, as they do not affect the question. The investigations we may enter into, in treating this subject, must not be considered as historical truths, but only as mere conditional and hypothetical reason-

---

[1] Rousseau, *op. cit.*, p. 161.

ings, rather calculated to explain the nature of things, than to ascertain their actual origin; just like the hypotheses which our physicists daily form respecting the formation of the world. . . ." [1]

(Note the attempt to bolster up the respectability of the method by the analogy with the method of natural science.)

So far so good. We are here left in no doubt as to the purely ideal, non-historical nature of the inquiry. But it is not very long before the discussion is conducted on the assumption that the attempted reconstruction of a remote past in the dearth of actual evidence is of an actual historical past. The account of the growth of inequality among mankind may be based on deductive conjecture, but for all that it does purport to give an account of what *actually* happened.

> " I confess that, as the events I am going to describe might have happened in various ways, I have nothing to determine my choice but conjectures: but such conjectures become reasons, when they are the most probable that can be drawn from the nature of things, and the only means of discovering the truth. The consequences, however, which I mean to deduce will not be barely conjectural; as, on the principles just laid down, it would be impossible to form any other theory that would not furnish the same results, and from which I could not draw the same conclusions." [2]

And then continuing his observations on the nature of the historical knowledge with which he regales us in the *Discourse*, he comments on

> " its being within the province of history, when two facts are given as real, and have to be connected by a series of intermediate facts, which are unknown or supposed to be so, to

[1] Rousseau, *op. cit.* Cf. the first draft of *The Social Contract* which explicitly rejects the historical character of the Contract, and treats it solely as an idea of right. " There are a thousand ways of grouping men together; there is only one way to unite them. That is why I give in this work only one method for the formation of political societies; although, in the multitude of aggregations which actually exist under that name, there are not perhaps two which have been formed in the same manner, and not one after the fashion that I establish. But I seek right and reason, and do not dispute over facts." (C. E. Vaughan, *The Political Writings of Rousseau*, 1915, Vol. I, p. 462.)

[2] Rousseau, *A Dissertation, op. cit.*, p. 190.

supply such facts as may connect them; and on its being in the province of philosophy when history is silent, to determine similar facts to serve the same end; . . ." [1]

The result of this confusion between ideal and actual history is apparent in the notorious opening passage of *The Social Contract*, where Rousseau proclaims the paradox that " Man is born free; and everywhere he is in chains." " Man " here is the ideal, conceptual model, " man in general," concerning whose essential nature it is asserted that freedom is an indispensable constituent. In other words, the normative claim is being made to the effect that man is born for freedom, that that represents Nature's ultimate destiny for him, and alone makes his life meaningful in terms of Nature's purpose; and in support of this normative claim, the ideal history of this " natural " man is invoked to demonstrate to us how in the primitive and earliest stages of his career, when his nature was to be seen at its purest, he enjoyed the freedom in question. In the light of the value criterion thus established, how sharp and effective is the contrast with the actual " chains " which, Rousseau alleges, are the main characteristics of man's life in the corrupt and inglorious present. But then, after the first shock of that revolutionary challenge, we read on, only to discover that we have apparently drawn the opposite conclusion to that which Rousseau intended us to draw; for, so far from proceeding to indict the " chains " which bind us, he claims instead that he thinks he is able to justify them. " How did this change come about? " he asks. " I do not know. What can make it legitimate? That question I think I can answer." [2] And the reason is that already, before the ink can have dried on the first sentence, the ideal history of natural man (the implicit idea lying behind the opening sentence), has given way before the actual history of men as they are, the idea of which is now uppermost. And in this history Rousseau sees men emerging according to a natural law of progressive development from a pre-moral, pre-social condition of life to the life of civil society, where he is able to live in the new dignity conferred upon him by the rule of law, sanctioned by the general will, and thus become the moral creature, capable

[1] Rousseau, *op. cit.*, p. 191.   [2] Rousseau, *The Social Contract*, Everyman ed., p. 3.

of freedom, which Nature intended him to be. "We might, over and above all this, add, to what man acquires in the civil state, moral liberty, which alone makes him truly master of himself; for the mere impulse of appetite is slavery, while obedience to a law which we prescribe to ourselves is liberty."[1] And thus, on this second view of history, the history of man is one of progressive development. This, perhaps, explains the fact that Rousseau is claimed as a supporter both by those who believe in a natural law of progress, and those who believe that man's career represents a retrogression from a golden age in the past.

This same two-fold interpretation of Nature's law is almost exactly paralleled in Diderot's *Supplement to the Voyage of Bougainville*, composed in 1772 (although not published until 1796) after Bougainville had published his account of his world voyage, from which he had returned in 1769. The central purpose of the *Supplement* is to hold up the life of the primitive Tahitian, and in particular his free sex life as a model of the ideal or natural, in contrast with which the life of the contemporary European, as described by the ship's chaplain to Orou, his Tahitian host, shows up in a very poor light indeed. The principles whereby the islanders conduct their lives are more natural than ours because they more truly conform to our essential and unchanging nature, to "man in general," that is.

> "Do you wish to know," asks Orou, "in all times and all places, what is good and bad? Then attach yourself to the nature of things and of actions; to your relations with your fellow creatures; to the influence of your conduct on your particular utility and the general good. You are out of your mind, if you think that there is anything, on high or below in the universe that can add to or take from the laws of nature. Her eternal will is that good be preferred to evil, and the general good to that of the individual. You may order the contrary; but you will not be obeyed."[2]

Further, Diderot asserts that this life that is natural in that it conforms to nature's laws or purposes, is to be found in the primitive rather than the civilized state.

---

[1] Rousseau, *op. cit.*, p. 16.   [2] Diderot, *Œuvres*, 1821 ed., Vol. II, pp. 383–84.

" I would willingly believe the most savage of the earth's peoples, the Tahitian who has held scrupulously to the law of nature, to be nearer to a good legislation than any civilized people." [1] The actual history of man is one of degeneration. It is the story of the decline from the age of innocence and bliss of unspoilt nature to the present artificiality of civilization.

> " Do you want to know the story in brief of almost all our wretchedness? Here it is. There existed a natural man: there has been introduced inside this man an artificial man; and there has arisen in the cavern a civil war which lasts the whole of life." [2]

And finally,

> " . . . ought we to civilize man or abandon him to his instinct? . . . If you propose to be his tyrant, then civilize him; poison him as best you can with a morality contrary to nature; make him shackles of every kind; embarrass his movements with a thousand obstacles; attach to him phantoms which terrify him; make the war in the cavern last for ever, and see that natural man is always in chains under the feet of moral man. Do you want him happy and free? Then don't interfere in his affairs: . . ." [3]

Yet, at the same time, when all this has been said, it remains true that in reading the *Supplement*, it is difficult to resist the impression that the author is also employing the Tahitian model as an example of the early stage in the life of a species which has subsequently developed to constitute a more advanced civilization. And even if we are wrong about this, it is certainly true that the primitivism which admittedly is the dominant note in the *Supplement* is amply belied elsewhere in Diderot's writings. Contrast, for example, with the present notion of an abiding, essential and universal human nature the following characteristic passage from his *Interpretation of Nature*.

> " Man praises the Eternal for his own petty views; and the Eternal who hears from the height of his throne, and who knows his own intention, accepts man's silly praise and smiles at his vanity." [4]

[1] Diderot, *op. cit.*, pp. 409–10.   [2] *Ibid.*, p. 417.   [3] *Ibid.*, p. 418.
[4] *Ibid.*, p. 212. (*Pensées sur l'Interpretation de la Nature* (1754), LVI.)

Or, more remarkable still, contrast with the principle of a fixed, unchanging human nature of the *Supplement*, the crude evolutionary theory of the species, anticipatory of Darwin, contained in his *Letter on the Blind*.[1]

The confusion in Diderot arose from the same source as in the case of Rousseau. At one moment the life of the Tahitian is considered as a factual state, illustrative of a stage in the development of mankind, and based on empirical anthropological evidence, provided in this case by Bougainville. The next moment, the life of the Tahitian is treated as a purely ideal, conceptual one, illustrative of the life of natural man, of man in general, and is accordingly essentially normative.

> " . . . in all ages," wrote a modern anthropologist, " philosophers who set out to define the *nature* of the State, have become involved in speculations about its *origin;* . . . historians in their researches into its origin, have been forced into conclusions as to its nature; . . . in both cases every belief about the nature of the State has been found to involve a belief about a state of nature." [2]

There precisely is the cause of the trouble, and it could not be more clearly stated, although Myres himself does not appear to be critical of this persistent and traditional attempt to derive norms from empirical inquiry, which was the source of so much confusion in the seventeenth and eighteenth centuries. Even Hobbes and Locke, who for their different ends were primarily interested in the purely conceptual or hypothetical state of nature, were also apt to consider it as an empirical stage of actual human history. Hobbes, for example, wrote:

> " It may peradventure be thought, there was never such a time, nor condition of warre as this; and I believe it was never generally so, over all the world: but there are many places, where they live so now. For the savage people in many places of *America* . . . live at this day in that brutish manner, . . ." [3]

This identification of the life of the contemporary savage with the life of the " state of nature," that is, of the early stages

[1] Diderot, *op. cit.*, Vol. I, pp. 328–31.
[2] J. L. Myres, *op. cit.*, p. 7.
[3] Hobbes, *Leviathan*, Everyman ed. (1937 reprint), p. 65.

of development of the human species, was important in that it implied a uniform series of stages in the development of mankind. The navigators and explorers of the Renaissance had made possible an enormous extension in the breadth of men's horizons and their knowledge of the planet's inhabitants. An ever increasing number of travellers gradually brought back to Europe first-hand accounts of life in the ancient civilizations of India and China, of the life of the African south of the Sahara and, above all, of the life of the natives of the New Indies in the West. At the same time, the discoveries of the Renaissance in the field of scholarship had enormously increased the extent of men's knowledge of life in the ancient civilizations of Palestine and Egypt, Greece and Rome, as revealed through the records compiled by historical scholars. It is no matter for surprise therefore, that in the light of the new scientific interests it should have occurred to contemporaries to look for similarities in the cultures of the past and those of primitives in the present. The Cartesian method consisted essentially in seeking for uniformities amid the apparent flux and diversity revealed by sense perception of the external world. And it was not difficult to find similarities, when the field was so vast as that of comparative cultures and the evidence was so general and vague as it often was both in the historical and anthropological fields. This characteristic interest of the eighteenth century is nowhere better exemplified than in the writings of the Jesuit, Joseph Lafitau, who after spending five years in a mission with the Iroquois in Canada, and drawing upon the sixty years' experience of a colleague among many different tribes, published in 1724 a massive two-volume work entitled *Manners of the American Savages, Compared with the Manners of the earliest times.*

" I have not been content," he writes in his Introduction, " to get to know the character of savages, and to inform myself of their customs and of their practices. I have sought in these practices and customs to find traces of the remotest Antiquity. I have read carefully those of the most ancient authors who have treated of manners, laws, and customs of peoples of whom they had some knowledge. I have compared these customs with each other, and I confess that if the ancient

authors have given me light to support some happy con-
jectures touching the savages, the customs of the savages have
enlightened me to understand more easily and to explain
several things which are in the ancient authors." [1]

And again,

" Of all forms of government, that which has appeared
most curious to me, is that of the Hurons and the Iroquois,
because it is most like that of the ancient Cretans and Lace-
dæmonians, who had themselves preserved the longest the
laws and customs which they had received from earliest
Antiquity. Although this form of oligarchic government is
peculiar to them, the manner of carrying out business is fairly
general in all the States of barbarous peoples: the nature of
business pretty much the same, as well as their public assem-
blies, their festivals and their dances." [2]

The weakness of this attempt at a comparative and deductive method lay in the fact that the inquirers were only too
apt to find what they wanted to find. Holding firmly to basic,
preconceived ideas about the essential nature of man, they
readily found evidence of it in their researches into current
anthropology; and anxious to establish similarities with ancient historical cultures, it was human enough to overlook
evidence which did not tally with the conclusions they wanted
to draw, and to emphasize such evidence of similarity as there
was. Not that contemporaries were unaware of the problem
of subjective bias in the field of social studies. Lenglet du
Fresnoy, for example, in his widely read and widely translated
Method of Studying History, admirably stated the difficulty.
Voltaire in a characteristic epigram somewhat cynically
described history as " a pack of tricks (*un ramas de tracasseries*)
that we play on the dead." While it may have been the case
that the widely differing conceptions of the " state of nature "
reflected to some extent developments in anthropological
evidence,[3] it seems more probable in the cases of Hobbes,
Locke and Rousseau that their different conceptions were

[1] Lafitau, *Moeurs Des Sauvages Ameriquains, Comparées Aux Moeurs Des Premiers
Temps*, Paris, 1724, Vol. I, pp. 3–4.
[2] *Ibid.*, p. 20.
[3] Cf. J. L. Myres, *op. cit., passim.*

largely determined by the political conclusions that they wished to establish. In the case of Lafitau, the writer, naïvely enough, makes no bones about the fact that he has a theological axe to grind, which would not permit him to find in his anthropological inquiries evidence of such a character as to jeopardize the true faith.[1]

So far we have been discussing the conception of the natural in deductive history as held by writers whose central interest was the construction of a theory of moral and political obligation. We find, however, the same kind of confusion and contradiction in the theories of the natural, manifesting itself in history, in writers whose main interests lay in other directions. This may be illustrated from the work of two of the ablest French thinkers of their time, Condillac in the field of psychology, metaphysics and epistemology, and D'Alembert, who, though primarily a mathematician, shared with Diderot the main burden of the *Encyclopædia*.

Condillac's declared intention was to " determine the extent and boundaries of our knowledge and to remake the human understanding altogether." He was therefore concerned, on the one hand, with a purely factual inquiry into the origins and development of the operations of the understanding, and then, on the other, he conceived for his task the normative one of diagnosing the errors whereby our understanding has been misled, and of prescribing the remedies whereby human intelligence might attain to its natural or maximum capacity. We are accordingly given a descriptive account of the *actual* genesis of the human understanding along strictly Lockeian lines on the one hand, and on the other an essentially Cartesian, non-empiricist, non-historical account of the normative criteria whereby we *ought* to remake the human understanding, as Nature intended us to do. The basic cause of human

---

[1] Lafitau, having in mind, no doubt, Locke's observations that there are atheists in Soldania, Brazil, and the Caribbee islands (*Essay Concerning Human Understanding*, Book I, Ch. IV, § 8) wrote, " Now what an argument does one not therewith furnish the atheists? One of the strongest proofs that we have against them of the necessity and the existence of a religion, is the unanimous consent of all peoples to recognize a superior Being. . . . But this argument falls, if it is true that there is a multitude of diverse nations, brutalized to the point that they have no idea of a God . . ." (Lafitau, *op. cit.*, p. 6.)

error, Condillac attributes to the defects and confusion that
have arisen in the language that we have developed to express
our ideas of the world.   Instead of appreciating what exactly
it is that we are doing when we make abstractions, we are apt
to mistake the abstraction for something which has actual
existence, instead of seeing that it is merely a name which we
attach to a certain amalgamation of specific qualities.   Using
words, the exact meaning of which we have never properly
thought out, inevitably entails confusion and error in our
reasoning about the nature of the world in which we live, and
is therefore productive of false knowledge.   The source of our
error will therefore be seen if we attempt to reconstruct the
conditions in which human thought originated and developed.

" Still children, incapable of reflection, our needs are all
that occupy us.   However, objects make on our senses impressions the more profound as they find there less resistance.   The
organs develop slowly, reason comes more slowly still, and we
are filled with ideas and maxims such as chance and a bad
education present them.   Arrived at an age when the mind
begins to put order in its thoughts, we still see only things
with which we have long been familiar. . . . Hence this indifference to know things to which we are accustomed, and
these movements of curiosity for all that appears new." [1]

This then is Condillac's explanation of the course which the
human understanding has actually followed.   If it be objected
that this " history " does not rest on adequate empirical
evidence, Condillac contends that the logical order of science
is the order in which things are actually generated in the
course of time, and are therefore capable of being deduced.

" Perhaps one will take all this history for a novel; but one
cannot at least refuse it probability.   I find it difficult to
believe that the method that I have followed has often caused
me to fall into error; for I have had for my object to advance
nothing save on the assumption that a language has always
been imagined on the model of that which has immediately
preceded it. . . . In a word, I have, it seems to me, demonstrated after a sensible fashion, that the things which appear

[1] Condillac, *Essay on the Origin of Human Knowledge, Œuvres*, 1822 ed., Vol. I,
pp. 343–44.

to us the most singular have been the most natural in their time, and that there has happened only that which had to happen." [1]

Accompanying this supposed actual history, however, and never clearly distinguished from it, is the ideal history of what Nature intended us to do. After making his diagnosis, Condillac proposes as the remedy that we should return to the origin of our ideas, and instead of being " prejudiced in favour of accredited opinions," we should seek to reconstitute our language without regard for custom. Our guide should always be Nature herself, for " the natural order in the thing can never hurt." " Nature has begun all things, and always aright: this truth cannot be too frequently repeated." By proceeding according to the method of " analysis " we shall be enabled to perceive the natural (normative or ideal) history of the human understanding, and this history is not the history of actual individuals, but of the ideal man in general. In Condillac too, this conceptual man, the essential, natural man raises his head in the guise of " a man that God would create."

> " It is in childhood that we are imbued with prejudices which retard the progress of our knowledge, and which cause us to fall into error. A man that God would create of mature character, and with organs so well developed that he would have from his first moments a perfect use of reason, would not find in the search for truth the same obstacles as we. . . . Thus, imagining words only after having formed the ideas, his notions would be always exactly determined, and his language would not be subject to the obscurities and to the equivocacies of ours. Let us then imagine ourselves in the place of this man, let us pass through all the circumstances in which he ought to find himself; let us see with him what he feels; let us form the same reflections; let us acquire the same ideas; let us analyse them with the same care, express them with similar signs; let us make, so to speak, a quite new language." [2]

The truth is that Condillac, like most of his contemporaries, unaware of the basic contradiction between the two concep- tions of history, the actual and the ideal, could not succeed in

[1] Condillac, *op. cit.*, pp. 340–41.   [2] *Ibid.*, pp. 365–66.

reconciling the two. If Condillac's norms for remaking the human understanding were universal and unchanging, natural in that they were available to the mind of man anywhere and at any time, then the difficulty of explaining why we should not in fact merely ape our forefathers, is insuperable. On this ideal supposition, it becomes impossible to explain the problem presented by the undeniable existence of evil and error. If, on the other hand, a purely empiricist and strictly historical interpretation of norms is rigidly adhered to, then it is difficult to see any justification for Condillac's optimism that mankind can be expected to turn over a new leaf. A natural law of historical progression is irreconcilable with an essentially anti-historical, rationalistic notion of a universal, abiding law of nature, which is accessible to all men by virtue of their powers of reason. Radical empiricist though he consistently strove to be, Condillac did not succeed in ridding himself of the Cartesian conviction that it should be possible to establish an " unassailable first principle " of a non-historical character, although he himself sought it not in the intuition of thought but in the original data of human sense experience.

While the distinction between natural history and actual history is in Condillac no more than implicit, in D'Alembert it is fully acknowledged and worked out in detail in his famous *Preliminary Discourse* to the *Encyclopædia*. The purpose of this introductory essay is to give the reader some idea of the organum of knowledge, as conceived by contemporaries, in order to explain the relations between the different subjects of the sciences, and the method according to which the *Encyclopædia* is planned. This task is accomplished from a three-fold point of view. First, our knowledge is broken down into its primary elements, and the order of its genesis is indicated. The method of deduction is here based on what is conceived to be the necessary order from a psychological point of view, much as it was conceived by Locke and Condillac. We are next given an " encyclopædic tree " of knowledge, along Baconian lines, from a strictly logical point of view, and we are specifically warned that this logical order is not to be confused with the order in which these branches of knowledge have actually been developed by the human mind in history.

> " Although the philosophic history we have just given of the
> origin of our ideas, is very useful to facilitate such a work, it
> must not be thought that the encyclopædic tree ought or even
> can be slavishly subjected to this history. The general system
> of the sciences and the arts is a sort of labyrinth, a tortuous
> path, where the mind is engaged without knowing too well the
> road to which it should keep." [1]

The contrast is between the order in which, through the workings of chance, our knowledge has in fact developed amid the
contingencies of history, and the ideal history on the other
hand of the genesis of the knowledge of a purely conceptual,
rational man, whom D'Alembert designates " the isolated
mind " (l'esprit isolé).

> " When one considers the progress of the mind since this
> memorable epoch [the Renaissance], one finds that these
> advances were made in the order that they ought naturally
> to have followed. . . . This order differs in truth from that
> which should be observed by the man abandoned to his own
> reason, or limited to communication with his contemporaries,
> such as we have mainly considered in the first part of this
> article. . . ." [2]

Finally, the essay concludes with an historical account of the
modern developments in knowledge since the revival of learning at the Renaissance. In this order, differing from the
order which " the isolated mind " left to itself would take, the
sciences of erudition came first, as a result of the immense
prestige which the achievements of the ancient classical
thinkers had acquired in contrast to the long barbarous ages
which had succeeded them. And so we are eventually brought
up to date with an account of the almost contemporary
achievements of those giants of intellectual endeavour, Bacon
and Descartes, Locke and Newton.

Inadequate as is this summary of a powerful piece of analytic
writing, it should suffice to show that in D'Alembert too the

[1] D'Alembert, Œuvres, 1805, Vol. I, p. 230.
[2] Ibid., p. 248.

old Cartesian distinction between a universal and unchanging reason on the one hand, and a developing historical order on the other, is maintained. The difficult and unsolved problem that this separation entails is that of explaining how it has come about that man has finally acquired the requisite enlightenment, or alternatively how he ever contrived to stray so far from the path that Nature intended him to follow. As an American writer has well said,

> " The emergence of science became either the product of a revelation, a sudden discovery without historical antecedents, and carrying its own certificate of validity, or it became the culmination of a process in which all evil was not really or finally evil, and all errors were necessary steps in the improvement of mankind. The harmonious order of nature emerged as a thinner version of Providence." [1]

It was more fashionable to speak of Nature than of Providence in an age whose secular temper caused it to feel somewhat embarrassed by the introduction of such an outmoded metaphysical term as Providence. To reveal the workings or laws of nature was, it was felt, in accord with the aims of the new science, whereas to attribute phenomena to the agency of Providence was, like all explanations in terms of final causes, worse than no explanation at all. Yet, that nature fulfilled an essentially similar role for the *philosophes* is evident when we see what are basically the same ideas regarding a historical law of necessary progress expressed in the older terminology by one like Joseph Priestley, who was still " naïve " enough to accept an explanation in terms of Providence. Yet, curiously enough, one of the few warnings that are to be found in eighteenth-century literature against the dangers of deductive, *a priori* reasoning in the field of history, are to be found in the pages of Priestley.

> " So important is this science of government," he writes, " that nothing can be more worthy of the study of those who have sufficient abilities, and who are friends of mankind; and the only foundation on which men who think, and who are not carried away by their own imaginations, will build any

[1] C. Frankel, *The Faith of Reason*, New York, 1948, p. 154.

conclusions is *historical facts*. Hypotheses built upon arguments *a priori* are least of all tolerable. Here observation and
experience are the only safe guides." [1]

Less surprisingly and with more justification than Priestley,
in view of the latter's practice, we find an even stronger *caveat*
in the writings of a Scottish philosopher, whose qualities have
been overshadowed by his more illustrious compatriots, Adam
Ferguson. Writing with Rousseau's *Essay on the Origin of Inequality* in particular in mind (as a footnote reveals), he says,

" The progress of mankind, from a supposed state of animal
sensibility, to the attainment of reason, to the use of language,
and to the habit of society, has been accordingly painted with
a force of imagination, and its steps have been marked with a
boldness of invention, that would tempt us to admit, among the
materials of history, the suggestions of fancy, and to receive,
perhaps, as the model of our nature in its original state, some
of the animals whose shape has the greatest resemblance to
ours." [2]

" If there was a time," he continues a little further on, " in
which he had his acquaintance with his own species to make,
and his faculties to acquire, it is a time of which we have no
record, and in relation to which our opinions can serve no
purpose, and are supported by no evidence. We are often
tempted into these boundless regions of ignorance or conjecture, by a fancy which delights in creating rather than in
merely retaining the forms which are presented before it: we
are the dupes of a subtilty, which promises to supply every
defect of our knowledge, and, by filling up a few blanks in
the story of nature, pretends to conduct our apprehension
nearer to the source of existence." [3]

As a corrective this was admirable and badly needed saying.
Yet, in stating his case, Ferguson if anything, overstated it,
and was less than fair to those who practised a method, which
as applied by most contemporaries Ferguson was certainly
right in deploring. The deductive method is not vicious in
principle, but it calls for much more caution in its use than
most eighteenth century thinkers, judging by their practice,

[1] Priestley, *Lectures on History* (1788), 1826 ed., pp. 39–40.
[2] Ferguson, *An Essay on the History of Civil Society*, 6th ed., 1793, p. 8.
[3] *Ibid.*, p. 9.

realized. Reliance on conclusions arrived at by deduction concerning past events will only be condemned in principle by those who reject entirely the scientific character of explanation in history. Such people, if they are consistent, will have to rest content with " explanation " of events in terms of " Providence," " predestined fate," " historic mission " and many forms of pseudo-explanation, unscientific indeed in that there is no means of verification available. By a scientific explanation I mean a group of empirically grounded statements to the effect that a given number of events occurred at a specific time and place, combined with another group of statements asserting a set of universal hypotheses, similarly empirically grounded, from which two groups of statements, a further statement asserting the occurrence of another event can be logically deduced. To give a simple example, if I know that a pan filled to the brim with water has been left on my lighted gas stove, and if I know further that water boils at 212° F., then I can deduce that the water will eventually pour over the sides of my pan, if not previously removed. In the interests of brevity, this is very crudely stated, but it should serve to concretize the abstraction of the analysis. And if we can predict what will happen in a given set of circumstances, we can " retrodict " [1] what set of circumstances must have gone to produce a given event, given of course the necessary data. But in the field of social and historical studies, that " given " is a very large conditional indeed. Rarely, if ever, are historical explanations capable of sufficiently complete and exhaustive statement to enable them to exhibit this predictive and " retrodictive " character. For example, if a given revolution is explained in terms of the economic exploitation of the majority of a community by a minority, and the consequent suffering and discontent of that majority, we are here clearly assuming the existence of some such universal hypotheses as " people revolt when they consider sufferings to be intolerable or when they consider they are being treated un-

[1] The term " retrodiction " has entered into general usage probably as a result of its revival by Professor Gilbert Ryle. Professor H. B. Acton, however, points out (*Mind*, 1953, p. 564) that the word was used in a similar context as early as 1895 by J. M. Robertson in *Buckle and his Critics*.

justly, etc.," but as our knowledge is insufficient to determine our meaning more precisely than is betrayed by the use of such vague and indefinite terms as " intolerable," " unjustly," etc., and as there are many other factors of equal complexity also involved, we cannot on the basis of these two groups of statements attempt any reliable prediction or " retrodiction".

In terms of the eighteenth century discussion, while agreeing with Ferguson that most of his contemporaries were inclined grossly to underestimate, if not to ignore entirely, the enormous difficulties in the way of " historical retrodiction," as against Ferguson we must agree with Hume that the method is not to be condemned in principle. Apart from the assumption that theism is the " truth " and polytheism " error," the principle of the following argument of Hume's, taken from the *Natural History of Religion*, seems to be sound.

> " As far as writing or history reaches, mankind, in ancient times, appear universally to have been polytheists. Shall we assert, that in more ancient times, before the knowledge of letters, or the discovery of any art or science, men entertained the principles of pure theism? That is, while they were ignorant and barbarous, they discovered truth, but fell into error as soon as they acquired learning and politeness. . . . It seems certain, that, according to the natural progress of human thought, the ignorant multitude must first entertain some grovelling and familiar notion of superior powers, before they stretch their conception to that perfect Being who bestowed order on the whole frame of nature. We may as reasonably imagine, that men inhabited palaces before huts and cottages, or studied geometry before agriculture; as assert that the Deity appeared to them a pure spirit, omniscient, omnipotent, and omnipresent, before he was apprehended to be a powerful, though limited being, with human passions and appetites, limbs and organs. The mind rises gradually, from inferior to superior: . . ." [1]

But Ferguson was certainly right in this that there was in the eighteenth century a great deal of " speculative " or *a priori* or " natural " history of a kind which merited only too well the criticisms to which he subjected it. From our point

---

[1] Hume, *The Natural History of Religion*, section I.

of view this development was exceedingly important, in that it gave rise to the widespread and deep-seated belief that there was at work in the universe a natural (teleological) law which had for its purpose the happiness and prosperity of our species; that this progression was destined to be realized through certain necessary (logically related) stages, and finally that by distinguishing the essential from the contingent in such information of an anthropological and ancient historical kind as we possess, we will be enabled to recognize the true (natural) universal history of mankind. To the attempt by genuine historians in the eighteenth century to write the universal history of the species in such a way as to reveal this natural law of progression, we must now turn our attention.

CHAPTER V

Universal History

MODERN WRITERS frequently distinguish universal history from philosophy of history by describing the former as a compendium of historical knowledge of the different peoples of the earth throughout recorded time, whereas the philosopher of history is concerned not simply to recount what has happened but to discover in the historical process significant trends or even laws of development. Once in possession of this knowledge, we are in a position to know what role history has decreed for us, what in fact is our appointed task according to our position on the road along which history is marching. In this way, history contributes directly to philosophical knowledge. The distinction is valuable in that it guards against the error of confusing two terms, which though closely related, are none the less distinct. Universal history should not be confused with philosophy of history. At the same time, we should not assume too rigid a distinction which may well preclude us from seeing that no universal history can be written without containing implicitly within it a philosophy of history of some sort. The writer need not himself be conscious of the fact that he has or could legitimately have any notion of any law of historical direction. Nevertheless, it will be here contended that some such assumption, however unconscious, is indispensable to the carrying through of the task of writing what purports to be a universal or world history.

A person who sets out to write an autobiography or history of himself has no difficulty in deciding his standard of relevance in selecting the material from which he may construct his narrative. His criterion of relevance is furnished by his own personality or ego, that bundle of memories, needs, desires and ideals which taken together enable him to conceive of the existence of a separate, individual self. It is the existence of this focal point, used as a constant criterion of relevance that lends unity to his narrative. If, at any point in his narrative, our author found himself shifting the focal point of his history from his individual self to any of the objects with which that self had as a part of its development identified itself, the village church, the trade guild or cricket club, for example, we would then say that the author had deserted his original autobiographical subject for a history of the church, guild or club, as the case might be. The important point is that if our author did substitute for his original project that of writing the history of a particular society or community, his new history would not stand in relation to his first one as that of a small-scale map of a large area to that of a large-scale map of a small one. His history of society, that is to say, would not be a synthesis emerging from an amalgamation of the accounts of the individuals who constituted that society. This will be at once apparent if we ask ourselves of what the history of our own country consists. Although men and women of all geographical areas within the country may be expected to contribute to the national history both as individuals and as members of many societies, the history of the country does not consist of a bird's eye view of the activities of all the individuals and societies existing within it. The inhabitants of these islands, sharing a common culture and something of a common purpose, are conscious that one level of their individual experience could be designated as falling within the definition " national," as opposed to personal, local or continental. This sphere is doubtless not easy to define at all clearly, but for all normal people this represents an important element in their experience of living. Abstracting, then, this element in our experience, the historian of Britain uses it as a criterion of relevance in selecting the kind of material he needs to construct an account of the development of the nation.

The case is quite otherwise, for the would-be historian of the world. If the inhabitants of the globe enjoy a characteristically planetary culture, they cannot be aware of the fact, since they know of no other such culture with which to contrast it. Nor is there any element in their experience at the " world " level to correspond to the existing sentiments and allegiances at the national level. For there is, as yet, no sphere in which men feel that they are co-operating in a common enterprise, actively shared and undertaken by all the members of the human family. On the other hand, the universal, " man," is an abstraction that is widely and firmly established in the minds of men. Although men have achieved citizenship, they have not as yet achieved " manship." Yet this does not prevent them from cherishing and using the generic abstraction as though it expressed an element of existing experience parallel to that expressed by the term " citizen." The result is that when men conceive the enterprise of writing the history of " man," they tend to regard it as parallel to the history of the American, the German or the Russian, being differentiated the one from the other as a small scale map is from a large one. In fact, the historian of the English, for instance, finds himself attempting to describe the conditions out of which emerged an empirically recognizable set of characteristics, which together constitute the quality of " Englishness." It is true that in the present state of knowledge, it is extremely difficult, if not rash, to generalize about the characteristics of national or continental traits, but they are at least phenomena subject to present investigation. To quote an American sociologist,

> " The assumption that a social character exists has always been a more or less invisible premise in ordinary parlance; and it is becoming a more or less visible premise in the language of the social sciences." [1]

The historian of man, on the other hand, finds himself dealing with an abstraction, which covers every known variety of human animal. Under these circumstances, the temptation under which every historian labours, of writing history to illustrate his own beliefs about the " ultimate purpose " of human life, is unavoidable for the universal historian. A metaphysical belief about the essential or true nature of man, is for him a prerequisite of those criteria of selection, without which a unitary and significant narrative would be impossible. This " metaphysical belief " may be supplied quite unconsciously, for there are many, even among historians, whose

[1] David Riesman, *The Lonely Crowd*, Yale University Press, 1950, pp. 4–5.

faith about the ultimate nature of man goes so deep that they are unaware of their uncritical assumption of what they would regard as self-evident, if not authenticated by a higher authority. In this way, then, the writer who sets out to give a strictly empirical account of universal history, is compelled to select and arrange his material according to a unifying or organizing concept that is in principle unverifiable, and normally emerges from the writer's own " philosophy of life."

If we may define universal history as the attempt to recount in outline, bare or detailed, the story of the human species arranged in a unitary, chronological sequence, then the history of universal history is an old one. Bodin, writing in 1565, included in his bibliography of writers of universal history a list of thirty-six separate entries, ranging from Moses who flourished in 1519 B.C. to Luther who flourished in A.D. 1519, and others of his own time, including Melanchthon, Bullinger and Mercator. Although Bodin did not himself attempt to emulate these writers of history on the grand scale, the publication of his *Methodus* [1] represents an important landmark in the history of historical writing in general. It is true that it is in many respects a characteristic product of late mediæval scholarship, particularly representative of the Platonism of the early Renaissance in its curious emphasis on the significance for human destiny of Pythagorean mathematics and the influences exerted by planetary constellations; yet, for all that, it contains within its peculiarly contemporary conceptions of the nature of causal relations the first recognizably modern treatment of historical method. He is, for instance, in contrast to both ancient and mediæval historians, as insistent as any modern that it is the historian's highest obligation both to his craft and to his public, to do his best to overcome the distortion inherent in his personal prejudices and predilections in ascertaining the truth of what happened in the past, and to abstain from passing judgment upon what has happened. " *Historia nihil aliud esse debeat quam veritatis et rerum gestarum veluti tabula.*"

It is this awareness of the difficulty of the problem of estab-

---

[1] Bodin, *Method for the Easy Comprehension of History*, 1556, English Translation of *Methodus ad facilem historiarum cognitionem*, by Beatrice Reynolds, Columbia University Press, 1945, The Records of Civilization series, No. XXXVII.

lishing an objective criterion of truth in the field of history
which directs his energies to the task of attempting to discover
if there are any discernible forces which operate as causal
factors in the rise and fall of empires and establish a common
direction of historical events. For possessed of such knowledge,
we would then be in a position to assess with a greater degree
of probability the general truth of any specific account of any
individual people.

> " Since, however, the disagreement among historians is such
> that some not only disagree with others but even contradict
> themselves, either from zeal or anger or error, we must make
> some generalizations as to the nature of all peoples . . . so that
> we can test the truth of histories by just standards and make
> correct decisions about individual instances." [1]

It is interesting to note that whereas by the nineteenth century
the main motive of the universal historians is the desire to
elucidate laws of development within the historical process,
Bodin is interested in such a possibility merely as a means of
establishing the general truth of historical accounts. His
interest in historical knowledge, once it is established on firm
ground, is like Voltaire's, essentially pragmatic; and this kind
of interest continued to dominate historical inquiry until well
into the eighteenth century. ". . . the greatest benefit of historical books," Bodin maintained, was " that some men, at
least, can be incited to virtue and others can be frightened
away from vice." [2]

The most constant and decisive factor in determining the
shape of the history of any particular people, according to
Bodin, is the character and manners of the people in question,
and these he believes to be determined largely by climatic
and geographical conditions. The detailed ethnological
analysis whereby he demonstrates this and shows that the
inhabitants of the temperate zone are superior to those of the
extreme northern and southern zones, is of no more than
historic interest. But although our characters are largely
shaped for us by forces outside our control, he does not deny

---

[1] Bodin, *Method for the Easy Comprehension of History, op. cit.*, p. 85.
[2] *Ibid.*, p. 9.

that education, if sustained over a long period, can to some extent modify character and habits. Consequently the door is left open for him to examine the art of government, which he believes to have played a crucial part in the rise and fall of historical empires. He concludes in favour of a monarchical institution administered in the general as opposed to the sectional interest, if a people is to frustrate the disintegrative tendencies within the State. In the last resort, however, it does seem that our own efforts can at best act only as delaying tactics, for Bodin stands firmly committed to a cyclical theory, in the classical tradition, of historical change. Empires have always crumbled away after reaching their apex of power; and so long and unbroken is this record of the succession of empire that enjoys its little day only to disappear as its predecessors, that our reason tell us that so far from this concatenation being fortuitous, it represents the working out of the Divine will. At this point, Bodin's susceptibility to the significance of numbers leads him to see in the perfect number 496 (perfect because it is equal to the sum of its factors) the crucial figure for the duration of empires.

It follows, then, that there is no room in Bodin's perspective of universal history for any notion of indefinite progress or of decay. Yet he does not regard evidences of progress and decay with equal indifference, as we might logically expect of a strict exponent of the cyclical theory. In his refutation of the prophecies of Daniel, interpretations of which still constituted a live issue in the sixteenth century, he not only defends the conception of progress in the past (though without suggesting that this will continue in the future) but roundly castigates those who sigh for a lost Golden Age. His remarks concerning the first vision of the four beasts which symbolize the number of empires before the end of the world, consist of a French patriot's polemic against Germans who had interpreted it to suggest the inevitability of the Roman Empire being superseded by a Teutonic one. Bodin argued that both on the grounds of size and strategic location it would be far more reasonable to suppose the Ottoman Empire qualified to fill the vacancy rather than the German. His discussion of the second vision of the image with the head of gold and the feet of clay, which had formed the basis of the myth of the four ages through which mankind was destined to decline from a golden age through the ages of silver and iron down to that of clay, is of greater interest to us. The original age of gold, he rejects on Scriptural grounds as being inconsistent with the evil ways we know men to have fallen into at the time of the Flood. Nor was the silver age of Rome in any important way superior to his own, as will be apparent to anyone who considers the consciences of men who could tolerate the cruel torture of the gladiatorial circuses. In contrast, the modern age, with its great discoveries in so many fields of knowledge, its voyages of exploration which have expanded the City State into a World State, above all else with its possession of the secret of the printing press, is immeasurably superior to previous ages. The following passage, in which Bodin good-humouredly explains the psychological source of the persistence of the golden age myth, also illustrates the quality of Bodin's prose.

> " Nature has countless treasures of knowledge which cannot be exhausted in any age. Since these things are so and since by some eternal law of nature the path of change seems to go in a circle, so that vices press upon virtues, ignorance upon knowledge, base upon honourable, and darkness upon light, they are mistaken who think that the race of men always deteriorates. When old men err in this respect, it is understandable that this should happen to them—that they sigh for the loss of the flower of youth, which of itself breathes joy and cheerfulness. . . . As though returning from a distant journey, they narrate the golden century—the golden age—to the young men. But then their experience is the same as that of men carried out of port into the open sea—they think the houses and the towns are departing from them; thus they think that delight, gentle conduct, and justice have flown to the heavens and deserted the earth." [1]

Mingled with many extravagances, destined very soon to be outdated, there was much in Bodin's treatise on history of enduring significance. First, there was an attempt to give an explanation in naturalistic terms of the determining factors of

---

[1] Bodin, *Method for the Easy Comprehension of History, op. cit.,* p. 302.

long term historical events in the shape of the natural character of the peoples concerned.   Secondly, he was not content merely to prescribe the duty of objectivity in historical writing, but himself strove consistently to implement it.   In an age of religious strife, of what we should to-day term the bitterest ideological conflict since the establishment of Christianity in Europe, his work is singularly free from any theological axe-grinding.   Thirdly, he was among the very earliest to espouse a theory of secular progression so far at any rate as the past was concerned.   And fourthly, although he himself did not attempt to write a universal history, he showed himself to be aware of some problems of method, in particular the problem of establishing a common and unitary chronological sequence in which to relate it from a non-national or even continental point of view.

The first major attempt to carry out what purported to be an empirical account of universal history along the lines and on the scale envisaged by Bodin, did not materialize for more than a hundred years, until in 1681 Bossuet published his epoch-making *Discourse on Universal History*.   The strength of the book lies in the magnificent way in which the vast historical panorama of the western world is unfurled before us in admirably balanced proportions down to the age of Charlemagne. (The author's intention subsequently to continue his history down to his own time was never fulfilled.)   Its glaring weakness lies in the apparent ignorance of the writer of the problem which Bodin clearly saw to be fundamental to the historian, the problem of objectivity.   This weakness which destroys much of the value of the book is a reflection of the author's own arrogance of mind and inability to doubt for a moment the absolute truth of his own cosmic faith.   Doubt of any sort concerning the nature of men's relation to God in heaven and the Church on earth was not simply weakness but impiety.

Bossuet's failure to subject to a critical examination the problems of method raised by the task he had assigned to himself, is already apparent in the brief introduction to the work. Defining the nature of universal history, he at once assumes the parallel of its relationship to lesser histories with that of a map of the world to larger scale maps of small areas.

" This type of universal history is in relation to histories of each country and of each people, what a general map is in relation to individual maps. In the particular maps you see all the detail of a kingdom or of a province in itself; in the universal maps you learn to place these parts of the world in their totality; you see what Paris or the Isle de France is in the kingdom, what the kingdom is in Europe, and what Europe is in the universe." [1]

He then proceeds to extend the parallel a stage further. Just as in our geographical knowledge we require to memorize certain large towns in relation to which we may envisage the position of the smaller ones, we need to erect similar landmarks in our historical studies in the shape of Epochs or stopping-places in order to give us a vantage point from which to survey the trend of events before and after. After this some-what cavalier treatment of the problems involved in period-ization, he proceeds arbitrarily to outline his own scheme of periodization. Although Bossuet himself attempts no justifica-tion of his scheme, it is shaped in all its essentials by his own theological teleology, which supplies the focal point or organ-izing concept of his history. The details of his three-tier periodization are readily apparent from the division of the chapters of Part I of the work. At the highest level, history is divided into three great periods: the life of man during the age when he had to rely solely on the law of nature for moral guidance; the advent of the second, being marked by the supplementation of that law by the written law received from God by Moses in the shape of the Decalogue on the tablets of stone; and the third, the period of Grace, being inaugurated by the birth of Jesus Christ. At the next level, history is divisible into seven ages, ranging from that of Adam to that of Christ; while the lowest and most detailed division consists of an expansion of the succession of ages into twelve epochs, concluding with the epoch of the Emperor Charlemagne.

This short summary of Bossuet's periodization will suffice to show the limitations of the book. In the first place, there is no attempt to take into account any evidence from the

[1] Bossuet, *Discours sur l'Histoire Universelle*, Les Meilleurs Auteurs Classiques, Paris, 1925, Introduction, pp. 6-7.

history of any parts of the globe other than those in which the Jewish religion originated and the Christian religion succeeded in taking root. Save for the intention stated in the title of the work and in the introduction, there is no universality in the treatment accorded to history.[1] The reason for this is plain. We discussed at the beginning of this chapter the need of the universal historian to supply some substitutes for the criteria of selection possessed by the national historian, for example, in the shape of the national characteristics and institutions of the people concerned. Not otherwise, we concluded, could the universal historian hope in his selection of material to construct a unified narrative in a unitary chronological sequence. In Bossuet's case, this unifying centre of interest, in the light of which the significance of all historical events was evaluated, was the establishment of Christ's kingdom in the institutional form of the Catholic Church on earth. With this firmly established as the final cause of all history, Bossuet quite rightly, according to his criteria, identified universal history with those events which had served to promote the accomplishment of that end. The history of those lands, whose peoples by their heathen beliefs fell outside the *civitas dei*, was not relevant to universal history, as he conceived it. This also is the explanation of his reliance on the Scriptures as his principal source of evidence, and his work is still an admirable if uncritical summary of the historical material contained within them.

Much as it may detract from the merits of his work, this lack of objectivity of treatment indirectly constitutes, however, the book's most important claim on our attention. Bossuet, like so many of his successors, in the art of universal history, was not primarily a historian so much as a propagandist. His intent was frankly polemical. In a world rife with the scepticism of such powerful intellects as Bayle's concerning the very existence of the workings of Divine Providence, Bossuet, in

[1] Cf. Voltaire, " She [Madame du Châtelet] complained that a man so eloquent [Bossuet] should forget in effect the universe in a universal history, and speak only of three or four nations which have to-day disappeared from the earth. . . . In the margin at the end of the discourse on the Jews is to be seen this note in her hand: Much may be said of this people in theology, but it deserves little space in history." (*Œuvres*, 1784 ed., Vol. 19, p. 367.)

the interests of sustaining a morality whose social sanction he believed to rest in a healthy respect for Providence, was determined to demonstrate the ways of Providence to man. Evidence of God's will is contained not merely in the Scriptures, not merely in the wonderful harmony of physical nature; it is equally apparent in the processes of human history, if we do but have the necessary patience and wisdom wherewith to seek it. Indeed, the *Discours* is best understood as an illustrative historical dissertation on the central theme of his Sermons in general and on the two Sermons on Providence in particular.

Although Bossuet admits that God operates in human affairs normally only through secondary causes, there is a great temptation to substitute for the thorough and painstaking investigation of these causes, which is required of the historian, a species of apologetics in terms of final causes only. Of no one is this more true than of Bossuet. It is not enough simply to recognize that

> " as in every affair there is that which prepares them, which determines the undertaking of them and which makes them succeed, the true science of history is to notice in each period those secret dispositions which have prepared the great changes and the important circumstances which have brought them about." [1]

We require the implementation of this principle. And in practice at every juncture where a causal explanation is required, we are referred to Divine agency. His introduction to his account of the rise and fall of the historic empires is typical in this respect.

> " These empires," we are arbitrarily informed, " have for the most part a necessary connection with the history of the people of God. God made use of the Assyrians and Babylonians to chastise this people; of the Persians to re-establish it; of Alexander and his first successors to protect it; of Antiochus the Illustrious and his successors to try it; of the Romans to sustain its liberty against the kings of Syria, . . ." [2]

The effect of the application of this technique when the explanation of great human disasters is in question, is one not

---

[1] Bossuet, *op. cit.*, Part III, Ch. II, p. 309.
[2] *Ibid.*, Part III, Ch. I, p. 303.

easily forgotten, as anyone who has read the account and explanation of the second destruction of Jerusalem at the hands of God's avenging instrument, Titus, will readily testify.[1] The very vividness of his masterly re-creation of the scenes he is depicting combined with the remorseless identification of the tragedy with the vindication of God's will, cannot but appal the reader who does not share the confidence of the author in the existence of a God, endowed with qualities of an anthropomorphism so crude.

Bossuet's final conclusion from his historical studies is not the less interesting for its being along the lines that we have consistently been led to expect. It is, in short, that nothing in human history is the result of chance (a word we use to cloak our ignorance), and that men fashion better than they know. Although men have their puny purposes and strive, vain creatures that they are, to execute them, the sum total of what happens is decided by no human power. The passage in which Bossuet advances this view is worth quotation both for the forcefulness with which it is stated, and for the remarkable similarity it bears to passages to be found in such different writers as Turgot, Engels and Bosanquet.

> " That is why all who govern feel themselves subject to a stronger power. They do more or less than they think, and their decisions have never failed to have unforeseen consequences. They are neither masters of the tendencies that past centuries have brought about in affairs, nor can they foresee the course that the future will take, still less can they force it. . . . Little did Alexander think that he was working for his captains or the ruin of his house by his conquests. When Brutus inspired in the Roman people an immense love of liberty, he did not dream that he was sowing in their minds the principle of that unbridled licence, by which the tyranny he wished to destroy was to be one day re-established in a harsher form than under the Tarquins. When the Cæsars flattered the soldiers, they had no intention of giving masters to their successors and to the empire. In a word, there is no human power which does not despite itself minister to designs other than its own." [2]

---

[1] Bossuet, *op. cit.*, *vide* Part II, Ch. XXI.
[2] *Ibid.*, Part III, Ch. VIII, p. 393.

Whatever blunders we may commit, however narrow and self-motivated our human designs, there is one who watches over all to secure the ultimate harmony of our conflicting individual wills according to his own designs. That is why however inexplicable and surprising particular events may seem to be, they do nevertheless continue to advance in a regulated progression (*une suite reglée*).

But Bossuet's "regulated progression" was to culminate in the supremacy of the Catholic Church, an institution which by its wholehearted devotion to the established order in France and by its persecuting intolerance of all dissenters, was provoking increasingly bitter resistance to its sway. Bossuet's reliance, moreover, on a knowledge of final causes to establish his case, ran counter to those strong currents in French thought shaped by the assumptions and methods of the new science. It is, therefore, not surprising that the *Discours* met among many with a reception not unlike that accorded the English Puritans by Queen Elizabeth, when she declared, " I see many over-bold with God Almighty, making too many subtle scannings of His blessed will . . ." [1] That, in fact, was the main burden of Voltaire's answering challenge. Bossuet had thrown down the gage to the spirit of the Enlightenment; it was only too willingly taken up little more than half a century later in the massive *Essai sur les mœurs et l'esprit des nations* (1745–1751). If Bossuet's work was an illustration of the theme of the Sermons on Providence, Voltaire's was no less on the theme of Locke's *Letter concerning Toleration*, although it was in no tolerant spirit that Voltaire castigated the spirit of intolerance.

Although Voltaire was careful to make no claim to be writing a universal history, the scale of his canvas was infinitely vaster and informed by a greater fund of historical scholarship than any previous historical work. Indeed, it still stands as one of the great monuments to human intellectual achievement. Its position in the field of history might properly be compared with that of *War and Peace* in the realm of fiction; nor, for that matter, are the respective subjects so very far

[1] The Queen's speech in Parliament, 1585, *Select Statutes and other Constitutional Documents*, 1558–1625, edited by G. W. Prothero, 1913 ed., p. 221.

removed from each other. As passionately didactic a moralist as Tolstoy, Voltaire too sought not simply to portray the doings of statesmen and generals, but to reveal the detail of customs and manners, of culture and opinion amid the variegated scene of human strivings in war and peace, in tribulation and joy. And never for a moment did he lose sight of his intention to edify. As historian, he regarded himself as one in the front line of battle in a war waged against what he regarded as the crimes, follies and superstitions of mankind. Writing his history ostensibly for Madame du Châtelet, who professed a contempt for the uncritical pettiness with which chroniclers and annalists had amassed vast compilations of dynastic and military events mixed with miracle and myth, he sought to sift the evidence to discover only the truth, and to relate only that part of it which was of importance in determining human destiny. And in the process, he appealed constantly against the wickedness of men as exposed in his historical record to the consciences of reasonable men everywhere.

> " Everything that is done does not deserve to be recorded. We shall therefore confine ourselves, in this history, only to what deserves the attention of all ages, to what may describe the genius and manners of men, to what may serve for instruction, and to enforce the love of virtue, the arts and our country." [1]

His history was to be a useful one, and by useful, he meant, " That which would teach us our duties and our rights, without appearing to pretend to teach us them." [2]   In his article on " History " in the *Encyclopædia*, he writes,

> " If you have nothing to tell us other than that one Barbarian succeeded another Barbarian on the banks of the Oxus and the Iaxartes, of what use are you to the public ? " [3]

Characteristic too of his essentially pragmatic interest in history, of his unrepentant urge to edify, is the following passage from his article on " Historiography " in the *Dictionnaire Philosophique*,

[1] Voltaire, *The Age of Louis XIV*, Introduction, *Œuvres*, 1784 ed., Vol. 20, p. 194.

[2] Voltaire, *Œuvres*, Paris, 1819 ed., Vol. XXXVI, p. 406.

[3] Voltaire, article on " History," *Encyclopédie, ou Dictionniar, Raisonné Des Sciences Des Arts et Des Métiers*, Vol. VIII (1765), p. 225.

" If an English Parliament has condemned an upright man
to torture, if an assembly of theologians has demanded the
blood of an unfortunate who thought not as they, it is the duty
of a historian to inspire in all the centuries to come a horror of
these juridical assassinations. The Athenians ought always to
have been made to blush for the death of Socrates." [1]

The supreme duty of the historian, he considered, is to teach
men the disastrous consequences which follow on their departure from the one immutable, natural law they possess:
Do unto others as you would wish to be done by. This law,
" God has sown in man to serve as a counter-weight to the law
of the strongest "; its defiance can lead only to the self-
destruction of our species " through war, chicanery and
scholastic theology." [2] With tireless reiteration, he inveighs
against the clerical forces of persecution of whatever denomina-
tion, wherever they raise their hand in the past or in the present. Intolerance, he recognizes as the chief scourge of mankind.

> " The only weapon against this monster is reason. The
> only means of preventing men from being absurd and wicked,
> is to enlighten them. To make fanaticism execrable, one has
> only to depict it. It is only the enemies of human kind who can
> say: You enlighten men too much, you write too much the
> history of their errors." [3]

It has been necessary to dwell at some length on this pragmatic, polemic aspect of Voltaire's history for two reasons. It
demonstrates that Voltaire held no " philosophy of history "
in the same way that Bossuet held a " theology of history."
That is to say, he made no serious attempt to substitute for
Providence an explanation of the whole historical process, to
establish laws of development. But it also shows that Voltaire
no less than Bossuet was compelled to introduce his own teleology in order to construct a unified narrative.

It may be objected to the first of these points that Voltaire
himself published in 1765 under the pseudonym of the Abbé
Bazin a work entitled *The Philosophy of History*. It is said that

---

[1] Voltaire, *Œuvres*, 1819 ed., Vol. XXXVI, p. 429.
[2] *Op. cit.*, Vol. XVI, p. 391.
[3] *Ibid.*, p. 383.

he was the first ever to use the phrase. But by this phrase he meant nothing more than history written " *en philosophe*," by a philosopher, that is, at once critical and rational, writing in the full spirit of the Enlightenment. In his review of Hume's history, he declared that " it belongs only to philosophers to write history." [1] In the problem of generalizing about the mechanics of historical change, he was never greatly interested. For one thing, he was generally content with a superficial explanation of the cause of events. Changes in opinion were ascribed to the gradual triumph of reason, political changes to a common-sense interpretation of human motives. But also he was too much of an empiric to be other than suspicious of a systematic periodization of history. It is true that in his Introduction to *The Age of Louis XIV*, he speaks of " only four ages in the history of the world," which he cites as the Age of Philip and Alexander, that of Cæsar and Augustus, that inaugurated by the Fall of Constantinople at the hands of Mahomet II, and finally, the Age of the Grand Monarch himself. But the basis of this periodization is, as he makes plain, no more than the effulgence of literary and artistic splendour which in certain periods seems to achieve its pinnacle, and then having exhausted itself, dies away. Nowhere does he elaborate upon this or ever attempt to write his history on this basis. Elsewhere he makes quite different suggestions, none of them altogether consistent with one another, not all of them meant with equal seriousness. For instance, in his Resumé of his general history, he says, " Three things never cease to influence the minds of men, climate, government, and religion: that is the only means of explaining the enigma of this world." [2] At the same time, he gives but short shrift to the climatic hypothesis in the form given to it by Montesquieu. Elsewhere again, he suggests:

> " It was noticed that since Charlemagne, in the Catholic part of our Christian Europe, the war of the empire and the sacerdotium was, until our own recent times, the principle of every revolution; there it is, we find the thread which guides us in the labyrinth of modern history." [3]

[1] Voltaire, *Œuvres.*, *op. cit.*, Vol. XXV, p. 513.
[2] *Op. cit.*, Vol. XVI, p. 336.
[3] *Ibid.*, p. 351.

It was then, he concludes, the history of opinion that it was necessary for him to write. But this does not prevent him from saying in a quite different context that force alone is really effective, or again in his treatment of heroes like Alfred the Great or Henry the Navigator from almost anticipating Carlyle's verdict that history is the history of its great men.

In fact, in Voltaire, for all his use of the term, we have not yet reached the philosophy of history as defined in this chapter. None the less, implicitly and embryonically it is there. Although Voltaire published no universal history as such, his *Philosophy of History* (which attempts to indicate the origins of races, religions, cultures), his *Essai*, his *Age of Louis XIII*, and his *Age of Louis XIV*, taken together constituted the most exhaustive attempt ever made by a single individual to write the entire history of humanity. Within the limits of contemporary knowledge, even the history of India, China and Japan was not overlooked, while the contributions of Islamic culture were fully recognized. Here are many distinct histories indeed, yet with a rare mastery of perspective, Voltaire contrives to give us a single unified narrative based on a single time sequence, in which every great nation seems unobtrusively and inevitably to play its appointed role at its appointed time. In the hands of so great an artist, we are almost ready to forget that the peoples whom the author has at any moment withdrawn from the world stage, have not on that account ceased to exist and to make history. The illusion that we are in fact reading an authentic account of the history of man, of a universal history of the world, is strong; and no greater testimony could be paid to Voltaire's genius. But for reasons already discussed, it is an illusion nevertheless.

Yet it is indisputable that Voltaire has given us a single History. If the subject is not " man," what, then, is the subject of his history? What is his constant criterion of relevance in his selection and arrangement of the vast material at his disposal? Is it not the unquestioned assumption of the Enlightenment in general and of Voltaire in particular, that the final cause and purpose of man in the abstract is the attainment of the supremacy of reason over emotion, prejudice, credulity and superstition? Only when men succeed in making their behaviour conform to standards of reason, will they realize their true dignity, that nobility which they are somehow " meant " to realize. The supreme goal of human effort, as dictated by Voltairean reason, is the attainment of happiness by every human being in this life here and now; the supreme obstacles to that end are the human proclivities to war, persecution, and belief in undemonstrable natural phenomena; the indispensable means to the overthrow of these obstacles are toleration, the enlightenment of the mind through freedom of thought, speech and writing, and the observance of Nature's immutable law for our species that the individual should do as he would be done by. Such were the cardinal articles of the liberal faith, and if they were held uncritically and dogmatically, their exponents could with some justification claim that the heat of the struggle to establish them in the face of the forces arrayed against them, did not permit otherwise. Voltaire at least was content to write militantly and confidently the general history of the emergence and perhaps, final triumph of these liberal values. I say perhaps, because Voltaire strikes a note of caution that was rare among contemporary writers. But wherever we choose to dip in the great history, we will find that this fundamental subject matter is always present, determining the selection and appraisal of the material. To take two obvious examples: the significance of China in world history is seen in the deism and tolerance of the educated Chinese in contrast to the warring persecution of the Christian Europeans; the Middle Ages are seen as the embodiment of the forces of darkness during which time Europe could only stand still and await through the long night the dawn of the Renaissance which eventually enabled her to march forward once more in the paths of Reason. There is, however, no truth in the widely held view that Voltaire was so blinded by prejudice as to be unable to evaluate positively any achievements in the Middle Ages. Witness, for example, his ready approbation of the work of Pope Alexander III.

Voltaire's history is ultimately a history of human progress, as he conceived it. But confident though he is that men will go on progressing, he is far from proclaiming his belief in a

historical law of progress. On the contrary, he is all too ready
to see the hand of Chance at work, whenever ostensible explanations of events are not readily accessible. Indeed, his
treatment of causation is often superficial and on this account
sometimes verges on the absurd. (An amusing illustration of
this is to be found in his *Memoirs*: " Charles VI died, in the
month of October, 1740, of indigestion, leading to apoplexy,
occasioned by eating *champignons*, and this plate of mushrooms
changed the destiny of Europe." [1]) But his progressive optimism
is tempered by an element of resignation and abiding imperfec-
tion. There are passages in Voltaire which remind us of
Pater's melancholy lines:

> " Given faultless men and women, given a perfect state of
> society which should have no need to practise on men's sus-
> ceptibilities for its own selfish ends, . . . there would still be this
> evil in the world, of a certain necessary sorrow and desolation,
> felt, just in proportion to the moral or nervous perfection men
> have attained to." [2]

Compare with this the following taken from Voltaire's Remarks
on the *Essai*:

> " Finally it is to be believed that reason and industry will
> always bring about new progress; that the useful arts will take
> increase; that among the evils that have afflicted men, pre-
> judices, which are not their least scourge, will gradually dis-
> appear in all those who are at the head of nations, and that
> philosophy, everywhere disseminated, will console a little
> human nature for the calamities it will undergo in all times." [3]

On Voltaire's reading of history, although manners and
customs differ enormously according to time and place, human
nature itself is in its fundamentals everywhere and at all times
the same. Hence it does not occur to him to question the
legitimacy of his projection of his own conception of the contemporary struggle between good and evil into the historical
past. Since Nature has implanted in the hearts of every
human creature " self-interest, pride, and all the passions,"
it should be no matter for surprise that human history at almost

[1] Voltaire, *Œuvres*, 1784 ed., Vol. LXX, p. 277.
[2] Pater, *Marius the Epicurean*, Everyman ed. (1934), p. 243.
[3] Voltaire, *op. cit.*, 1819 ed. Vol. XVI, p. 421.

any period represents "an almost continuous succession of crimes and disasters." But on the other hand, this long martyrdom of man is not the whole story; for there is also an abiding "love of order which animates in secret the human species," and saves it from itself. Even the religious impulse which has been fraught with such evil consequences over all the earth, is well intentioned enough everywhere, and the ethic, in contrast to the dogma, universally calls for peace and good will among men. Finally, he concludes in retrospect that in spite of all the retarding influences, during the period which he has surveyed since Charlemagne down to the present, " this part of the world is incomparably more populated, more civilized, more wealthy, more enlightened than it was then and that it is even much superior to what the Roman Empire was, Italy excepted." [1] And that, apart from a request to the reader to consider how much more progress even could have been made but for dynastic wars and the institution of monasticism, is his final word.

As the century advanced and the long torpor of the reign of Louis XV drew to its close, the pace of events gathered momentum. In America, the revolt of the colonies was hailed as a portent by all those struggling against the old order in Europe; the spirit of reform was everywhere in the air; even the absolute monarchs of the eighteenth century saw the wisdom of making some concessions to the aspirations of their middle classes. The infectious optimism thus engendered is, as we would expect, reflected in the writings of the latter part of the century; the note of caution, the element of resignation that we had occasion to notice in Voltaire, gave way to an optimism, not more robust or courageous, but more arrogant. That tide in the affairs of men of which Shakespeare spoke was hypostatized into the march of history; to the concept of progress was increasingly conjoined the notion of inevitability. Interest in and speculation about history, stimulated in part no doubt by the work of Voltaire as well as by the signs of approaching revolution spread rapidly. Turgot in France, Priestley in England, Kant in Germany began consciously to philosophize about the historical process as a whole; began

---

[1] Voltaire, *op. cit.*, p. 343.

to strive to discern laws of development.   In the craft of history writing proper, Britain alone produced contemporaneously such pioneering giants as Gibbon, Hume and Robertson.   In France, however, the centre of historical interest continued to focus on the wide sweep of general, if not universal history. With the exception of the Abbé Raynal's *History of the establishment of European commerce in the two Indies*, which, as Voltaire pointed out, contained as much political pamphleteering, as it did of history, two of the most widely circulated historical works of the last quarter of the century were the Chevalier de Chastellux's *De la Félicité Publique*, published in 1772, and Condorcet's *Sketch of an Historical Picture of the Progress of the Human Mind*, published in 1793.

Although Chastellux intended only, as his title indicates, an essay on the public welfare, illustrated from the facts of other nations and times than his own, in effect his work does not differ substantially either in form or subject-matter from the more ambitious undertaking (again judging by the title) of Condorcet.   Both writers, too, as one might expect from two such ardent admirers of Voltaire, wrote from an almost identical standpoint.   The master himself accorded Chastellux's work an unusually warm reception, and we are fortunate in possessing his carefully annotated edition of the work, in which the criticism consists largely of gentle rebukes restraining the exuberance and naïve under-estimation of difficulties frequently met with in Chastellux's pages.   " It seems to me that it is a crime of *lèse-humanité*," wrote Chastellux, " to relate an atrocious fact without consigning it to the horror of posterity." [1]   And the aged but indefatigable champion of the cause of "humanity," cheering on the younger apostles, comments in the margin " Bravo! Bravo! "   And again:

> " It is time to take in hand the too long neglected cause of humanity, to consider the people in the State, and to separate the idea of happiness from that of glory and success.   Wherever I see trophies, I shall think then of the blood they have cost: wherever I shall be shown vast and magnificent edifices, I shall deplore the sweat that has gone to their construction." [2]

[1] Chastellux, *De la Félicité Publique*, Paris, 1822 ed., Vol. I, p. 84.
[2] *Ibid.*, p. 57.

He is, in short, going to write history *en philosophe*, in the spirit of the Enlightenment.

To write in that spirit means for Chastellux to start from the conviction that all men enjoy the natural right of equality. The normative rule which he lays down for all governments is that they should pursue not the greatest happiness of their societies but the greatest happiness of the greatest number.

> " Our surprise," he says, " has diminished, but our affliction has increased, when we have assured ourselves that the governments the most esteemed, the legislation the most revered, have never held to this unique goal of all government: the greatest happiness of the greatest number of individuals." [1]

This is the fundamental assumption which he makes concerning the ultimate purpose of our earthly life; and this it is which determines the teleology of his historical synthesis. A general history is for him a history of human happiness, with the principle of equality taken for granted. His criteria for happiness are of a strictly material kind; and they are carefully defined. We must, he says, first resolve what is the maximum amount of work a man can do without injury to his well-being, and what is the minimum he must do for the necessities to preserve his life at a reasonable standard of comfort. This done, we are then in a position to know how much time a man has at his disposal without imperilling either his well-being or his subsistence. If the sovereign makes on his labour power economic demands in excess of this marginal surplus, then we may know at once that the majority of men in that society are unhappy.[2] Thus equipped with an embryonic labour theory of value and a crudely utilitarian conception of the public well-being, Chastellux is in a position to write his history of the public happiness. He is not wholly unaware of the objection that these assumptions will entail a flat, two dimensional history, in which the dynamic of history is assumed not to apply to the notions of what constitutes public happiness, by which fixed standards we are to evaluate all other historical events. But he does not attempt seriously to defend his position, since he regards it as self-evident that such phenomena

[1] Chastellux, *De la Félicité Publique, op. cit.*, Vol. II, pp. 70–71.
[2] *Ibid.*, Vol. I, p. 60.

as human ferocity, civil wars, plagues, famines, etc., must at whatever stage of human history they occur, be the symptoms of dire human suffering.

> " There is, therefore," he concludes, " nothing to prevent us from judging the ancients as we judge each other, and from applying to these great objects the best known principles of morals and politics." [1]

Few eighteenth-century historians paid less heed than Chastellux to Montesquieu's judicious warning,

> " To carry over into remote centuries all the ideas of the century in which one lives, is among the sources of error that which is the most fertile." [2]

In his historical survey he confines himself to Europe and, in the early period, to the cradle of European civilization in the Middle East. He begins by examining the records of the " old monarchies " of the Egyptians, the Assyrians and the Medes, and concludes that all governments had their origin not in any contract or treaty, but in force, oppression and guile. In the first ages of the world, institutions are mainly characterized by despotism and superstition, while all change is almost invariably the outcome of brigandage or usurpation. In the case of the Egyptians only does he attempt a direct application of his happiness test. After estimating the total population at a maximum of seven millions, and allowing for an army of over 400,000 together with a huge number of priests, he concludes that the whole of the net revenue was consumed by the king, the priests and the military; and that, accordingly, the people were unhappy. When we come to the age of Greece, " we are compelled to admit that what is called the beautiful age of Greece was a time of torture and punishment for humanity," [3] largely on the grounds that they massacred their prisoners, although the institution of slavery is itself sufficient to prove the case against the Greeks. The civilization of Rome stands similarly condemned on the basis of their ferocious cruelty to

[1] Chastellux, *De la Félicité Publique, op. cit.*, p. 161.
[2] *Montesquieu, De l'Esprit des Lois*, Book XXX, Ch. XIV, Classiques Garnier (1949), Vol. II, p. 314.
[3] Chastellux, *op. cit.*, Vol. I, p. 86.

their prisoners, as displayed in their circuses and games. Indeed, he " cannot maintain, in a matter of such a nature, the calm necessary for discussion." [1] He does, however, appreciate their achievements, and indeed in contrast to the Middle Ages, these days of classical times shine brightly.

> " Let one think of the darkness that has covered the earth from Constantine to the Medicis: a night of twelve hundred years has succeeded the brilliant days of Athens and Rome; . . ." [2]

The difficulty with this kind of progressive interpretation of history is, as Comte observed of Condorcet, that we are left with a standing miracle on our hands. If the history of humanity is one of travail and suffering, and if " all that is participates in what has been: . . . most of our modern régimes originating in the barbaric centuries and the unhappy eras . . ." [3] what grounds have we for believing that men will ever change? Neither Chastellux nor Condorcet provide a satisfactory answer to this problem. Convinced as they were of the unlimited power of reason, of " lumières," it sufficed for them that the miracle had occurred; and if anyone doubted it, then let them examine a little more closely the intellectual awakening of the Renaissance and its prodigious fruits in every aspect of Western life. On such an historical interpretation, the problem of periodization was of the simplest. There was the long age of darkness, and there was the age of light. The Stygian waters dividing the two were the sixteenth and seventeenth centuries; and the ferrymen who brought humanity to the Elysian fields were Bacon, Descartes, Newton and Locke. Chastellux's own metaphor was actually that of Noah loosing the dove after the universal deluge.

> " Weary of slaughter, of superstitition, of errors," he writes, " the peoples finally cease to close the ear to reason, . . . The words of tolerance, liberty, agriculture, industry are the first to be pronounced. They are making themselves heard over all Europe, and are resounding unto America. It is the seed thrown at hazard, which in some places is borne by the winds, but which in others bears fruit and prepares rich harvests:

[1] Chastellux, op. cit., p. 197.   [2] Ibid., Vol. II, p. 51.   [3] Ibid., p. 285.

happy progress the reality of which we have recognized, and
have wished to present as an object of consolation and encouragement to our contemporaries." [1]

When finally we come to examine the work of Condorcet,
we find that we have already anticipated much of what he
had to say. This is inevitable, since no single writer of the late
eighteenth century more fully embodied what Hazlitt was to
call " the spirit of the age." In Condorcet, all the streams of
the Enlightenment united in a single impassioned flow. A
shining faith in the perfectibility of man, in the inevitability
of historical progress, in the natural rights of man founded on
human reason, in the power of scientific methods to transform
man's knowledge of and control over himself and his society—
these were all among his profoundest convictions. In him
too we find at its most pronounced the tendency to reconstruct
a progressive ideal or conjectural history, the tendency to
utopianism, the tendency to interpret history as a struggle
between light and darkness in the shape of the forces of reason
struggling against those of clerical superstition. If Voltaire
was the Messiah of the Enlightenment, Condorcet was its
foremost disciple, saint and martyr. For the serenity of his
faith, his essential gentleness and nobility of character remained
inviolate even when at the end the forces which he had done
so much to evoke, were so cruelly turned upon himself.

Although Condorcet informs us that he is going to sketch
the history of the progress of the human mind, like Chastellux,
he does, in fact, confine himself to the history of the Europeans.
At first sight, he would appear to differ from Chastellux in the
detail of his systematic periodization. Condorcet divides his
history into ten periods: the first three, preceding the invention of alphabetic writing, are largely conjectural, and consist
of the formation of societies, the pastoral stage of development,
and the agricultural stage; there follow the ages of Greece
and Rome, the Middle Ages, divided into two by the Crusades;
then comes the period from the invention of printing to
Descartes, that from Descartes to the foundation of the French
Republic; and finally, the age of future progress. It will be
apparent from this summary that these divisions follow no

[1] Chastellux, *op. cit.*, p. 233.

consistent principle; that they are, in fact, no more than convenient stopping places in time. What purports to be the determining factor marking the beginning or end of an era is sometimes an economic phenomenon, sometimes a religious one, at others a political one. The effective periodization which determines the order and significance of the narrative is as simple as that of Chastellux. There is the age of barbarism, marked by despotism and ignorance, and there is the age of Enlightenment, when reason at last begins to be socially effective; and the dividing line is that which marks the beginning of the eighth period, according to the formal periodization, namely, the invention of the printing press, which for the first time enabled the philosophers to have direct access to the mass of mankind.

The really interesting and largely novel explanation of the nature of social change in history is advanced almost incidentally by the author in his attempt to meet the difficulty created for him, as for Chastellux, by the type of periodization discussed above. If history is the account of suffering and error, how is the suddenly acquired capacity for enlightenment and indefinite perfectibility on the part of men to be explained? Condorcet was aware of the inadequacy of ascribing such momentous developments merely to a technical invention, much as he appreciated its importance. The explanation that he advances, in that it emphasizes the gradual, developmental nature of progress, contrasts with his own actual writing of the history of that progress, where the *de novo*, cataclysmic aspect is much more in evidence. This explanation of historical change is, however, of remarkable interest in its own right, in view of later developments. We have, for instance, only to substitute economic for intellectual criteria, capitalist for priest, to see at once the embryonic affinities with subsequent Marxist doctrine.

The capacity of the individual mind to commit error, he argues, is as much a necessary and characteristic constituent of its make-up, as the capacity to reason correctly and discover truth. Now social progress consists of the elimination of error by a large number of individuals grouped together to form a society; and as nothing can break the continuity of the chain of history, " each present instant depending on what the preceding instants offered," it follows that the propagation of error among peoples is historically necessary in the sense that it is an indispensable condition without which the law of historical progress would not be fulfilled. We can go further than this even, and assert that " according to the general laws of the development of our faculties, certain prejudices had to arise at each period of our progress." [1] The initial committal of error, then, is necessary, but why does it persist so stubbornly? Why is it that " men still maintain the prejudices of their childhood, those of their country and their century, long after they have recognized all the truths necessary for the elimination of those errors "? [2] The reason is that everywhere and at all times the degree of enlightenment possible for any individual is determined by the profession he pursues. Thus reason and truth suffer perpetually at the hands of the philosophers themselves, who are blinded by intellectual vested interests; at the hands of the less intelligent group in society who are by nature conservative; and, finally, but by no means least, at the hands of " certain accredited or powerful professions " which have a vested material interest in opposing the forces of reason. It is above all in the exploitation or rather guileful deception of the mass of men by this third group, and in the struggle of the victims to escape from their intellectual bondage that Condorcet sees the decisive determinant of significant historical change. And we are left in no doubt as to who constitute the guilty party. They represent too permanent a feature of the sociological landscape for their significance to go undetected.

> " I mean that separation of the human species into two portions: the one destined to teach, the other to believe; . . . This distinction, of which, at the end of the eighteenth century, our priests still expose to us the remnants, is found among the least civilized savages; . . . It is too general, it is met with too constantly at every period of civilization, for it not to have a base in nature itself." [3]

[1] Condorcet, *Esquisse d'un Tableau Historique des Progrès de l'Esprit Humain*, edited by O. H. Prior, Paris, 1933, p. 10.
[2] *Ibid.*
[3] *Ibid* . pp. 18–19.

It is always to the interest of this class to keep men in essential
ignorance in order to rivet more firmly the chains by which
they keep them in tutelage.

> " These castes took possession of education, in order to
> fashion man to support more patiently chains identified, so to
> speak, with his existence, in order to take from him even the
> desire to break them." [1] *

The priests, however, in playing this Iago-like role, only
appear to the superficial observer to be playing an unprogressive role. In actuality, the role which history has allotted
them, is as necessary to the working out of the law of progress,
as the more obviously progressive role of the contemporary
liberal intellectuals. It is true that Condorcet is not anxious
to stress this point, but it is more than implicit in much of what
he says. For instance,

> " Then it will be seen that this stormy and painful passage
> from a crude society to the state of civilization of enlightened
> and free peoples, is not a degeneration of the human species,
> but a necessary crisis in its gradual march towards its absolute
> perfection." [2] *

The central thesis of this chapter has been to show by an
examination of the attempts to write what is generally regarded
as universal history during this period, some sort of philosophy
of history was always implicit in the mind of the writer,
although it was not yet consciously formulated as such. In
the case of Condorcet, it might appear that it had finally become quite explicit and fully conscious, but that would be an
overstatement of the case. Scattered passages have been
selected from the *Esquisse* in order to emphasize their significance in the light of subsequent developments. It must also
be stated that the extracts which have been asterisked cannot
with certainty be attributed to Condorcet's own pen.[3] There
is nevertheless quite sufficient evidence in the original text to
warrant the interpretation here given, although it does not at

[1] Condorcet, *Esquisse d'un Tableau Historique des Progrès l'Esprit Humain, op. cit.*,
p. 43.
[2] *Ibid.*, p. 26.
[3] For a discussion of the textual problems and the possibility of interpolations
in the original MSS., *vide* O. H. Prior in *op. cit.*, pp. xxiii–xxiv.

all follow that this aspect of his work would have loomed so large in Condorcet's own mind. There is no doubt that Condorcet had begun consciously to attempt on the analogy of the methods of the natural sciences to predict the inevitable course of the main stream of historical events, as the following passage shows.

" If man can predict, with an assurance almost complete, the phenomena of which he knows the laws; if, even when they are unknown to him, he can, according to the experience of the past, foresee, with great probability, the events of the future; why would one regard as a chimerical enterprise, that of tracing, with some verisimilitude, the picture of the future destinies of the human species, according to the results of its history? The only foundation of belief in the natural sciences, is this idea, that the general laws, known or not known, which regulate the phenomena of the universe, are necessary and constant; and by what reason would this principle be less true for the intellectual and moral faculties of man, than for the other operations of nature ? " [1]

The detail of Condorcet's own predictions we shall have occasion to discuss in the following chapter. Here we need only observe that according to his half-formed law of human progress, the present stage of human enlightenment guaranteed for Condorcet that the future of humanity would be immeasurably brighter than the past. The men of his generation were, he believed, fortunate not only in living at the time of one of the greatest revolutions in history, but also in possessing the knowledge which enabled them to recognize the peculiar significance of that revolution. It behoved them, therefore, to make good use of that knowledge in order to ensure that the promised happiness would be purchased at the minimum sacrifice, and disseminated as widely and rapidly as possible.

[1] Condorcet, *op. cit.*, p. 203.

CHAPTER VI

The Eschatology of Progress

CONDORCET, as we have seen, did not confine himself to delineating the past; he made so bold as to predict the future. His tenth epoch was the epoch of future progress. In this, as in so much else, he was the child *par excellence* of his time. There never was a period when intelligent students of politics felt themselves more completely out of sympathy with Milton's memorable advice to them in the *Areopagitica*.

> " To sequester out of the world into Atlantic and Utopian politics, which never can be drawn into use, will not mend our condition; but to ordain wisely as in this world of evil, in the midst whereof God hath placed us unavoidably." [1]

The history of utopia in the shape of an ideal commonwealth, in the light of which existing conditions may be measured, satirized and eventually reformed, is an old one reaching back at least as far as Plato's *Republic*. Following the example of More's celebrated *Utopia*, the seventeenth century, as Milton's words testify, saw a spate of accounts of fictitious states, which included Campanella's *Civitas Solis* (1623), Bacon's *New Atlantis* (1626), Harrington's *Oceana* (1656), Vairasse d'Allais' *The History of the Sevarites or Sevarambi* (1675), Jacques Sadeur's *A New Discovery of Terra Incognita Australis* (1693), Fenelon's *Télémaque* (1699), not to mention many other lesser known works on the model of Vairasse in particular. What is peculiar, however, to the works of this *genre* which appeared in the late eighteenth century is their setting. Unlike their predecessors, they are not set in " noplace," nor in remote or fictitious parts of the globe, nor in the past; they are deliberately set in the future. In the case of Mercier and

[1] Milton, *Areopagitica, The Prose Works*, Bohn ed., 1878, Vol. II, p. 74.

Rétif de la Bretonne, utopian works appeared under the titles of *The Year* 2440 and *The Year* 2000 respectively; while Condorcet, Volney and Godwin all describe in some detail the state of things to come.

Condorcet would, it is true, have repudiated any suggestion that he was engaged on a merely imaginative creation of how the world would be, if it were to be refashioned according to his wishes. For him, the " tenth epoch " of humanity represented a serious, if necessarily imperfect attempt at a scientific prediction on the basis of our knowledge of the past, of what course future history was in its broad outlines most likely to take. But in fact, Condorcet's attempted prediction was no different in kind from the many other contemporary daydreams of a golden future time. They testify not to the success of attempts to induce general laws of development in the historical process, but to the felt needs and wish fulfilments of the writers concerned, to the intensity of their frustration in the present, and to the urgency of their nostalgia to escape from it into the future.

De Tocqueville, writing more than half a century after the Revolution, observed of the pre-revolutionary writers on politics that they were completely divorced from the actual responsibilities of political administration. In contrast to England, he wrote,

> " in France the political world remained as one divided into two separate provinces, with no mutual intercourse between them. In the first, they administered; in the second, they established the abstract principles on which all administration ought to have been founded." [1]

It was this political frustration combined with a consequent failure to appreciate the complexity or the depth of the roots which political and social institutions necessarily have in the culture of a mature society, which explains the superficial aridity of much of the pre-revolutionary political writing.

After steeping oneself in the vapid pages of the pre-'89 utopians, it is with new-found sympathy that one turns to

[1] De Tocqueville, *L'Ancien Régime*, edited and translated by G. W. Headlam, 1925, p. 152.

Taine's brilliant indictment of what he termed *l'esprit classique* of the literary precursors of the revolution. Even the fiery polemic of Burke becomes more intelligible. Moreover, there is in Burke's pages the heart of the matter.

> " The science of constructing a commonwealth, or renovating it, or reforming it, is, like every other experimental science, not to be taught *a priori*." [1]

The trouble with Burke is that the insight he showed in his study of the political defectiveness of *a priori* utopianism is clouded over by the virulence of his partisanship. Such passages as the following:

> " We are not the converts of Rousseau; we are not the disciples of Voltaire; Helvetius has made no progress amongst us. Atheists are not our preachers; madmen are not our lawgivers." [2]

—invective of this order reveals the essential impotence of the understanding to grasp the causes of that which it fears. Burke's fears may have been well grounded, but he did not stop to inquire into the reasons why intelligent and sensitive men could have erred in their understanding of the true nature of the inner structure of political and social institutions. An uncontrolled, emotional overflow is no substitute for painstaking analysis.

Our understanding of the nature of the intellectual sickness of the *ancien régime* may be assisted by an analogy with the mental life of the individual. A frustrated person or one who has lost confidence in his power to make an adequate adjustment between his own needs and his limiting environmental possibilities, may compensate for his discouragement by seeking refuge in private phantasy. Withdrawing from the distressing task of wrestling with the actualities of his existing situation, he finds relief in diverting his externally dammed energies into the projection of an image of an idealized self, wholly emancipated from the frightening restrictions and

---

[1] Burke, *Reflections on the Revolution in France, Works,* Bohn ed., 1867, Vol. II, p. 333.

[2] *Ibid.,* p. 358.

disappointments actually experienced. Once this process of phantasy escapism has taken a firm hold, the gulf between actuality and the spurious ideal rapidly widens, since the withdrawal inevitably aggravates the individual's inability to cope with the external difficulties, which in turn drives him to take ever deeper refuge in the compensatory triumphs of phantasy. Moreover, the contrast between the deteriorating, external situation and the idealized image of it, grows increasingly painful. Present actualities occasion the deepest gloom; while the memories of past failure are no less humiliating. The present is something to escape from; the past something to expunge; the future, from the urgency of present frustrated needs, something devoutly to be wished, and yet from the nature of the case, something ever receding.

The parallel breaks down, perhaps, when we pass beyond diagnosis, and attempt to prescribe a remedy for this morbid condition. For in the case of the individual, therapy, though doubtless emotionally painful, would not normally require a surgical operation. While in the case of the pre-revolutionary reformist intellectual in France, the necessary catharsis could not be achieved under existing political conditions. As de Tocqueville has shown, Bourbon despotism had by the eighteenth century left little remaining of the ancient liberties and self-governing powers of the French people. If it was an exaggeration to say, as Law did, that France was governed by thirty *intendants*, it is yet true that France of the *ancien régime* was governed by a comparatively efficient and highly centralized bureaucracy. This new class had every incentive to compensate with privileges those whose powers and responsibilities they had usurped. For the institution of privilege possessed the additional advantage of increasing the existing animosities and jealousies dividing the separate classes of the nation, whose unity alone could have proved fatal to the reigning despotism. It was all very well for Burke to pontificate in the very different political conditions prevailing in England. Had he been cut off from all share in the responsibilities of government, as would have been his lot across the channel, his case would have been far otherwise. Given the contemporary conditions in France, it is not difficult to under-

stand the attitude of her political intellectuals. Their political
thought evinced some of the symptoms of political immaturity
and a lack of realism, but the degree of that distortion was the
direct outcome of the very real evils of the *ancien régime* in
France.

So far we have interpreted this belief in a future paradise in
terms of present emotional needs. But there was another and
more profound reason why Burke, for instance, was so wide of
the mark when he declared, " People will not look forward to
posterity, who never look backward to their ancestors." [1]
The belief in posterity combined with a detestation of the past
served also to fill a profound metaphysical need. The parallel
between the Christian eschatology and the eschatology of
progress in the religion of humanity has been so brilliantly
portrayed by Carl Becker,[2] that any subsequent writer must
remain deeply indebted to him.

There cannot be many human beings who, in those rare
moments when they contemplate the universe and their own
comparative insignificance succeed in remaining immune
from feelings of wonder and awe. When Margaret Fuller was
reported as saying that she accepted the universe, Carlyle is
reputed to have commented, " By God, she'd better ! " But
the lady's determination is interesting as evidence of the difficulty that some people find in accepting the human situation
for what it, at any rate ostensibly, is. Earthly human life is
comparatively insignificant in relation to the vast scheme of
things in which it is set; in relation to time it is no more than
a fleeting breath. Yet the conviction or at least, the hope,
persists that there is some more ultimate, transcendental
purpose fulfilled by our ephemeral strivings, and accordingly,
to find some such support, speculation begins.

For many centuries this need has been filled for most Western
peoples by the transcendental explanation of the human
drama provided by orthodox Christian theology. While
asserting the full moral responsibility of the individual for his
actions, it yet denied that the real significance of human

[1] Burke, *op. cit.*, p. 307.
[2] *Vide* Carl L. Becker, *The Heavenly City of the Eighteenth-Century Philosophers*,
1932, Ch. IV, " The Uses of Posterity," *passim*.

action was to be looked for in this life. All merely human action was necessarily imperfect, the life of man necessarily corroded by sin and suffering, but by the grace of the vicarious sacrifice and expiation through the Son of God, the sin of mortals was redeemed so that ultimately they could hope to be admitted to an eternal life beyond the grave, where the immeasurable love of God would finally be revealed. Such a faith raised the human struggle to a high dignity, gave it enduring significance, while to the participants in the struggle it gave ground for hope in the midst of despair. As such, it was not to be supposed that it would be lightly superseded in the power of its hold over men's imagination. If the *philosophes* were to succeed in their attempt to transfer mens' aspirations from the eternal to the temporal, it was necessary that they should at least continue to affirm that life was not devoid of purpose and that there was reasonable hope of that purpose being brought to an earthly fulfilment. That they did in fact continue to affirm that the human story is one with a happy ending, is a tribute not to their insight into the psychology of mass receptivity of ideals, but to the fact that their own fundamental assumptions had been irrevocably shaped by the very tradition they sought to repudiate. To none of the *philosophes* did it occur to question the purposefulness of life; but for them that purpose was destined to be realized not through the atonement of another, but through man's own capacity for perfectibility, while the final treasure was to be laid up not in heaven but on earth. If there could be no rational foundation for celestial immortality, there surely was for the earthly immortality of our own species. For Diderot, posterity is " l'Être qui ne meurt point," and therefore to live in the eyes of posterity is to achieve the only kind of immortality open to us and worthy of our aspiration. The religious quality of that faith in the temporal future of mankind is perhaps most clearly seen in action in the nature of Condorcet's *apologia pro vita sua* in the face of death. It is in the contemplation of future progress that the philosopher finds his salvation.

> " It is there that he finds the true recompense of virtue, the pleasure of having achieved a lasting benefit. . . . This contemplation is for him a refuge, where the memory of his perse-

cutors cannot pursue him; where, living in thought with man re-established in his rights as in his natural dignity, he forgets that which greed, fear or desire torment and corrupt; . . ." [1]

When the valiant, reasonable ones die at the hands of the avaricious and the superstitious, when the *philosophe* is hounded to his death by the forces of tyranny or priestcraft, faith in the cause of reason demands assurance that the dead shall not have sacrificed themselves for nothing. And so in Reason's court, Posterity was conveniently though sincerely invoked as the final seat of judgment before which Right would be vindicated.

> " O posterity," prayed Diderot, " holy and sacred! Stay of the unhappy and the oppressed, thou who art just, thou who art incorruptible, who avengest the good man, who unmaskest the hypocrite, who draggest down the tyrant, may thy sure faith, thy consoling faith, never, never abandon me! Posterity is for the philosopher what the other world is for the devout ! " [2]

In fine, future generations of men constitute at once our refuge in the present and our ultimate judges. The fact that *our* actions in the present may shape *their* destiny in the future provides for men the only purpose that they need with which to make of life a significant and meaningful event. The fact that those future generations will be fully " enlightened " means that our norms in the present must be shaped by the knowledge of the obligations we are under to pass successfully before the bar of their judgment. One of the best statements of this view is to be found in the writings of another pre-revolutionary figure in our own century. The reader of Chekhov may recall how desperately the three sisters, in the play of that name, long to escape from the tediousness of their life in the present in a small provincial town to a life in the future in Moscow, where they are convinced that life will be completely transformed for them. The pathos of this illusion is admirably brought out by the author, but in the process one of the characters, Vershinin, is made to say,

---

[1] Condorcet, *op. cit.*, p. 239.

[2] Quoted by Morley, *Diderot*, 1886, Vol. II, p. 284, from Diderot, *Œuvres* (1876), Vol. XVIII, pp. 100–101.

" After two or three hundred years, after a thousand—the actual time doesn't matter—a new happy age will begin. We, of course, shall not take part in it, but we live and work and even suffer today that it should come. We create it—and in that one object is our destiny and, if you like, our happiness." [1]

There is no doubt of the compelling power of this mirage which persists so stubbornly in spite of the disillusion of the successive generations of those who hunger and thirst after righteousness and are yet unable to find any consolation in the present.

So far we have confined ourselves to a discussion of the psychological and metaphysical roles of the eschatology of progress. It remains to inquire what was the nature of this " last state " ($\check{\epsilon}\sigma\kappa\alpha\tau\sigma\varsigma$) of humanity. Whither was progress leading men? To review the different pictures that were constructed of the future of human society in the second half of the eighteenth century would be a tedious and profitless task. Yet while there is an infinite variety of detail, differing according to the personal predilections of each writer, there is a fairly clearly defined pattern, common to them all, which gradually emerges. I refer to a common passion for the principle of equality and probably as a corollary to this, for a rigorous regulation of the life of the community, down to the minutest detail. Although the principle of liberty receives occasional honourable mention, it is for the most part left to take care of itself in the anxiety to ensure that human nature, still apparently suspected of being wayward, shall be kept securely on the path of equality.

Already in the writings of Morelly at the turn of the half-century the claims of equality in the State override all others.[2] All private ownership of property is abolished, since individual ownership is " the mother of all crimes, which are the children of despair and of raging poverty." [3] The State, as the single permissible employment agency, is accordingly responsible for the maintenance of all its citizens. Each individual must

[1] Chekhov, *The Three Sisters*, English Translation by Julius West, 1916, Act. II.

[2] The main source for Morelly's egalitarianism is the *Code de la Nature*, 1755, but it should be noted that two years earlier Morelly had published a long utopian poem, entitled *Naufrage des Isles Flottantes, ou Basiliade*, informed by similar principles.

[3] Morelly, *Basiliade*, Vol. I, p. 204.

contribute to the common fund " according to his strength, talents and age," while in the enforced absence of all private buying and selling, distribution, to be determined by the single criterion of need, personal and professional, will be conducted exclusively through publicly-owned warehouses and shops. The highly centralized system of administration is organized on strictly mathematical lines, each administrative unit being made up of multiples of ten of the subsidiary unit. In the interests of equality and uniformity, there are detailed regulations which severally restrict the field in which any freedom of choice is left to the individual. These regulations extend to marriage and divorce, to education and choice of vocation, even to the subject of dress. Marriage is compulsory about the age of fifteen; divorce is not permissible until ten years have elapsed; consistent with austerity, there is freedom of choice in dress after the age of thirty, but before that age everyone is to be dressed uniformly in colours appropriate to their profession; domestic education is closely regulated, while after the age of ten, all children must proceed to the workshops in which moral, political and religious instruction is compulsory; the numbers of persons authorized to apply themselves to the arts and sciences is to be fixed by law. Finally there are laws of studies, designed to prevent what are euphemistically termed the " égaremens de l'esprit humain et toute *rêverie transcendante*."

The modern reader, familiar with the nightmare utopias of *Brave New World* and *Nineteen Eighty-Four* may be forgiven if he detects an ominous ring in State worship of this order. But when he comes to examine L. S. Mercier's *The Year* 2440 he may well wonder whether Orwell at any rate did not draw some of his inspiration from this forgotten utopia. In Chapter X, for example, we are introduced to a man with a mask, which he wears, we are told, " to hide his shame " for having written a book of dangerous principles " contrary to sound morality." " Every day he is visited by two virtuous citizens to combat his erroneous opinions with the arms of gentleness and eloquence, to listen to his objections, reply to them, and engage him to retract as soon as he is convinced. Then he will be rehabilitated; he will acquire from the very confession of his error a greater glory; . . ."[1] The test, moreover, of a "bad book" is the verdict of the general public, in whose hearts the principles of universal morality are engraved. "Who is the man who would dare to judge a book before the public had done so?"[2] Since nothing is calculated to lead the mind farther astray than such works, censorship is not confined to the writings of living authors. All pernicious works require to be expunged from the memory of the human race, and accordingly a great burning of the books has taken place. "We have abridged what seemed of most importance; the best have been reprinted: the whole has been corrected according to the true principles of morality."[3] Among those whose works have been destroyed *in toto* are Bossuet and, among English philosophers, "those dangerous sceptics who had wanted to shake the foundations of morality."[4] Voltaire survived in stringently abridged and bowdlerized form, his offence consisting of his disrespect for Rousseau whose works are preserved entire. The only works among the condemned to be reprieved are volumes of theology, which "pestiferous works" are preserved in cellars to be hurled against the enemy in the event of war, since the ideas they contain are much more dangerous than mere cannon. Finally, the man who has written a bad book or whose cause is otherwise unjust, according to the law of the land, will find no advocate to defend him. For all defence attornies are incorruptible, by which is meant that

> "they are answerable for their honour for the causes they undertake. They abandon the guilty man, already condemned by their refusal to defend him, to appear trembling, without an advocate, to excuse himself before his judges."[5]

Intolerance of this order represents, it is true, an extreme case, but it is not unrepresentative in that it shows how much more concerned the *philosophes* in general were with the problem of privilege than they were with the problem of power. They too easily assumed that with equality and enlightenment, the

---

[1] L. S. Mercier, *L'An Deux Mille Quatre Cent Quarante*, p. 51 (English Translation entitled *Memoirs of the Year Two Thousand Five Hundred*, London, 1771).
[2] *Ibid.*   [3] *Ibid.*, p. 199.   [4] *Ibid.*, p. 204.   [5] *Ibid.*, p. 79.

problem of power could be safely left to take care of itself. The major social evils of their time were universally ascribed to the twin vices of acquisitiveness and ignorance; with the vice of arbitrary power they seemed but little concerned. In their unqualified faith in the power of institutions to make men good, the utopians at any rate merited the rebuke that Dostoievsky reserved for the men of '89.

> " If there be brethren, there will be brotherhood. But if there are no brethren no ' institution ' will ever produce brotherhood. What is the sense of establishing an ' institution ' and inscribing on it: Liberté, Egalité, Fraternité ! Nothing will be achieved by an ' institution ' . . . and brethren will start chopping off the heads of their brethren in order to achieve brotherhood through ' the civic institution '." [1]

Government was for most of them an immensely powerful instrument for good, once the people were enlightened enough to realize that they were dupes of those who perverted government to their own sectional ends. In this matter Godwin was the exception among contemporary utopian thinkers; but while he had no love for any form of government, he simply assumed that the institution was destined to vanish.

> " There will be no war, no crimes, no administration of justice as it is called, and no government. These latter articles are at no great distance; and it is not impossible that some of the present race of men may live to see them in part accomplished." [2]

Insistence on equality is likewise the keynote of Condorcet's vision of the future. The direction of future progress lay primarily in the destruction of inequality among nations and between classes. All men everywhere, Condorcet believed, are equal in rights by virtue of their common humanity. The American and French Revolutions are portents in the history of the recognition of this principle; even in Britain the friends of humanity are advocating the abolition of slavery. Soon the imperialist exploitation of the coloured peoples by the Europeans will be swept away by the universal recognition of the

[1] Dostoievsky, *The Diary of a Writer*, 1949, Vol. II, p. 1002.
[2] Godwin, *An Enquiry Concerning Political Justice*, 1793, Vol. II, pp. 871–72.

brotherhood of man. The only combination of circumstances which could prevent this revolution would be by a new invasion of Asia by the Tartars, and Condorcet believed this disaster to be henceforth impossible. Of course, equality among nations could not be expected to come about so long as nations themselves were riven from top to bottom by internal dissension based upon class inequality. This social inequality rested partly on disparity of wealth and of education, but its roots went deeper, Condorcet was shrewd enough to see, in that it was a necessary concomitant of the existing economic structure of society. So long as the system of production depended for its organization on the existence of a large number of men who had nothing to sell but their labour power, and of a small number possessed of a margin derived from " either land revenue or interest on capital almost independent of their industry," [1] then class inequality was inevitable. The means whereby this internal inequality was destined to be rooted out of the life of nations lay in vast social welfare schemes inaugurated by the State, whereby the national income would be drastically redistributed; and secondly, in the introduction of equality of opportunity to participate in a general education, the methods of which were to be specifically designed to bring knowledge within the reach of the understanding of every normal citizen. In fine, although Condorcet did not share the thoroughgoing communizing of property and education of Morelly or Rétif, he would have approved in spirit the motto which Rétif had inscribed in all languages on the principal gate of the ideal city: " *Sans l'égalite parfaite, point de vertu, point de bonheur.*" [2]

So much of the future Condorcet felt sufficiently confident to predict in comparative detail. But beyond that relatively proximate stage, he hinted at future developments of a scope not yet possible to anticipate. Human life itself, he believed with Godwin, if not destined to achieve physical immortality, would almost certainly prove capable of enormous prolongation. In Godwin's words, " Generation will not succeed generation, nor truth have in a certain degree to recommence

---

[1] Condorcet, *op. cit.*, p. 212.
[2] *Vide* Rétif, *La Découverte australe par un homme volant ou le Dédale français*, 1782.

her career at the end of every thirty years."[1] Moreover, on the
implicit assumption that both thinkers made of the inherit-
ability of acquired characteristics, the intellectual and moral
faculties of men would prove capable of indefinite improvement. " Mind, in a progressive view at least, is infinite." [2]
Consequently, in the long run, it is impossible for any of us to
attempt to prescribe any foreseeable limits to the ultimate
achievements of the human intellect. And this fact was important in that it constituted the essential answer to pessimists of
the Malthusian kind. Whatever might appear to the comparatively limited intellects of the present generation as an insuperable obstacle to the future establishment of a terrestrial
paradise, was the result of the fallacy of assuming that future
generations would only be equipped with the same puny
faculties as ourselves, with which to meet the anticipated
problems. [3]

So far we have discussed the means whereby the acquisitiveness or rapacity of human beings is to be eliminated in the
future. There remains the compelling evil of ignorance to be
overcome.

> " Yes, ignorance and the love of accumulation! these are the
> two sources of all the plagues that infest the life of man! They
> have inspired him with false ideas of his happiness." [4]

Much the most forceful and imaginatively vivid account of the
future elimination of ignorance (by which is meant principally
faith grounded on " evidence " of an unverifiable nature) is
to be found in the pages of the above quoted work of Volney.
Five years before the revolution broke out, the author made a
journey through provinces of the Ottoman Empire which had
formerly constituted the kingdom of Egypt and Syria, whose
decaying ruins now occasion in the writer gloomy speculations
of the fate of empires. From this morbid condition he is
rescued by the appearance of the " Apparition " or " Genius,"
who after informing him that man makes his own destiny and

---

[1] Godwin, *op. cit.*, p. 871.

[2] *Ibid.*, p. 866.

[3] Cf. Godwin, *op. cit.*, p. 871, and Condorcet, *op. cit.*, p. 222.

[4] Volney, *The Ruins: or, A Survey of the Revolutions of Empires*, (1791) English
Translation, n.d., probably 1879, p. 20.

that empires crumble because men choose to depart from the laws of nature, whisks his spirit away into the uppermost regions above the atmosphere, whence he is given a bird's-eye view into the future of our planet. The oppressed multitudes of the earth first throw off the yoke imposed upon them by the tyranny of the privileged class, and then proceed to elect legislators to investigate the true principles of morality, by consulting all those who profess knowledge thereof. One by one, representatives of all the world's great religions state their doctrines and their claims to be true, as a result of which no two doctrines among the prodigious number examined are found to agree. Moreover, the evidence adduced by each in favour of the absolute truth of its doctrines is similar in kind to the credentials of all the rival disputants, and is accordingly bitterly repudiated by all except in their own case. Miracle is hurled against miracle, martyr cited against martyr, the revelation of the one pitted against the divine scriptures of another, until in despair the people turn to the legislators for a solution of this problem of contradictions. The solution follows from the statement of the problem, and as the reader must have anticipated, is along thoroughly positivistic lines such as Comte himself could scarcely have excelled. After developing as a criterion a correspondence theory of truth, the legislators enunciate the principle that this " resemblance " between our ideas and their models can be secured only in those cases where

> " the objects of our inquiry can be referred to the testimony, and subjected to the examination, of our senses. Whatever cannot be brought to this trial is beyond the limits of our understanding; we have neither rule to try it by, nor measure by which to institute a comparison, nor source of demonstration and knowledge concerning it." [1]

From which it follows that in the general interests of peace, men should consent not to pronounce on issues where grounds for reasonable belief are inadequate.

> " . . . we must draw a line of demarcation between such as can be verified and such as cannot, and separate by an inviolable

[1] Volney, *op. cit.*, p. 142.

barrier, the world of fantastic beings from the world of realities: that is to say, all civil effect must be taken away from theological and religious opinions." [1]

The principal cause of strife among men, namely the intolerance arising out of ignorance will thus be remedied in the future.

Having thus completed our outline picture of the future destiny of mankind according to the late eighteenth-century utopians, there remains one further question to ask. The pictures we have drawn are not simply representative of the dreams of individuals, anxious to tell us how they personally would set about remoulding the world in accordance with their desires. Such they are, it is true; but they also purport to be predictions of the future. The question we must raise, therefore, is this: on what grounds are these forecasts made? Only in the case of Condorcet is there any suggestion that his predictions are warranted on the basis of our knowledge of laws of nature operating within the historical process.[2] With the others, the argument is a frankly teleological one. Man by his nature is born into the world to achieve certain ends which are defined by nature. Sooner or later, men will realize those ends, because they are somehow meant to do so. How do we know what those ends are? Since they are rational ends, since the universe is run on rational lines, we need only consult our reason to discover what they are. In practice, even in Condorcet's case, in spite of his scientific pretensions, this kind of assumption provides the effective determinant of his reasoning and his conclusions. Trained in the use of his reason, he tells us, man discovers that " his rights are written down in the book of nature." " Every political system ought to be based on natural right: it is the unique base of civil society," wrote Mercier. The legal code drawn up by Morelly is, he tells us, a " Model of legislation conforming to Nature's intentions." Finally, in the pages of Volney, the doctrine receives its classic statement.

[1] Volney, *op. cit.*
[2] Cf., however, Condillac, " Knowledge of the past will lift the veil which hides the future from you." But his discussion of the subject is exceedingly superficial. *Vide* Condillac, *Œuvres*, 1822 ed., Vol. 15, pp. 15–16.

" Man is governed, like the world of which he forms a part, by natural laws, regular in their operation, consequent in their effects, immutable in their essence; and these laws, the common source of good and evil, are neither written in the distant stars, nor concealed in mysterious codes; inherent in the nature of all terrestrial beings, identified with their exist- ence, they are at all times, and in all places, present to the human mind; they act upon the senses, inform the intellect, and annex to every action its punishment and its reward. Let man study these laws, let him understand his own nature, and the nature of the beings that surround him, and he will know the springs of his destiny, the causes of his evils, and the remedies to be applied." [1]

But at the very moment when this belief in the natural rights of men grounded on an appeal to rational self-evidence was being most loudly proclaimed; when the belief constituted the official philosophy of the men who carried through in its name the great social and political revolutions which occurred in America and France; when, in short, it seemed to be assured of well-nigh universal acceptance, its very foundations were in the process of being undermined by the most devastating attack to which it had ever been subjected. And to an examination of this counter-thesis we must now turn, if we are to understand aright the intellectual conditions out of which the philosophy of history finally emerged full-fledged.

[1] Volney, *op. cit.*, p. 15.

CHAPTER VII

The Decline of Natural Law

" Nor did I deem that thou, a mortal man,
Could'st by a breath annul and override
The immutable unwritten laws of Heaven."

THE VOICE is that of Sophocles' Antigone, the period that of
Periclean Athens. The tradition of a belief in a law of nature
as a norm to which men may appeal when dissatisfied with the
content of positive law, is a very ancient one. It is true that
Antigone in her repudiation of the laws of Creon was appealing
not to a universal law of reason, but to customary religious
practices whose observance the positive law had violated.[1]
Nevertheless, the significance of this appeal from positive law
to an allegedly higher authority was not lost on contemporaries.
Aristotle expressed his disquiet in the following terms in the
Rhetoric:

" For it is evident that, if the written law is counter to our
case, we must have recourse to the general law and equity, as
more in accordance with justice; . . . (this is why Antigone in
Sophocles justifies herself for having buried Polynices contrary
to the law of Creon, but not contrary to the written law: . . .)." [2]

But although the Sophists' antithesis between nature and convention was repudiated by Aristotle, with the passing of the
City State the doctrine strengthened its hold over men's minds
as a result of its development at the hands of the Stoics.[3]

All mankind, it was held, women no less than men, barbar-

[1] Professor Kitto reduces still further the significance of Antigone's appeal by
emphasizing the strength of her purely personal motives. " Face to face with
Creon's legality she indeed answers legally . . . but essentially she is doing much
more than championing one code against another; she is giving her whole being
for her brother's honour." (H. D. F. Kitto, *Greek Tragedy*, 1950 ed., p. 127.)
[2] Aristotle, *Rhetoric*, I, xv. 4–6 (Loeb Classics, 1947 reprint, p. 153).
[3] The Cynic, Antisthenes, who together with Diogenes exerted a considerable
influence over the early Stoics, is said to have been a pupil of the Sophist, Gorgias.

ian as well as Greek, the slave equally with the freeman, were alike possessed of the divine spark. God was no entity that dwelt on Olympus, but (in the metaphor of Zeno) pervaded the universe as honey runs through a honeycomb. Already in Aristotle, we find Empedocles quoted to similar effect; viz. that killing is not right for some and wrong for others, "But a universal precept, which extends without a break throughout the wide-ruling sky and the boundless earth."[1] Nature is the totality of the universe and everything in it bears the mark of the infinite Creator who sustains it. Man, a part of this scheme, is distinguished from the rest of nature by his ability to recognize the element of rationality in the cosmic process. Nature was identified with Reason and Reason with God. It followed that there was a normative Natural Law, susceptible of intuitive discovery by every rational man. It also followed that this universal or common law was binding upon all men, both rulers and ruled; and that since it was obligatory on men to ensure that positive law conformed as nearly as possible to natural law, the appeal lay open against the tyrant to the higher court of natural law. If the doctrine contained within it revolutionary implications, they were, in fact, never fully worked out by the Stoics. Indeed, one of the principal channels through which Stoic ideas gradually permeated European thought was the Roman law, and no Roman jurist would have asserted that (in the famous words of Suarez) an unjust law is not law. This conservative emphasis of the upholders of Natural Law was, moreover, strengthened by the development of the theory at the hands of the early Christian Fathers.

With the growth of the Church, the Stoic conception of a world state [2] of men bound by a common adherence to a divine law of nature began to take on actual institutional shape in the form of the Catholic Church, the Augustinian *Civitas Dei*. The Cynics' belief in the human descent from an original Golden Age was transmuted into a theology of Original Sin. In the Garden of Eden, where human nature was free from the taint of passion, man stood in no need of the

---

[1] Aristotle *op. cit.*, I, xiii. 2. (Loeb, p. 141.)

[2] "The poet says, Dear city of Cecrops;" wrote a later Stoic, the Emperor Marcus Aurelius, "and wilt not thou say, Dear city of Zeus?"

regulation of law, the later necessity for which reflected the sinfulness of man, as a result of the Fall. On this view secular law represents at best an unavoidable evil, necessitated by man's sinful nature; while the law of the Church is the reflection of the divine law of the Kingdom of God, of the Garden of Eden, of man's estate before the Fall. This was in effect to set up a dual system of Natural Law, that to which the positive law of secular princes approximated, whose function was the repression of the disorder consequent upon man's unbridled passions; and secondly, a law of nature closer to the divine law itself, a law of higher authority, the earthly interpreter of which was the Church. The effect of this doctrine, so long as the twin swords of imperium and sacerdotium were harmoniously balanced, was to strengthen the conservative character which the Natural Law theory had assumed in the Roman Law tradition. The theory, thus developed, underwrote the sacrosanct character of the positive law rather than the existence of certain natural rights, inherent in the individual as such, which remained rights whatever the positive law might state.[1]

In this way the radical, individualist tendencies of Natural Law theory remained no more than latent. But if the mediaeval synthesis conceived of law as the instrument for the bridling of human passions in respect of property, convention and well-tried institutions, it also clung tenaciously to the idea that law is the source of power and that accordingly might alone can never make right. Tyranny was defined as that state where law was the creature of power. Although secular rule was sometimes indistinguishable from the terror imposed by the most ruthless of contemporary over-lords, and though the City of God sustained the indignity of the " Babylonish Captivity " and the Great Schism, yet for over a thousand years there survived intact the notion that power over men represented a sacred trust, whose tenure was conditional upon the exercise of moral responsibility.

Moreover, the radical, individualist seeds within the Natural

[1] Cf. Ernst Troeltsch, *The Ideas of Natural Law and Humanity in World Politics*, 1922, § 2 in O. Gierke, *Natural Law and the Theory of Society*, Cambridge, 1934, Appx. I.

Law tradition were never totally extinguished, and in the later Middle Ages they bore fruit. Neither Ockham nor Marsiglio can be said to have interpreted Natural Law in a conservative or authoritarian fashion; while in the modern period, although the two strains continue to run through the political thinking of the time, in the secularized version of the theory developed by Bodin and Grotius, it is the radical strain which gradually emerges as the most characteristic. If the theory of Natural Law was used by Filmer to defend the Divine Right of Kings, it was Locke's development of the theory to vindicate the right of the people to repudiate their rulers, which made by far the more profound and enduring impression. So much so, that to-day we tend to identify historically the protagonists of Natural Law theories with movements of social protest and political reform. In the modern era, there have been countless occasions when at a time of political crisis in the affairs of nations the appeal has gone forth to the sanction of Natural Law. However vulnerable to critical analysis the foundation of the belief may be, the emotive power of the idea is to this day far from spent; while as a matter of history it would be difficult to exaggerate its effectiveness as a social force in sustaining the spirit of the oppressed in time of adversity.

This very brief résumé of the role of Natural Law theory in the development of European political thought should suffice to enable us to draw certain conclusions. First, its function was no less than to provide the original and fundamental premise from which the central tradition of European values was derived. Secondly, the age and continuity of that tradition was without parallel in the history of thought, extending as it did unbroken from the Stoics in the third century B.C. down to the eighteenth century. Thirdly, in the later period especially, it played the leading role in radical, progressive movements in the shape of an individualist belief in the natural rights of man. And finally, it is clear that any attack on this tradition resulting in a weakening of belief in the self-evidence of rights grounded on Natural Law, would necessarily leave a wide hiatus concerning the fundamental status of moral and political values. To the question of the nature and direction of this attack on Natural Law, culminating in the root and branch assault of David Hume, we must now turn; although it may assist us to a clearer understanding of the issue, if we precede the historical narrative by a brief analysis of method. For the theory of Natural Law is inseparable from the application of a specific method, which was no less decisive for its uncritical acceptance in the field of political theory. Political thought was indeed well advanced before theorists showed any real awareness that possible alternatives of method constituted a problem at all.

The traditional method of moral and political philosophers was largely determined by the particular conception of the function of philosophy, or rather of the nature of the philosopher's task, which flourished in the ancient world. I refer to the conception of the philosopher as an ascetic recluse, who by his victory over distracting passion and by the calm serenity of his synoptic wisdom may be expected to reveal to us a vision of the purpose of life, a knowledge of inner reality inaccessible to normal sense experience. Through the inward spiritual quality of such experience, knowledge may be obtained which passes beyond the limits set by mere phenomenal experience to include the noumenal world of the essence of things, of " things in themselves."

> " Then dawns the Invisible; the Unseen its truth reveals;
> My outward sense is gone, my inward essence feels;
> Its wings are almost free—its home, its harbour found,
> Measuring the gulf, it stoops, and dares the final bound."

The political philosopher, adopting this method of approach, may thus furnish himself with the necessary value premises concerning the nature of the good life, and on the basis of these premises proceed to erect an ideal State, by the canons of which existing institutions may be measured. The prototype of this highly rationalistic method is, of course, to be found in *The Republic* of Plato, but it is characteristic also of Aristotelian method[1]; and this mode of approach tended to establish itself

---

[1] Aristotle, it is true, claimed that his political treatise was based upon an analysis of the constitutions of no less than 158 contemporary states. But his primary classification of states is determined by the assumed Platonic conception of the true state as an institution ordained by Nature for the promotion of " the good life " for all its " citizens." Cf. A. C. Bradley, *Aristotle's Conception of the State* in *Hellenica*, edited by E. Abbott, 1898 ed., pp. 166–222.

as virtually self-evident in the Western tradition of political thought.

Now, the relationship between this method and the doctrine of Natural Law was so close that the one could not come under attack without the other. For the fundamental characteristic of all theories of Natural Law has always been an appeal from something that *is* to something that *ought* to be, from that which is imperfect to an absolute norm or standard of perfection in the light of which existent defects may be measured. The belief in Natural Law is essentially a dualistic doctrine, in which the *is* is contrasted with the *ought*. And similarly, the rationalist in method insists on drawing a sharp distinction between the realm of fact and the realm of value. Since, it is urged, the status of ultimate aims is a question of value and not of fact, it is impossible to set up as a criterion of the validity of values an empirical test as to what values are in fact held by the majority at any one time or even by the alleged consensus of opinion of the " best " men of all times, without assuming some such principle as the divine right of the majority. This is why even so convinced an empiric as Locke held that there must in the nature of things always be a legitimate sphere for the philosophy as well as the science of politics. On this view, the scientist may analyse, classify, even try to induce such generalizations as may hold in the field of actual political institutions, but he cannot *qua* scientist prescribe what ends we ought to pursue as opposed to describing the ends we do in fact pursue. He may prescribe the requisite means to achieve a given end, but it is for the philosopher to prescribe the end itself. The philosopher may well give due consideration to the scientist's evidence of the actual, but only in order to assist him in the prosecution of his own special task—the enunciation of the principles which should determine our ultimate moral and political values.

The conflict inherent in the dualism of the rationalist's position has not unnaturally always evoked an antithetical monism, which has been strengthened by the effectiveness of the developing technique of Baconian scientific method. Those who have been impressed by the reliability and universality of the criteria of verification of science, have emphasized the dangers of identifying internal experience, however seemingly genuine, with a knowledge of eternal moral principles. These principles, it is pointed out, are susceptible of no criteria of proof other than appeal to personal or rather subjective experience, whose variations according to time and place, even from individual to individual, are notorious. The tendency to erect into universal and eternal principles normative standards which are historically and geographically conditioned, is understandable in view of the human desire for certainty and permanence; but it should not be permitted to blind us to the facts of the proper limits to human knowledge. The rationalist is in the empiricist's eyes guilty of a lack of humility concerning the human capacity to discover truth, to which the counter charge is levelled that the empiric protesteth overmuch that knowledge is power.

Without necessarily asserting that the rationalist's separation of fact from value represents a false dichotomy, the empiricist will urge that, in view of the difficulties involved in the appeal to rational self-evidence, the validity of any hypothesis in the field of political thought should depend on the results of measuring the consequences of the supposed truth of the hypothesis on established human needs. To take a concrete example, if we assert that "All men have the right to life, liberty and the pursuit of happiness" or, more modestly, "All men should stand equal before the law," are there really any grounds for believing with Jefferson and the founding fathers that these generalized moral imperatives are entitled to a universal validity, by virtue of their self-evidence to rational men everywhere? A generation which has lived through a world war of six years' duration, arising ultimately out of a conflict of moral values, should stand in need of no further amplification of the dangers of relying on the appeal to rational self-evidence as the foundation of values. So, the empiricist would urge, we should treat such assertions not with disrespect, but also not with uncritical reverence. Rather should we regard them as inductive propositions of a hypothetical nature, subject to such tests as their internal consistency with other propositions, and their effectiveness in enabling us to satisfy what appear to be profound needs of our nature. Most empirics will, in fact, be found to rest their basic values on utilitarian or pragmatic assumptions.

Criticism of this order emphasizes the practical difficulties attaching to the Natural Law position in the absence of agreement as to methods of procedure and verification. But historically, the attack on Natural Law, when it began to emerge, went much deeper in that it challenged its fundamental dualism. Implicitly at least, attempts to eliminate the dualism of the *is* and the *ought* can be traced as far back as the Sophists. In the Platonic Dialogues, for instance, we find Thrasymachus maintaining that the only legitimate authority in the State is that which has the power to enforce its *diktat*; that right is dependent not on any abstract conception of justice but in the last resort on might alone. We find a similar approach to politics in the writings of Machiavelli in the sixteenth century, but it is not until Hobbes published his *Leviathan* in 1651 that we see the construction of a systematic theory of political obligation, based on premises independent of a normative Law of Nature. As his thought is developed within the framework of the current contract theory of the State, he retains, it is true, the old terminology and frequently speaks of " natural laws " and " natural rights "; but he uses these terms empirically to describe what he regards as the inevitably atomistic position of men divorced from the obligations of civil society. Following in the footsteps of Machiavelli, Hobbes attempts to found a theory of the State entirely on naturalistic, pragmatic assumptions. His is the first thorough-going attempt, and by far the most logical, to substitute for abstract, intuitive conceptions of natural law and justice, a psychological theory to explain the basis on which authority does in fact rest in society; and to that authority he is prepared to grant no validity other than its power to assert itself.

On this view, the political philosopher may legitimately point out to any ruling authority the advisability of attempting to satisfy the needs of his people, of knowing when it is expedient as well as graceful to make concessions to demands from below. What he is not entitled to do, however, is to tell governing authorities that their power is conditional upon their ruling in accordance with the precepts of justice or, negatively, on their refraining from violating the ancient canons of Natural Law. Hobbes' logic is far too consistent to permit him the luxury of maintaining a theory of sovereignty in the State side by side with a theory which sets distinct limitations to that "sovereignty." This, as he points out, is to render the concept meaningless. In reply to Hobbes, we are, of course, entitled to object to the consequences of his theory in the field of actual political institutions; but that does not detract from Hobbes' achievement in attempting to break away from the traditional dualism of Natural Law by employing his logic to deny the validity of a presumed conflict between the *is* and the *ought* in regard to ultimate ends. For Hobbes, those ends are already defined for us by the nature of man's psychological make-up, and it is the function of the philosopher or scientist to study the empirical evidence of those limiting psychological factors. The fact that his own psychology was crude and *a prioristic* in the extreme, while detracting from the persuasiveness of his conclusions, does not deprive his work of its interest to the student of method in political thought.

The foundations of the whole structure of Natural Law were still further undermined by Rousseau in the following century. Although he too still lacked the courage to emancipate himself completely from the tradition of the social contract and the state of nature as the basis of his theory of the State, they represented in his treatment of them no more than the old bottles out of which the new wine was bursting. He himself would seem to have been aware of this, judging by the attack he made on Natural Law in the unpublished first draft of *The Social Contract*, and subsequently dropped in the writing of the authorized text. I quote from the second chapter of Book I of the first draft:

> " Indeed, if the notions of the great Being and of the natural law were innate in every heart, there would be no need to teach explicitly the one and the other. That were to teach us what we already knew. . . . If they were not [innate], all those to whom God has not given them are dispensed from a knowledge of them. As soon as specific instructions were necessary for that, each people has its own that are proved to

be the only good ones, and from which are derived slaughter and murder more often than concord and peace." [1]

For Rousseau, the appeal against what he regards as social injustice is not to an abstract sense of justice, manifest to right reason everywhere; nor is it, despite his preservation of the language of the contract, an appeal to a supposedly original agreement between ruler and ruled; the crucial appeal is to the general will, " *le moi commun.*" It is, of course, possible to argue, as many have done, that this is merely to substitute one metaphysical conception for another; that we have no more adequate criteria for verifying the nature of the alleged general will at any given time than we have of verifying the alleged precepts of Natural Law. Nevertheless, the consequences of Rousseau's theory, strictly rationalist though it was in method, were to shift the reformer's gaze from Natural Law as the ultimate normative sanction to the possibility of attempting to validate his ideals by appealing to a general will, theoretically, at least, susceptible of an empirical examination in terms of existing beliefs and aspirations.

By Rousseau's time, signs were multiplying that the time was ripe for an overt attack on the main fortress of Natural Law. Machiavelli, Hobbes and Rousseau had each in his distinctive way burrowed under the outer walls, but before the eighteenth century no one had attempted a direct assault on the hard core of the Natural Law position by questioning the epistemological validity of the very possibility of rational self-evidence in this field. This service it was left to Rousseau's great contemporary, Hume, to perform. For good or ill, Hume's analysis, despite the pains which subsequent thinkers have been to in order to refute it, dealt a powerful blow to the whole edifice of Natural Law. It is on the basis of Hume's analysis that the entire structure of positivistic thought in the nineteenth and twentieth centuries has been reared; for which reason alone no political theorist can fail to take account of it. But from our present centre of interest, its importance lies in the challenge it presented to those concerned with the problem

[1] *The Political Writings of Jean Jacques Rousseau*, edited by C. E. Vaughan, 1915, Vol. I, p. 451.

of the status of values. That challenge was taken up in more quarters than one, but not least of the attempts to meet it was to be found in that school of opinion which concerned itself with the knowledge of history's laws.

The common assumption made by the upholders of the system of Natural Law was, as we have seen, the belief that there exist universally and eternally certain moral truths obligatory upon all men to follow, which are directly intuited by right Reason, as it operates in all normal men. Now Hume attacked this assumption at its roots by analysing the precise nature of the role played by reason in the formulation of the ethical beliefs which influence human motives and intentions, aid in shaping human character and inspire certain courses of conduct. In contrast to the common-sense view that certain modes of conduct are in themselves good or evil as the case may be; that good and evil are actual properties of things in themselves quite independently of how men observe them or whether men in fact respond to them, Hume, like Spinoza, held that ethical terms are the vehicles whereby we predicate the existence of certain relations between objects and ourselves. In Hume's view, a thing is only rendered good or bad in so far as it is perceived to have consequences favourable or unfavourable in terms of human desires or aversions. This does not mean that every time a value judgment is made, the evaluator consciously makes a hedonistic calculation of the possible consequences of what he is judging; it means rather that in the first instance some such process was enacted, and from this beginning a tradition established. Certain things have thus through force of habit and custom come to be approved or disapproved by the majority of mankind; and through a constant usage the majority of us (all except the freak moral psychopaths, the existence of whom Hume is doubtful [1]) come to respond habitually and mechanically on moral issues.

On this view, then, the relations predicated by ethical terms are defined solely in terms of a psychological theory concerning

---

[1] " Absolute, unprovoked, disinterested malice, has never, perhaps, place in any human breast . . ." (Hume, *An Inquiry concerning the Principles of Morals, Works*, 1854, Vol. IV, p. 291.)

the nature of human emotions. Human beings are so constituted, Hume maintains, that they respond favourably to
and thus approve actions and qualities which they perceive
to have pleasant consequences to themselves or to others or
are judged to be instrumental in the promotion of pleasure.
Moreover, other things being equal, as he puts it, meaning
provided the individual concerned is not distracted by some
such powerful emotion as jealousy, spite or revenge, then the
human psychic structure is such that he will experience
emotions of approval in the knowledge of the happiness of his
fellow creatures. And, conversely, he will disapprove of conditions which render them subject to misery or misfortune.
'Would any man,' he asks rhetorically, 'who is walking alone,
tread as willingly on another's gouty toes, whom he has no
quarrel with, as on the hard flint and pavement?' [1] His
hedonism is not egoistic in the narrowest sense, but rather a
benevolent one; he does, in fact, posit the existence in human
beings of a moral sentiment of Benevolence or Humanity, the
evidence for which is of a strictly empirical kind.

We are now in a position to raise the question of how, on
this view of the status of ethical norms, we are to distinguish
between right and wrong in a given instance. Hume, it
should be noted, is not asserting that moral questions are to be
decided simply by reference to an individual's subjective
sentiments and tastes, the evidence for which can by their very
nature only be the unverifiable statement of the person concerned that he does in fact experience certain emotions of
approval or disapproval towards a given action. If this were the
case, there would be no point in discussing moral issues in the
hope thereby of making a truer appraisal of the distinction
between right and wrong on rational grounds. Whereas on
Hume's view, there is a means, a very simple means, of deciding
the issue in any moral controversy. When in doubt as to the
ethical terms we ought to apply to a given action or quality,
it is only necessary, Hume correctly argues on his assumptions, to discover what actions in fact do evoke sentiments of
approval in the majority of mankind and what actions evoke
their disapproval.

[1] Hume, *op. cit.*, p. 290.

" The hypothesis which we embrace is plain. It maintains that morality is determined by sentiment. It defines virtue to be *whatever mental action or quality gives to a spectator the pleasing sentiment of approbation;* and vice the contrary. We then proceed to examine a plain matter of fact, to wit, what actions have this influence: we consider all the circumstances in which these actions agree; and thence endeavour to extract some general observations with regard to these sentiments." [1]

In this way does Hume overcome the conflict between the *is* and the *ought* in the field of morals and politics. To find out what we ought to do, it is only necessary to find out how the majority do as a matter of fact react in their moral sentiments to the issue in point.

The main consequence of this analysis was to unseat Reason from the place it had long been supposed to occupy as the arbiter of and authority for our ethical knowledge. True, it had not altogether been banished from the scene by Hume's logic, but it had been reduced, as he himself said, to the status of passion's slave. " Reason is, and ought only to be, the slave of the passions, and can never pretend to any other office than to serve and obey them." [2]   In the complex human situation Reason is necessary to calculate the balance of fortune or misfortune likely to result from a proposed course of action, to effect an adequate adjustment between means and ends, but by itself it is powerless to determine that we should incline our efforts to the achievement of any ultimate end whatever. That we do in fact tend to prefer to direct our efforts towards the realization of ends of a benevolent kind rather than the contrary is the result of our emotional constitution, of our desires and passions, of our innate moral sentiments. Reason is indispensable in pointing the way in which we may arrive at our goal, but the larger task of prescribing the goal itself lies beyond its scope and capacity, except for the menial statistical task of determining the direction of the moral sentiments of the majority of mankind.

Moreover, even this limited role assigned to Reason in

---

[1] Hume, *op. cit.*, pp. 357–58.
[2] Hume, *A Treatise of Human Nature,* Everyman edition (1949 reprint), Vol. II, p. 127.

determining the morality of a course of action, is only granted by courtesy of our naturally determined inveterate habits. It is not only against the confusion of Reason with the ascription of value that we must be on our guard. Reason is and can only be concerned with matters of fact, and accordingly there are no grounds for sharing the general belief that Reason is capable of intuiting the existence of a necessary causal connexion where actually it perceives nothing more than the fact that within our sense experience event x has always in the past been succeeded by event y, whose only relationship to one another is not a logically necessary one but one based purely on the deep-seated and ineradicable habits of human sense experience. As Hume puts it, his hypothesis is " that all our reasonings concerning causes and effects, are derived from nothing but custom; and that belief is more properly an act of the sensitive, than of the cogitative part of our natures." [1] Reason is, in fact, tacitly defined in such a way as to confine it to the function of deductive inference, to the function of ratiocination in the strictest sense. But the effect of the analysis is to make even the adjustment of the means-end relationship which Hume allows is the legitimate function of Reason in the definition of ethical terms, to rest on no more sure foundation than that of inveterate human habit, which fortunately for our sanity Nature decrees shall hold us in perpetual thrall.

Complete rational scepticism could scarcely go further than in the following celebrated passage from Hume, who, whatever his faults, could never be accused of lacking the courage of his logic.

" Where a passion is neither founded on false suppositions, nor chooses means insufficient for the end, the understanding can neither justify nor condemn it. It is not contrary to reason to prefer the destruction of the whole world to the scratching of my finger." [2]

We may well feel that the attack on rational self-evidence had over-reached itself. It had not been Hume's original intention to assault the gates of Reason itself, yet to this point his logic would seem to have carried him. If, as Hume says. " Morals and criticism are not so properly objects of the

[1] Hume, *op. cit.*, Vol. I, p. 179.   [2] *Ibid.*, Vol. II, p. 128.

understanding as of taste and sentiment," [1] and if, as he says elsewhere, " Truth is disputable, not taste " [2]; then the gap between the *is* and the *ought* has only been closed at the cost of the extrusion of the judgment from the sphere of norms. But if questions of moral taste are not subject to rational judgment, it is difficult to see how belief in this field can be other than at the mercy of caprice, impulse, prejudice or habit. The only sense in which one man's taste in these matters may be said to be inferior to another's is that in which is meant that he is outvoted by his contemporaries. If I prefer the atomization of London's inhabitants to a life of prosperity for them, my appraisal of this moral situation cannot be said to be incorrect in terms of an intelligent choice of values, but only in terms of being a minority sentiment. Empiricism of this order goes beyond the repudiation of the rationalist's belief in the existence of an unseen realm of eternal, universal values; it leaves the formation of a sound judgment concerning what is desirable and worthy—generally regarded as the basis of human character—to the mercy of such forces as immediate emotional impulse, crude self-interest or class prejudice, passive acquiescence in custom or any one of the social forces which operate when intelligence abdicates.

If Hume is right, then it is true that the objectivity of values has been saved from the subjectivism of interpretations of an alleged Law of Nature, subject to no known means of verification. But we may well feel that this advantage has been dearly bought if the price is the denial that value is an integral part of our experience to be judged experimentally in terms of consequences. Hume argues that if you push a man to the utmost limits of inquiry concerning the reasons why he does something, you will eventually press him to an ultimate end, beyond which no reference to any other object is possible; and that accordingly that ultimate something must be desirable on its own account, the only reason being that human sentiments are for the most part so constituted. Apart altogether from the logical status of the question concerning the ultimate end (Cf. pp. 247–249 below), this reasoning assumes

[1] Hume, *An Inquiry concerning the Principles of Morals, Works,* Vol. IV, p. 187.
[2] *Ibid.*, p. 231.

that the main task confronting a rational judgment in matters of morals consists of a clear-cut choice between competing monisms, good and evil. But, as Hume himself acknowledges, the moral psychopath is an extremely rare animal; there is virtual unanimity among human beings to-day that kindness is preferable to cruelty, for example; yet this fact scarcely diminishes the urgency of the moral problems which beset us. For human beings seek many goods which are often mutually incompatible; and a moral choice usually consists in determining the wisdom of wanting some goods in preference to others. If value is to be identified with enjoyment or satisfaction as such; if ethical terms are relational predicates defined exclusively in terms of a psychological theory regarding our wants and desires; then it follows that judgment is excluded from the field of value.

In practice we all act on the assumption that some goods are worthier of cultivation than others. If we equated value with the satisfaction of sentiment, irrespective of other consequences attached to the pursuit of that satisfaction, then indeed there would be no problem of conflicting wants. In actual fact, it is precisely this problem which constitutes the hard core of most moral issues, in the solution of which lies the truest test of human judgment. Merely because the will is impotent by direct action to transform the sentiments, it does not follow, as Hume believed, that Reason is impotent to act upon the sentiments. If, for instance, an individual discovers through introspection and reasoned reflection that certain of his wants are the product of forgotten but determinant conditions, and that his repressed wants now conflict with and frustrate other wants, he is frequently thus enabled to bring his wants under intelligent control. It is, in other words, only when the intelligence has judged of his conflicting wants in terms of their causes and effects that he is able to make an effective rational choice between them. At this point and at this point only are wants transformed into values. Hume's mistake lies essentially in the identification of satisfaction or enjoyment (on the part of the majority) with value.

The consequences of Hume's analysis in the history of European thought were manifold. Certainly it provided a natural bridge for the passing of the Enlightenment into the nineteenth century's Romantic reaction against it. Never have the weapons of Reason been more skilfully or more destructively turned upon itself than in Hume's trenchant pages. For all his religious scepticism, his mordant analysis of the foundations of the miraculous, the offence he gave to the pious as well as the pietistic, in the last resort Hume is on the side of the angels. Reading him, one is reminded of a similarly nihilistic analysis made by Dostoievsky more than a century later in his *Notes from Underground* (sometimes translated as *Letters from the Underworld*).

> " Where are the primary causes on which I am to build? Where are my foundations? Where am I to get them from? I exercise myself in reflection, and consequently with me every primary cause at once draws after itself another still more primary, and so on to infinity. . . . I said that a man revenges himself because he sees justice in it. Therefore he has found a primary cause, that is, justice. . . . But I see no justice in it, I find no sort of virtue in it either, and consequently if I attempt to revenge myself, it is only out of spite. Spite, of course, might overcome everything, all my doubts, and so might serve quite successfully in place of a primary cause, precisely because it is not a cause. But what is to be done if I have not even spite. . . . In consequence again of those accursed laws of consciousness, anger in me is subject to chemical disintegration. You look into it, the object flies off into air, your reasons evaporate, the criminal is not to be found, the wrong becomes not a wrong but a phantom, something like the toothache, for which no one is to blame, . . ." [1]

Dostoievsky's own way out of the impasse was to embrace a profoundly mystical form of Christian faith, since premises built on reason were no more than illusion. It is also not without significance, perhaps, that out of the fanatical Russian nihilism of the 'sixties was eventually born a no less fanatical faith in Marxism.

In the case of Hume at any rate, there is no doubt that his destructive analysis left many people profoundly disturbed.

[1] *The Novels of Fyodor Dostoevsky*, English Translation by Constance Garnett, London, 1918, Vol. X, pp. 62–63.

If the bolder among contemporary intellects were stimulated to rouse themselves from their " dogmatic slumbers " the more timid experienced the anxiety associated with the shifting of ancient and familiar intellectual landmarks. It was these misgivings which provided the slowly emerging philosophy of history with its opportunity, particularly in Germany. Hume had undermined belief in the rational foundations of values; the philosophy of history represents on the part of its exponents one very influential attempt to restore those foundations. Only if we view it in this light, may we hope to understand its full historical significance and the reasons for its still enduring influence.

CHAPTER VIII

The Philosophy of History

IN THIS chapter we shall consider the emergence of the philosophy of history, conceived as an attempt to read a message into history or to derive a scheme of values therefrom. It may be that in principle the philosopher of history in this sense is merely doing what Aristotle did when he claimed that the *polis* was the final cause of man, in that it represented the end process of his " natural " development. The difference is that the modern philosopher of history claims to have discerned a given course of direction in history, independently of any speculation, but as a result of a careful investigation of the principal facts of history. The difficulty with this claim, however, is, as we saw in our analysis of the attempts to write a universal history, that the historian in his need to tell a philosophically significant story or at least to give unity to his narrative, is either compelled to have recourse to an explicit teleology or unconsciously smuggles in his own values as organizing concepts.

Examples of teleologists, viz. those who believe that the historical process is a developmental series of events through which the true nature of man's final perfection is destined to be realized, are Aristotle, Kant and Hegel. While the teleologist is under no necessity to claim that the developmental series has realized its final form in the present, there is a strong temptation for him to do so. Neither Aristotle nor Hegel succeeds in resisting this temptation, and even Kant, who aspires to a universal peace which only too obviously had not yet been realized, believes that man has reached the stage where the conditions are ripe for the assault on this " last " stage of our progress. In the case of men like Comte and Marx, where the teleological method of approach is at any rate not explicit, and where it is not pretended that the whole course of history has reached its end station in our own time, we still find that the present happens to fall into a unique category in the succession of the ages. This is most glaring in the case of Marx. All history, he tells us, is the record of class struggle. But the present class struggle in which living protagonists are engaged, is destined by history's laws to be the final one, from which will ultimately emerge a classless society. The illusion that the present occupies a special, if not unique place of honour at the banquet of history, is one that dies hard. Men persistently aspire to elevate the significance of the role they play in the attempt to give added stature to their own struggles and ambitions.

It must not be thought that we are attempting to impugn the legitimacy of the appeal to history in order to increase the persuasiveness of proposed courses of action in the present. We may well join with Burke in so far as he restricts his argument to the appeal to maintain intact institutions which are claimed on historical grounds to have served men well in the past; or, on the other hand, we may consider Marx's historical demonstration of the ineffectiveness of capitalist institutions to be sufficiently convincing to warrant our joining him in a struggle to concert the overthrow of those institutions. The philosopher of history, however, is not content with such a modest claim. For Burke, the wisdom of the species as revealed by a study of history is interpreted as a reflection in some measure of divine purpose, and as such mandatory upon us to cherish. For Marx, the capitalist phase of society is doomed to dialectical transformation by historical necessity. The philosopher of history does not say to us, " These are the facts of history as I read them. If you are wise, you will take them into account in shaping your present aims." Rather does he say to us, " This is the direction of history, as revealed by an empirical study. Whether you as an individual will it or not, your generation is historically determined to continue this line of direction."

It is not difficult to see why there exists a temptation to write history in this fashion. A feeling of confidence regarding one's capacity to play a significant and, it is hoped, successful role in the conditions in which one finds oneself, is for many a necessary condition of their facing the future without a sense of futility.   The assumption that a previous generation, vanquished in some past decisive struggle, was nevertheless on the right track or in the main course of historical development, and that we in the present are running up a kind of historical cul-de-sac, is apt to be psychologically demoralizing to those involved in the present struggle.   When George Orwell in his *Nineteen Eighty-four* makes Big Brother establish in his revolutionary State a department for the constant rewriting and falsification of history to accord with the new " line " as it switches this way and that, we are sufficiently aware of the temptation to make his satire frighteningly convincing.   Certainly European history, as written by English or French liberal historians, must make depressing reading to a patriotic German who has lived through twelve years of Nazism, if he finds those histories convincing.   True, he may now take heart for the future from them, but the psychological temptation to write a history which will not culminate in his own self-abasement must be considerable.   The problem is admirably seized by the Swiss historian, Walther Hofer, in a discussion of the task confronting contemporary German historiography.

> " That is why it is important to search out those men and those ideas which warned that the wrong path had been taken, and sought to direct the German spirit back to its true historic mission.   These men and these ideas, however, were forced aside by the main stream of development.   Hence, in the traditional picture of history, they have been given only an insignificant place, or indeed no place at all.   We must now take up the search for the wasted opportunities." [1]

Historians, in fact, being human, are predisposed to put a premium on success in their historical writing.   In a brilliant analysis of what he terms " Whig " history, Professor Butterfield has shown how in the field of historical writing as elsewhere nothing succeeds like success.   Those movements in the past which, whatever the motives or intentions of their protagonists, are ultimately considered to have been successful in

[1] *German History: Some New German Views*, 1954, edited by Hans Kohn, pp. 204–205.

the sense that they led to the establishment of those things we now value, tend to be sympathetically emphasized by present historians. For example, although Luther and his followers cared as little as their opponents for the principle of religious toleration, the eventual outcome of the Protestant challenge from the point of view of to-day, predisposes us to look with more sympathy on the reformers than on the " reactionaries." Or to cite a more ironic example of Butterfield's,

> " the significant case arises when the very men who opposed votes for women until the vote could be withheld no longer, are unable to see in the opponents of the Great Reform Bill anything but the corrupt defenders of profitable abuses; . . ." [1]

The desire to eliminate the apparently pluralistic character of historical events, to make history coherent or intelligible, leads to the setting up, sometimes unconsciously, of a system of inevitabilities or of a single organizing concept wherewith to interpret history as a unity. The difficulty is that even where this is done deliberately as a tool of inquiry, where the organizing concept is put forward tentatively as a hypothesis to be confirmed or otherwise by empirical investigation, history is so rich and many-faceted that plausible confirmation is easily available. Whether our hypothesis be that the monistic key to history is the realization of liberty or the development of reason, or whether we suppose that the crucially determinant factor in history is climate or economic structure or the careers of event-making heroes, there is ample evidence to confirm any or all of these theories, if favourable evidence is selected carefully enough.[2] Even if we succeed in stating what conditions, if realized, we should consider to invalidate our hypothesis, it is always possible to " get round " unfavourable evidence with some degree of plausibility by claiming that we are guilty of taking too narrow a view, that we should survey events or conditions on a larger scale or over a vaster period of time. Similarly when the line of direction

---

[1] H. Butterfield, *The Whig Interpretation of History*, 1950, p. 30.

[2] This does not mean that all these theories are of equal value. In studying a particular society, it is obviously more important to investigate the economic structure than, for example, the extent to which bean consumption predominates in its dietary habits. (Cf. Feuerbach.)

in a developmental series of events appears to be broken, the period during which this change of direction is observed, is declared to be not significant or merely contingent, or that it is in effect a blank period representing no more than the ephemeral ebb of the tide. The Dark Ages for example are thus periodized by virtue of their failure to fit into a line of development, in which free inquiry is deemed of definitive significance. Similarly, in order to preserve intact the illusion of an onward march towards the realization of a given goal, the histories of entire civilizations are ignored as irrelevant or inessential. Or if not ignored entirely, they are, as in the case of Hegel, invoked at an appointed time in their story, only to be dismissed again into the shades of oblivion and irrelevance, once their significant contribution has been made, the test of significance being the idea of human freedom as conceived by Hegel. The subjectivism of Hegel's criteria of periodization may seem evident enough to us today, but European history is still written as though the familiar periods were in some curious way inherent in the events themselves, instead of being convenient pegs which serve to break up the narrative intelligibly in the light of European values. This element of uncritical subjectivism in our historical perspective is sufficiently strong in most of us to bring us up with a salutary jolt when we read a passage like the following, taken from the work of a Muslim historian. Discussing the invasion of France by Musa in A.D. 712, he writes:

> " Standing on the Pyrenees, the dauntless Viceroy conceived the project of conquering the whole of Europe. . . . The cautious and hesitating policy of the Damascene Court lost the glorious opportunity, with the consequence that Europe remained enveloped in intellectual darkness for the next eight centuries." [1]

The effect of the geographical and cultural standpoint of the writer in determining his scheme of periodization is here apparent, to the European eye at least. The effect of the time factor is, of course, even more important, since the sense of

[1] Quoted by F. J. Teggart, *Theory of History*, Yale University Press, 1925, p. 40, from Ameer Ali, *A Short History of the Saracens*, 1899, p. 111.

perspective in periodization is dependent upon the distance at which we stand from the historical events in question. Our sense of the " totality " of history, and of its line of development in a single time series is inseparable from our own beliefs in the present concerning what is of most enduring significance in life. And accordingly we shall expect to find that the philosophy of history as here understood is necessarily based upon recourse to the teleological method, whether it be explicit, as in the case of Kant, for example, or suppressed as in the case of Comte.

> " If the philosophy of history," wrote Professor Flint, " be merely a scientific representation of universal history as a process of progressive development, Turgot has probably a better claim than anyone else to be called its founder." [1]

Certainly no man can claim to have exerted so far-reaching an influence on so slender a basis at so young an age as did Turgot in this field. Although his short fragmentary *discours* [2] have assuredly received their due meed of recognition,[3] their influence, if not their originality, has not been exaggerated. Reflecting on the one hand the empiricist tradition of Locke and Condillac, they combine on the other hand a profoundly Christian faith in the workings of Divine Providence, strongly reminiscent of Bossuet. And similarly, if we look forwards instead of backwards, they foreshadow both the positivism of Comte and the teleology of Kant.

The study of history, Turgot maintains, is differentiated

[1] Robert Flint, *History of the Philosophy of History*, 1893, p. 282.

[2] The two lectures delivered at the Sorbonne in 1750, at the age of 23, are entitled *On the Advantages which the Establishment of Christianity has Brought to Mankind*, and *On the Successive Progress of the Human Mind*. The second is much the more suggestive of the two. In addition, there are two other important fragments, of uncertain date, subsequently published under the title, *Plan of Two Essays on Universal History*. All these works are to be found in Vol. I of the *Œuvres de Turgot*, edited by Gustave Schelle, Paris, 1913.

[3] It is significant that perhaps the most lavish of the many ecomiums that Turgot has elicited from subsequent writers is that of Professor A. J. Toynbee in our own time.

" Yet in these immature and fragmentary essays he has made a greater permanent contribution to the understanding of history than Acton succeeded in making by devoting a long and laborious life to historical industry." (A. J. Toynbee, *A Study of History*, 1934, Vol. I, p. 46 n.)

from the study of natural phenomena by virtue of the fact
that the latter are subject to constant laws, operating within
" a circle of unchanging revolutions," whereas when we turn
to the succession of men, we find that there is endless and un-
repetitive variation. This difference of subject matter is
reflected in the difference of technique which we apply to
them. In physics we *describe* the rules of uniformity, in history
we *relate* a story. Nevertheless every historical age is insepara-
bly linked to all its predecessors by an unbreakable chain of
cause and effect, and it is the philosopher's task in narrating
the events of universal history, to study the conditions and
effects of necessary causal laws. Universal history includes
an account of all the stages of human progress from the first
beginnings of life, as outlined in the Scriptures in default of
any surviving evidence, through the process of the forming
and subsequent mixing of races, through the process of
language, of morals, customs and the sciences, through the
rise and fall of empires and religions, until we reach the
present stage of humanity's onward march to perfection, the
glorious reign of Louis XV. But in addition to this task of
narration, universal history must supply us with the key to
the mysteries of historical causation.

> " To reveal the influence of general and necessary causes,
> those of particular causes and the free actions of great men
> and the relation of all that to the very constitution of man;
> to show the springs and the mechanism of moral causes by
> their effects; that is what history is in the eyes of a philo-
> sopher." [1]

Montesquieu's attempt to explain national differences in
terms of climatic conditioning, he rejects as precipitate and
exaggerated, because he himself sees no evidence to justify
any such correlation, and because as an axiom of method he
believes it to be sounder not to attempt to evaluate physical
factors until we have exhausted our efforts to provide an
explanation in terms of moral causes. Turgot's own guiding
principle which enables him to explain the nature of the forces
moving nations is, of course, the principle of inevitable progress.

[1] Turgot, *Œuvres*, Vol. I, p. 277.

This derives from the peculiar characteristic of human beings, viz. the faculty of language which enables them to transmit their pool of knowledge to their successors as a cumulative heritage. The faith is, once again, in the perfectibility of man, based on the power of the freely inquiring intellect; and, as we would expect, Turgot's bird's-eye view of human progress culminates in pæans of praise to Galileo, Kepler, Bacon, Descartes, Newton and Leibnitz. But progress also requires the service of the passions as well as of reason; and here Turgot implicitly repudiates the notion of a simple mechanical progression. Evil and error are necessary for the realization of progress, which emerges out of conflict. The idea which Kant and Hegel were to develop into a central tenet is clearly stated by Turgot, although he does not give it the same emphasis.

> " Interest, ambition, vainglory change at each instant the scene of the world, submerge the earth with blood; and in the midst of their ravages, customs are softened, the human mind is enlightened; isolated nations approach each other; commerce and politics finally reunite all parts of the globe; and the entire mass of humanity, by alternations of calm and agitation, of good and evil, proceeds continuously, if slowly, towards a greater perfection." [1]

And elsewhere,

> " It is only through turmoil and destruction that nations expand, that civilization (*police*) and governments are in the long run perfected; . . ." [2]

Similarly in the pursuit of truth, error so far from proving an obstacle to enlightenment, as we might expect, has proved to be a necessary condition for the discovery of truth, since men need to make mistakes in order to distinguish the true.

This fact that progress requires for its realization not only reason but reason's antithesis, " tumultuous and dangerous passions," is also important in furnishing us with the clue to the problem of why certain nations after making early advances have ceased to maintain them and become static, as in the

---

[1] Turgot, *op. cit.*, pp. 215–16. [2] *Ibid.*, p. 285.

cases of Egypt, India and China.   The immediate causes of these phenomena are explained in terms of such factors as excessive awe of authority, the restrictions of the limits of free inquiry, the slavery of subjects and the despotism of princes. Although the principles of human character do not vary, yet certain intellects are exceptionally endowed and bear rich fruit provided that they find the requisite conditions to develop and mature.   ". . . and from the infinite variety of these circumstances there arises the inequality of the progress of nations." [1]   But the ultimate causes of these instances of retarded growth are much more deep-seated.   They lie in the absence of the necessary invigorating forces of the seemingly anti-social passions.   China was in effect stifled through an excess of reason and justice.   It is the passions which multiply our ideas and extend our knowledge, " in default of the reason whose time had not come and which would have been less powerful if its reign had been sooner."

> " That which is never perfect ought never to be entirely fixed.   The tumultuous, dangerous passions have become a principle of action, and consequently of progress.   All that which draws men out of their condition, that puts beneath their gaze varied scenes, extends their ideas, enlightens them, animates them, and, in the long run, guides them to the good and the true, whither they are led by their natural bent. . . ." [2]

Just as the distillation of a good wine requires a strong fermentation, so hatred and vengeance and other terrible passions are required to generate out of these explosions the gentle passions.

It does indeed appear that everything is for the best in the best of all possible worlds.   The difficulty, of course, with this view that everything is inherently and inevitably progressive, that no event is wasted but contributes directly or indirectly to the realization of perfection, is that it is logically impossible to apply any test of progress to any given development. Turgot is, for instance, loud in his acclamation of the Christian contribution to civilized values, particularly during the dark ages of barbarism.   He could not pass by in silence, he says,

---

[1] Turgot, *op. cit.*, p. 217.   [2] *Ibid.*, pp. 283–84.

" this new light which, while the Empire advanced to its ruin, was spread throughout the universe; a light a thousand times more precious than those of letters and of philosophy. Sacred religion, could I forget you?" [1]   But, on Turgot's view of necessary progress, it is morally meaningless to single out the Christian contribution for laudation, since the ferocity of the barbarians was somehow equally necessary if only to create the opportunity for the Christian role and our evaluation of it. The historical process is for Turgot, as for Bossuet, controlled by Providence. The difference is that Turgot's Providence acts not arbitrarily, but uniformly according to discoverable laws. And he is concerned to discover the conditions under which progress is realized. Here once again we meet the view that since no single individual or group is consciously striving to promote that which actually emerges in the long run, therefore there must be some plan or law which they are fulfilling in despite of themselves.

> " And ambitious men themselves, in forming the great nations, have contributed to the designs of Providence, to the progress of enlightenment, and accordingly to the increase of human happiness, an end which concerned them not at all. Their passions, even their rages, have led them, unbeknown to themselves, to where they were going. I believe I see an immense army whose every movement is directed by a mighty genius. . . . Each part makes its journey in face of obstacles without knowing what can be the outcome; only the general sees the effect of so many combined marches: . . ." [2]

The question remains to be asked: where are we to look for the key which will enable us to apprise the fundamental direction of progress. It is not, as we might expect, in the field of morals, in the development of man's conception of right and wrong. For the principles of morals are unchanging and are susceptible of intuition by all men equally, independently of their reason.

> " . . . this instinct, this feeling for the good and the upright, which Providence has imprinted in all hearts, which precedes

---

[1] Turgot, *op. cit.*, p. 228.   [2] *Ibid.*, p. 283.

reason, which often carries it along in its own despite, leads the philosophers of all times back to the same fundamental principles of the science of morals (*Mœurs*)." [1]

In the realm of morals, the " sacred religion " has for all time laid down the truths that men need. It is in the field of knowledge that we must look for the key to human progress. For the unspoken assumption of Turgot's essays is the Baconian maxim that knowledge is power. Through knowledge of the causes of the phenomena that affect human life, the range of control over those phenomena can be extended. And so Turgot is led to enunciate the three stages of development of the human understanding, which Comte was later to adopt as the basis of his system. The three stages, which Comte defined as the theological, the metaphysical and the positive, are defined very clearly by Turgot in the following terms:

1. " Before men were able to understand the connection between physical effects, nothing was more natural than that they should suppose that they were produced by intelligent beings, invisible and similar to ourselves; for what would they have resembled? Everything that happened, in which human action had no part, had its god, . . ."

2. " When the philosophers had recognized the absurdity of these fables, without however having acquired true insight into natural history, they thought to explain the causes of phenomena by abstract expressions, like essences and faculties, expressions which nevertheless explained nothing, . . ."

3. " It was only very late, in observing the mechanical action that bodies have on each other, that from this mechanism were drawn other hypotheses, which mathematics could develop and experience verify." [2]

From this analysis, there emerged the inescapable conclusion that now that the anthropomorphic and speculative stages of human curiosity had at last been superseded, and the principles of inquiry had finally been established on firm ground, progress in the future would be guaranteed at a constantly accelerating rate.

Turgot's faith in Providence operating uniformly according to discoverable laws in history as well as in the realm of physical

---

[1] Turgot, *op. cit.*, p. 224.   [2] *Ibid.*, pp. 315–16.

phenomena, is strikingly paralleled in the thought of his English contemporary, Joseph Priestley. Although Priestley's enduring fame is based on his scientific discoveries,[1] he exerted a considerable influence in his own day as an indefatigable publicist in theology, philosophy and history. Of particular interest to us in the present context are his observations on history, which are to be found scattered in his *Lectures on History* (written for teaching purposes, while he was still a tutor in the Warrington academy, and eventually published in 1788) and in short tracts like the *New Chart of History* (1770).

It may, he writes, be thought presumptuous for man to think that by a study of history, he may hope " to scan the ways of God in the conduct of human affairs." But this objection could be urged with equal force, he justly observes, against the attempt to discover God's purposes as revealed in the evidence of the physical world. And yet no one would any longer seriously question the legitimacy of these methods of studying physical phenomena. And the methods are similar in principle and intent.

> " Both methods are equally attempts to trace out the perfections and providence of God, by means of different footsteps which he has left us of them, differing only in this, that the one is much more distinct than the other." [2]

It is true that the principles of nature's uniformities, as a result of countless observations by generations of mankind, are far more clearly understood. The main reason for this wide discrepancy in the measure of success in the two fields in discovering uniformity amid apparent irregularity is the availability of the experimental method to the student of the works of nature, and its denial to the student of history. Whereas the former student can, owing to the constancy of nature, whose operations are more completely exposed to observation, repeat his experiments as often as need be, the student of human affairs is concerned with events which under Providence happen but once. And even then, the record of all the attendant circumstances which constitute the indispensable evidence

---

[1] Priestley was described by Cuvier, the great French naturalist, as " the father of modern chemistry who would not acknowledge his daughter."

[2] Priestley, *Lectures on History, and General Policy*, 1826 ed., p. 551.

for the study of causal relations, is only imperfectly bequeathed to us by history.

Nevertheless, we should not permit the admitted difficulties of the enterprise to make us despair of the attempt. Certainly we have no cause to doubt that history jointly with nature's works, " is, in reality, an exhibition of the ways of God." On what other conceivable assumption could we account for the undoubted fact that great and important ends are so frequently realized in history through means which appear to us either as unconsidered trifles or as being of a totally different order of events from that of the end which they are subsequently seen to have promoted? Would the unsophisticated ever have dreamed of supposing that the amours of Henry VIII could have led to such a momentous historical change as the Reformation? [1] Is not a correlation of cause and effect of this order in itself convincing evidence that amid all the flux, variety and seeming chaos of history, there is in reality a grand design working itself out. To discover the principles of this design and reveal the conduct of Providence underlying the confusion and perplexities of history, is " the noblest object of the attention to an historian."

Priestley's own attempt to elucidate these principles is, however, disappointing and his philosophy of history is little more than an exegesis of biblical prophecy. After drawing up a chart of the principal revolutions in the rise and fall of the great historical empires, he is compelled to admit that such a survey cannot but give rise to somewhat melancholy reflections. Yet while we naturally deplore a depravity which has led to the shedding of so much human blood, we should not allow this to blind us to the fact that wars and revolutions, with all the suffering that they entail, " have been, upon the whole, extremely favourable to the progress of knowledge, virtue, and happiness." Indeed, the more clearly we realize the ingenuity of the benevolent Author of history in contriving so consistently to bring forth the most desirable conditions from the greatest disasters, the more freely will flow our gratitude, and the more solicitous shall we be to advance by our efforts the ends He has in mind. Moreover, we must remember

[1] Priestley, *op. cit.*, p. 53.

that it will not be long now before the age of war and revolution finally passes away, and the chart of history will no longer be so shockingly disfigured. On the basis of " evidence," [1] the curious naïvety of which is rather reminiscent of Bodin two centuries earlier, we are finally assured that the day cannot be far distant when the " wretched governments " of the present shall be swept away, and " the happiness of mankind be placed upon the most solid foundation."

It was not, however, in England but in Germany that the belief that history moved according to fixed principles, most firmly took root, and bore a rich crop of philosophies of history. Although others besides Hegel produced work or speculated in this field (e.g. Lessing, Schiller, Schlözer, Fichte, Schelling), there appeared while Hegel was still in his teens two works which merit our particular attention. In 1784 there appeared the first of Herder's four volumes on the philosophy of history (*Ideen zur Philosophie der Menschengeschichte*, 1784–91), and in the autumn of that year, Kant, stimulated by his disagreement with Herder to turn his own energies into this field, published a slight but important article on this subject in the *Berliner Monatsschrift*. And it is to an examination of this article, entitled *Idea of a Universal History in a Cosmopolitan Sense*,[2] that we must now turn.

Although Kant admits that his interest in universal history is inspired by the desire to see the achievements of a Kepler and a Newton emulated in the field of history,[3] he himself

---

[1] " It is only the toes of Nebuchadnezzar's metallic image that now subsist, and we are assured, that Christianity, represented by the little stone which was cut out of the mountain without hands, shall fall upon them, and, utterly destroying all the remains of the image, become a great mountain filling the whole earth." (*A Description of a New Chart of History, containing a view of the principal Revolutions of Empire, that have taken Place in the World*, Inscribed to Benjamin Franklin, 1770, pp. 21–22.)

[2] Kant, *Idee zu einer allgemeinen Geschichte in weltbürgerlicher Absicht, Kant's gesammelte Schriften, Königlich Preussischen Akademie der Wissenschaften* edition, Berlin and Leipzig, 1923, *Band* VIII. A modern French translation of this article is to be found in *Kant—La Philosophie de l'Histoire*, edited by S. Piobetta, Paris, 1947.

[3] " We wish to see whether we can succeed in finding a clue to such a history, and then we shall leave to Nature the task of producing the man capable of writing history on this principle. Did she not thus produce a Kepler, who in unexpected fashion, subjected the excentric orbits of the planets to fixed laws; and a Newton who explained those laws in terms of a general principle of nature? " (Kant, *op. cit., Band* VIII, p. 18.)

does not hesitate to have recourse to a teleological method of interpretation. Indeed, it is not too much to say that every page of Kant's essay bears the stamp of Aristotle, although Kant's own conclusion is, of course, very different from that reached by Aristotle. And yet it is Kant's merit to have realized the dangers implicit in a thoroughgoing teleology when applied to the writing of history. The development of the ninth and final proposition of the essay leaves the impression that there was a suspicion in his mind that his method, rigidly applied, would result in cutting the ground from under the historian's feet. At any rate, he found it necessary to issue a caveat against *a priori* history, lest it should mistakenly be supposed that he was claiming to usurp the task of the historian.

> " To believe that I with this idea of a world history, which possesses to some extent an *a priori* guiding thread (*Leitfaden*), wished to supplant the study of actual, mere empirically constructed history, would represent a misconception of my intention." [1]

He grants that it may appear a strange, indeed absurd notion to write history " according to the idea of the course the world must follow if it had to conform to certain and reasonable goals." [2] One might be forgiven for supposing that no more than a novel would result from such an assumption. Nevertheless, he insists to the end that this idea that Nature, herself playing an indispensable role in the working out of human freedom, is acting according to her own final purposes, is a very useful one. Although it does not as yet permit us the insight to penetrate very far into the secrets of the mechanism of Nature's plan, it does at least furnish us with the clue to reduce to some semblance of order what would otherwise be a formless, arbitrary agglomeration of human actions.

The essay begins by summarily and effectively disposing of the argument that the possession by human beings of the capacity for free will precludes any attempt to find in human behaviour evidence of uniform laws operating here as in other natural events. Whatever metaphysical assumptions we choose to adopt concerning the autonomy of the will, there

---

[1] Kant, *op. cit.*, p. 30.   [2] *Ibid.*, p. 29.

can be no doubt that the results of our willing (" the phenomenal manifestations ") are no less determined than other
natural phenomena. The conclusive test of this is to be found
in our ability, through the collection and study of vital statis-
tics, to predict with a high degree of accuracy the number of
marriages, births and deaths in a particular society over a
specific period, despite the fact that no act could well be more
voluntary than the act of marriage in a free society. It is true
that the agents of these actions, considered as individuals,
little think that in fulfilling their own wishes, which even on
occasion conflict with the aims of their fellows, they are nevertheless conspiring to carry out Nature's design for her. Nor
if they did realize this fact, would the knowledge be in the least
likely to deflect them from their goals.

What, then, according to Kant, is Nature's law of human
development? That the Kantian scheme derives not from a
prior study of history, but from a teleological conception of
human nature is evident from the tenor of his whole argument.
Indeed, it is not until the end of the essay that any reference is
made to actual history. He then suggests that if we take as
our starting point the history of Greece (as our most ancient
source of authentic history) and proceed via the Romans and
the barbarians down to our own time, we shall observe a
steady course of improvement in the Constitution of Europe,
the significance of which lies in the fact that these States will
probably one day give laws to all others. The actual foundation on which the Kantian philosophy of history is reared,
consists as it did for Aristotle of a major and a minor premise
concerning (a) the nature of man, and (b) the nature of Nature,
or rather the principle of her operation. The essential
argument may be neatly summarized in syllogistic form in the
following terms. First, uniquely distinctive of human nature
is the endowment of reason and free will; secondly, Nature
makes nothing in vain; therefore, the natural end of man is
the realization of those conditions in which reason and free
will can achieve their maximum development. But whereas
for Aristotle those conditions were realized in the city state,
for Kant they would not be realized until men had established
a Society of Nations.

Unlike many contemporary upholders of the doctrine of progress, Kant is aware of the objection to the theory that it takes for granted a willingness on the part of the generations to work and sacrifice themselves for benefits which will accrue not to themselves, but to those whose only merit it is to have been born at a later time. Although this may appear at first sight unjust, men submit because Nature has decreed that only as a species, not as individuals, can men develop reason to the full. For this task far exceeds the life-span of any individual. Reason needs time in which to experiment, and history is essentially the time-frame in which reason proceeds along her appointed path of progression. But how could Nature be sure that man would use his reason to this required end? In the first place, man was so constituted that he was not self-sufficient, independently of reason. He was, for instance, furnished neither with horns, nor claws, nor fangs, but only with hands. But this alone was not sufficient for Nature's purposes, since reason would only have been developed to the extent that man's survival and minimal comfort demanded. Therefore, in order to ensure that man would emerge from the state of the Arcadian shepherd, Nature divided human nature against itself, so that out of the conflict of warring elements, man would be tested to the utmost, and would be driven relentlessly forward. Thus was established the supreme paradox of human nature, at once man's greatest challenge and the instrument of his continual advancement, his " unsocial sociability " (*ungesellige Geselligkeit*). Turgot's " tumultuous and dangerous passions " have their counterpart in Kant's anti-social forces of antagonism, selfishness, greed, vanity and lust after property and dominion, for which vices, we are assured by both writers, we should thank Nature, since without them we should be doomed to stagnation.

For Kant, then, the law of human progress rests upon the necessity which man is under to labour in the testing fire of human conflict. " Man wills concord," he says, " but Nature knows better what is good for his species; she wills discord." [1] This is, after all, not peculiar to man. We have only to observe the trees of the forest to see that it is those which have

---

[1] Kant, *op cit.*, p. 21.

to struggle most fiercely for the conditions of survival, which
become the straightest and most beautiful. The importance
which Kant attached to this principle is seen in his insistence
that this law of conflict is a necessary condition of all the culture
and art which man has produced. These glorious achievements are the fruits of human " *Ungeselligkeit*." In his
Critique of Judgment, Kant develops this principle to give us a
social analysis, which foreshadows in a most striking fashion
Marx's subsequent analysis of the class struggle, although, to
be sure, Kant does not draw a similar revolutionary conclusion.
The passage is worth quoting at length as well for its own sake
as for the fact that we know that Marx studied Kant carefully
during his first year as a student at Berlin.[1]

> " Skill cannot be developed in the human race except by
> means of inequality among men; for the great majority
> provide the necessities of life, as it were, mechanically, without
> requiring any art in particular, for the convenience and leisure
> of others who work at the less necessary elements of culture,
> science and art. In an oppressed condition they have hard
> work and little enjoyment, although much of the culture of
> the higher classes gradually spreads to them. Yet with the
> progress of this culture . . ., their calamities increase equally
> in two directions, on the one hand through violence from
> without, on the other hand through internal discontent; . . ."

So far Marx would find little with which to quarrel in this
analysis. With the advancement of bourgeois culture, the
dispossessed proletariat find their position deteriorating as a
result of the sharpening of the class war within the nation,
and the struggle of the nation to protect bourgeois interests
abroad from the pressure of other bourgeois cultural groups.
It is Kant's conclusion, which follows immediately from the
above-quoted passage, which contrasts with that of Marx.

> ". . .; but still this splendid misery is bound up with the
> development of the natural capacities of the human race, and

---

[1] *Vide* Karl Vorländer, *Kant und Marx—Ein Beitrag zur Philosophie des Sozialismus*,
Tübingen, 1911, pp. 35–36, for a discussion of the letter, dated November 10th,
1837, from Marx to his father, in which he discusses Kant in relation to his own
intellectual development.

the purpose of nature itself, although not our purpose, is thus attained." [1]

The miseries of the " oppressed " like war, that other " undesigned enterprise of men," are necessary, and as such we should accept them in good heart in the knowledge that they are Nature's indispensable scourges to achieve our final liberation. This, at least, would appear to be the logical conclusion, but, in fact, he says in the article on universal history that " it seems, we are capable by our own reasonable disposition of accelerating (*schneller herbeiführen*) the attainment of this epoch, so happy for our successors."

We have now seen how Nature works and what instruments she chooses for her purposes. It remains to ask what is this final purpose. What, in short, is to be the ultimate outcome of all the wickedness, lust for destruction, childish vanity and folly which would appear to be man's principal contribution thus far to the pages of history? Following Rousseau, Kant argues that man entered society because he found the state of licence a state of slavery to the anti-social passions. His desire to give expression to his *gesellig* dispositions led him to submit to the rule of law, the only solution to the problem presented by man's inveterate temptation to make an exception in his own case. Man finds true freedom only when he voluntarily submits to a will that is universally valid; but so far, the area over which this has been achieved, extends not beyond the confines of the nation state, with the result that in the sphere of inter-state relations the forces of *Ungeselligkeit* still prevail. Man has found a master, but, since this master is necessarily human, he too needs a master. To effect some solution of this problem is the last and most difficult of all the tasks which confront mankind; and it is as a small contribution to this end that the present essay and the better known *Zum ewigen Frieden* are intended.

It is man's ultimate destiny to achieve complete freedom through the suffering of war and the poverty and exhaustion inseparable from constant preparation for war. Finally, all passion spent, the chastened nations will be made aware of

[1] *Kant's Critique of Judgment*, English Translation by J. H. Bernard, 1914 ed., p. 356.

the necessity, under which Nature has laid them, of sacrificing their claims to national sovereignty that they might submit to the universal law prescribed by a Society of the Nations. This, we are assured, is no visionary dream, but a statement of man's final cause, the evidence for which consists of that part of Nature's plan already executed in history. If as yet we have only a hazy perception of the shape of that plan, that is no cause for surprise when we consider how short is the course which history has yet run. With so large a stretch of the circuit yet to run, we can no more expect certainty of prognostication than we can as yet hope to plot precisely the course of the sun and its satellites in the planetary constellation.

In actual practice, as has been noted, Kant makes little pretence of deriving his theory from a prior examination of the facts of history. He made no claims to being a historian. In Kant we see the skeleton of the philosophy of history with its characteristic methods laid bare. We see the dependence of historical monism on teleology, and we see the essential circularity of the argument revealed. Man ought to seek self-control (*Selbstgesetzgebung*) through submission to a universal supranational law. Why? Because this is Nature's plan for the course of human development. How do we know? Because suffering the consequences of human *Ungeselligkeit*, we value that which makes for *Geselligkeit*; and with these values firmly established, those facts from universal history which are relevant to a struggle, defined in terms of these values, are selected to demonstrate an inevitable historical progression to the ultimate end of freedom under universal law.

Herder's massive work on the philosophy of history is extraordinarily difficult to summarize. The ingredients are many and the mixture curious. We are regaled with an immense display of learning concerning the social customs and ethnic characteristics of many diverse races of mankind, ranging from the Eskimo and the Hottentot to the Indian and the Chinese. Scrupulous as to sources where recorded history is concerned, he yet does not hesitate to follow the Old Testament account of the origins of the world and the creation of man. But while his Christian piety dictates his acceptance of the Scriptures, his faith in Reason, affronted by much of the detail, demands that he rationalize and modernize the ancient myths. It is significant, too, that the biblical account is accepted not on the basis of divine revelation, as is the case with Turgot, but on the grounds that the Mosaic account represents the most ancient of all the human traditions on this subject. Moreover, in his interpretation of history, Herder, for all his respect for the facts and the carefulness of his research, is singularly free from any scholarly inhibitions concerning the legitimacy of speculation. Few writers of repute have in fact permitted themselves to give rein so freely to speculation so grandiose or analogies so fanciful.

No less than the thinkers already discussed in this chapter, Herder believed that the essential function of the historian was to learn to scan the ways of God for man, as revealed in the record of the past.

> " There is no nobler use of history than this: it unfolds to
> us as it were the counsels of Fate, and teaches us, insignificant
> as we are, to act according to God's eternal laws." [1]

Nor is he any less convinced than they that the course of history is a progressive one. Of significant interest, however, in the case of Herder, is his frank confession of the psychological motives at the roots of this belief.

> " It is a melancholy prospect," he says, " to behold nothing
> in the revolutions of our Earth but wreck upon wreck, eternal
> beginnings without end, changes of circumstance without
> any fixed purpose. The chain of improvement alone forms a
> whole of these ruins, . . ." [2]

It may well seem a melancholy prospect to many men, but the mere need to feel conviction concerning the chain of improvement, does nothing to establish the truth of the belief. On the contrary, our knowledge of our own need to feel satisfied on this score, should predispose us to examine all the more critically evidence which appears to confirm that which we wish to establish.

---

[1] Herder, *Outlines of a Philosophy of the History of Man*, English Translation by T. Churchill, 1800, p. 467.

[2] *Ibid.*, p. 230.

The novelty of Herder's teleological interpretation of history lies in the fact that he relates human life to the world of nature, out of which it emerged. Herder's view of the universe is thoroughly organic in character, so that each part of the whole is considered as an organism whose purpose it is to prepare for a higher phase of development. The order of development *ab initio* lies through the solar system, the earth, vegetable life, animal life down to human life. Each is a means to a higher end, realizing its final function when it produces that perfect example of its kind, which crystallizes into a new species.[1] But in the sense that everything is the product of previous growth, a part of the great chain of being, it is true to say that everything was potentially created in the first act of Creation. For Nature is self-generating.

> " Nothing in nature stands still: every thing exerts itself and pushes on. . . . When the door of creation was shut, the forms of organization already chosen remained as appointed ways and gates, by which the inferior powers might in future raise and improve themselves, within the limits of nature. New forms arise no more: . . ." [2]

Man, however, is unique among natural phenomena in that he represents the end to which all other forms are subservient means. He is also unique because, as the most perfect of beings, he is also the most perfectible. As he represents the culmination of all natural processes, so is he the first in another higher series of development. He is, so to speak, the connecting link between the lower physical world from which he has emerged and a future state of spirituality, in which the spirit of man is immortal. It is not altogether clear to what extent the new sphere of existence that lies in the future is capable of realization on this earth, this " inn for travellers." [3] The Earth, he says, " is only a place of exercise " and this life

---

[1] It would seem that Herder is committed to a theory of evolution which would exclude an independent act of creation for human life, as described in the Book of Genesis. Yet although he draws many comparisons between human and animal life, his distinction between man and the primates is as sharp as any drawn by Bishop Wilberforce, for example, in the famous Darwinian controversy.

[2] Herder, *op. cit.*, p. 114.

[3] *Ibid.*, p. 127.

a state of preparation. But as a species, man is here on earth gradually leaving his animal nature further behind. On his mind, God has imprinted religion and humanity; and by means of a growing tradition, capable of absorption by the organic nature of man, man is educable along the path of historical progress leading ever nearer to a likeness of the divine image.

What evidence does Herder adduce in support of the law which has promoted and will continue to promote the progress of humanity in our species? Again the picture that emerges is not at all clear. On the one hand, it is pointed out that the number of destructive geniuses is steadily diminishing; that no empire since Rome has based itself on war and conquest; that we no longer dream of building pyramids or of indulging in gladiatorial games; that we no longer live as troglodytes or cave dwellers. We have succeeded in bringing the forces of Nature increasingly under control; while even the invention of gunpowder has had the favourable result of transforming a savage trade into " the most honourable art of crowned heads." Like his predecessors, of whom we have spoken in this chapter, Herder sees beneficent purpose at work in violence and bloodshed.

> " Only by opposing struggles against false pretensions can the sweet labours of man be victorious . . . the seed germinates more beautifully in a subsequent period from the ashes of the good, and when irrigated with blood seldom fails, to shoot up to an unfading flower." [1]

From which he concludes that revolutions are as historically necessary as waves are to a stream, if it is not to become a stagnant pool.

On the other hand, Herder has no patience with those who maintain that life in the State necessarily represents any progress for the happiness of men over that which they enjoyed in the state of nature. On the contrary, the noble savage, reminiscent of Rousseau's first love, acquires more merit in Herder's eyes than the unreal figure of the lover of humanity. " The savage has room in his poor hut for every stranger.

---

[1] Herder, *op. cit.*, p. 231.

. . . The deluged heart of the idle cosmopolite is a hut for no one."[1] We must learn to look for our happiness and improvement not to the State, still less to a supra-national State, but to ourselves. After all, millions of our species live in ignorance of the arts of government, and are yet much happier than those who have made sacrifices for the illusory advantages of the State. Kant's belief in the final goal of the Society of Nations for humanity, as can be imagined, gets very short shrift. Such contrivances are dismissed as artificial, inorganic mechanisms unsuited to the vigorous vitality of human beings.

> " Nothing therefore appears so directly opposite to the end of government as the unnatural enlargement of states, the wild mixture of various races and nations under one sceptre."[2]

The reference to " the wild mixture of various races " is significant, for Herder's frank selection of European culture as the arch-exemplar of historical progress, is based on an ethnological theory of a kind with which we have since become distressingly familiar. In so far as Herder realized the un-wisdom of hypostatizing an abstract human nature, uniform and universal, this was all to the good. But his insistence on fundamental racial differences went far beyond the fruitful exploration of environmental influences on the character structure of different ethnic groups. He maintained that races were differentiated by innate defining peculiarities, implanted by Nature in a way analogous to that in which she differentiates the oak from the elm, for example. If certain races have remained in a static condition, it is because it is in their nature to do so. Europeans enjoy a progressive culture within a historic society, essentially because of the superior qualities with which Nature has endowed them. While the institution of slavery and the exploitation of the African by the European is deplored by Herder, he does not attempt to conceal his belief in the natural inferiority of the Negro. It is impossible to exaggerate the mischief which has been caused by specious generalizations of this kind, based as they are on simple but false analogies. Herder has sometimes been called

---

[1] Herder, *op. cit.*, pp. 222–23.   [2] *Ibid.*, p. 249.

the father of modern anthropology. If this be so, it is difficult to resist the conclusion that few sciences can have been more unfortunate in their paternity.

The criticisms which have been levelled against Herder's predecessors apply with even more force to Herder. In his case, for all the Enlightenment's vaunted respect for the methods of science, his ineradicable taste for speculation and facile analogy found in the pages of history ample scope for an expression, wholly unclouded by the empiricist's characteristic caution in induction and zeal in verification. If in the pages of Turgot, we were able to perceive the roots of Comte; if Kant and Condorcet, both children of the Enlightenment for all the gulf that separates them, were nevertheless seen to join hands in their foreshadowing of Marx; then it may be said with equal truth that from Herder the road lies wide open to Hegel. All these thinkers shared in common the belief that the historical process was governed by ascertainable law. All with the exception of Comte attached vital importance to the significance of human conflict in determining the course of human development. And finally, as we shall see, both Hegel and Marx at least were logical enough to believe on their premises that the status of values was determined by a knowledge of a historically determined system of inevitabilities.

CHAPTER IX

Hegelianism

It is a contention of this book that the emergence and increasing influence of Marxism in the nineteenth century were closely related to the disillusion accompanying the collapse of the belief in self-evident natural rights. By the nineteenth century sufficient time had elapsed to allow the educated mind to absorb to the full the implications of Hume's destructive criticism; and consequently a climate of opinion began to form in which the necessity for a new synthesis of thought, in which the precepts of Natural Law could no longer be assumed as universal premises, was taken for granted. We must, of course, guard against the fallacy of treating thought as though it were a process developing in a vacuum. The momentous events of the French Revolution and the Industrial Revolution separate the nineteenth from the eighteenth century, and of course separate Marx from Hume. It might well be argued that the disillusion which came as the aftermath of the Revolution in France in the shape first of the excesses of the revolutionaries themselves and, secondly, of the arbitrary despotism of Napoleon, did more to weaken the faith of the run of mankind in the self-evidence of natural rights than a thousand Treatises on Human Nature could ever hope to do. Moreover, Hume, living as he did in a cultured and leisured, oligarchic society of almost Augustan splendour, the peace of which was troubled by scarcely a ripple from below, could afford to take a positivistic attitude towards values more difficult for those inured to the class warfare and social strains of a harsher age. To those possessed of imagination and a social conscience, who lived under the shadow and shame of the exploitation of children, women and men, on the scale revealed in such documents as the Report of Sadler's Committee on the conditions of child labour in the factories (1832)—to such men and women as these, Hume's view that moral experience which enables us to ascribe value, so far from being a form of knowledge or apprehension is a form of feeling or sentiment, appeared to be destructive of the very basis of our ethical judgments.

The fact remained that Hume had been responsible for creating a kind of hiatus in philosophy—a gap which would be filled either by the aggressive and undisguised irrationalism of the Romantics or by something else. In accordance with the English empirical tradition, the Utilitarians under the leadership and inspiration of Jeremy Bentham and James Mill proceeded to develop the utilitarianism latent in Hume on the basis of the Hartley-Hume psychology. But as the nineteenth century wore on, and the consequences of holding *laissez-faire* economic assumptions about the role of government in an age of fierce industrial expansion were ever more clearly revealed, the inherent conflict of the Utilitarians became increasingly evident. Nowhere is the crack down the middle of the utilitarian structure, the attempt to reconcile logical incompatibles in psychology, ethics and politics more tragically revealed than in that incomparably candid philosophical confession, given to us by John Stuart Mill in his *Autobiography*.[1] There remained for those who still placed their faith in reason and who rejected both the traditional structure of self-evident natural law and the utilitarian attempt to evade self-evident values by introducing a synthetic psychological hedonism, the Marxian synthesis.

Yet it is impossible to discuss Marx without first examining the Hegelian reaction against the materialism of the eighteenth century. For, paradoxically enough, the most immediate and influential source of the ideas of Marx, the materialist, was the idealism of the Romantics. That this movement should have raised its head first in Germany is scarcely surprising. Awakening from an intellectual torpor which had afflicted her since the devastation of the Thirty Years War, she experienced her intellectual resurgence at a time when Europe as a whole was

---

[1] *Vide* R. V. Sampson, " J. S. Mill: An Interpretation," *The Cambridge Journal*, January, 1950.

beginning to react against the first flush of revolutionary enthusiasm, and when Prussia herself was smarting under the humiliation of Jena and the subsequent contempt which she met with at the hands of Napoleon. In the circumstances, it was hardly to be expected that the Germans would evince enthusiasm for everything French, least of all for the ideas of the Gallic *Illumination*. Our concern here, however, is not with the strident German nationalism which disfigured Hegel's later career so much as with the general climate of disillusion which did so much to determine the direction of his thought in his early life. Since the French Revolution had appeared to have succeeded, and since the ideals of liberty and equality yet remained as elusive as before the Bastille had fallen, a certain scepticism among those who conducted the inquest into the reasons for the failure to win social freedom, is not to be wondered at.

The eighteenth-century philosophers, impressed by the extraordinary successes of Kepler and Galileo, Descartes and Boyle and Newton aspired, as we have seen, to apply the methods of natural science to the social studies, in the hope of claiming for them a parallel authority as an exact instrument of predictive capacity. They accordingly regarded the individual as another type of machine, working according to fixed principles, complete in itself, and intelligible in terms of psychological law explaining the emotions, motives, inclinations, habits of the individual. Once these laws had been formulated and verified, since society was no more than the aggregate of its constituent individuals, all social problems would yield to the diagnosis inherent in the new knowledge, even as the laws discovered by Newton enabled him to specify the conditions under which bodies fall to earth and the planets revolve in the heavens. For Condillac, D'Alembert or Diderot, Helvetius or Holbach, the individual, although differentiated from the animals by possession of self-consciousness and the power to make moral judgments, was nevertheless no more than an object in nature. For any Voltairean, the criteria of significance for any statement about the real world consisted as for Hume, in an appeal to the observable and verifiable experience of sense data. The existence of the world they took largely for granted, and such questions as they did raise regarding its origins were pursued by methods of retrodiction hewing as close as possible to the canons of empiricism. Thus individualistic and intellectualistic in temper, atheistic and naturalistic in belief, radically but mechanistically empirical in method, they stressed the values of liberty, equality and fraternity in an age which embodied the denial of these things in every avenue of its social life. In practice, their intellectualism and excessive, almost naïvely optimistic faith in the power of reason outran their empiricism and thus paved the way for the reaction which succeeded the waning of the high hopes they had raised in the hearts of the revolutionaries.

Hegel, sceptical of the validity of methods which he held to be as dogmatic as the metaphysics for which they were substituted, conducted a frontal assault on the proposed application of naturalistic method to the social studies. Rejecting the materialist assumptions, his view of nature as well as of man developed along profoundly metaphysical and rationalistic lines. Thought and being were identified in an attempt to claim for the Spirit, for intuitive Reason as monistic a function as the materialists had claimed for matter. Reality, as the emanation of the Creator no less than the human minds which seek to know it, informed by the same Reason as operates in human thought, is susceptible in its inmost essence of direct apprehension by human reason. The real world as perceived by the human percipients is simply the thought content of the Absolute Idea, of Divine Reason which has existed through eternity outside time itself and independently of our own world. The clearest evidence of this Absolute in its progressive unfolding is to be found in the immense and awe-inspiring story of human destiny. And it is accordingly to history that we must turn for the clearest insight into the workings of eternal and universal reason. Since that history reflects in its externals an inward Reason, what may appear to the uninitiated as the idle play of chance or as fortuitous events does in reality conceal the workings of divine law, " the march of God in the world." And the philosopher's highest task is by his insight to reveal a knowledge of the laws of Reason which are history's laws. On the basis of this reasoning, Hegel claimed to have substantiated the principle that " the real is the rational and the rational is the real." As a central tenet, it suffered from a fatal ambiguity, since conservative Hegelians emphasized the first half of the statement, while the radicals laid stress upon the second half. Nevertheless, there is no denying that no more radical attempt had ever been made to overcome the dualism inherent in the conflict between the *is* and the *ought*, between fact and value. For once we have knowledge of the laws behind the historical process, developing progressively under the impetus of its own logic, it would be an act of cosmic impiety on our part to seek to defy laws expressing a Reason greater by far than that possessed by any finite intelligence. For the laws of history are no merely human projection or arrangement imposed on events so as to make a pattern intelligible to human reason, but are immanent in the events themselves, independently of their being grasped by the actors in the process, who may or may not be aware of the laws of their destiny, who may or may not (that is to say) be free. For the only true freedom lies in the recognition of Necessity and so adjusting our aims to harmonize with the superior Reason represented by that Necessity.

> " For Law is the objectivity of Spirit; volition in its true form. Only that will which obeys law, is free; for it obeys itself—it is independent and so free." [1]

The problem of freedom was for Hegel inseparable from the dynamics of social change. Freedom like the other values held by many to be self-evident, Hegel refused to consider as absolute in its embodiment in the human conception of any particular period. It was constantly developing through time towards the final goal of the Absolute, and consequently to the philosopher living in the flux of history, the dynamic element in culture was the crucial element. The mistake of the eighteenth-century materialists had been to view the world as substance instead of seeing it as a constantly developing process, a perpetual becoming. Thus overlooking the significance

---

[1] Hegel, *The Philosophy of History*, English Translation by J. Sibree, New York, 1944, p. 39.

of dynamic change, they were led to oversimplify and mistake the nature of causation.   Certainly in the domain of social studies, explanation in such terms as laws of individual psychology, climatology or ethnology was to be rejected as specious. For if this kind of explanation were valid, there would be no need of any historical inquiry into a people's past to discover their characteristics.   Whereas in fact, the legacy of the past, the collective memory of common traditions constantly renewed and growing anew is crucial to the understanding of any people at any period.   To suppose that methods which had been successful in the natural sciences could on that account be bodily transposed to humanistic disciplines was to mistake fundamentally the inner logic of these last.   The basic conditions were different.   In the humanities there was no recurring, uniform sequence of events susceptible to experimentation and measurement.   For human beings are historical animals, entities which are always developing, learning, changing entities which are unique and unrepeatable.

To understand this dynamism aright, it was essential to grasp the organic nature of society.   For the processes of growth of society parallel those of the individual.   A society, and in particular the modern nation state, has a character or soul even as the individual has.   When we seek to define the dominant characteristics of the English Restoration or the Italian Renaissance, the activity is of the same logical category as when we describe the defining peculiarities of the character of John Smith.   And this spirit is determined by laws of growth of which societies have so far dwelt in ignorance.   The different elements that compose a nation's culture are as complex and as closely inter-dependent as are the constituents of individual personality, so that in the one case no less than in the other is it possible for one element to respond to new experience and changing circumstance without automatically affecting the other elements.   It is as absurd to examine the jurisprudence or the art or the economics or the music of a given culture in isolation from one another as to seek to understand a single personality trait of an individual divorced from his total character structure.   Although each worked in a different medium, Trollope, Huxley, Bagehot, Rossetti are by their mere contemporaneity as easily recognizable as mid-Victorians as are Purcell, Wren, Clarendon and Newton similarly branded as products of the Restoration. Historians had hitherto erred in studying the different elements of societies, as if they existed in self-sufficient, water-tight compartments, intelligible as autonomous units, instead of recognizing that cultural events are members one of another.[1]

The advance made by this awareness of the unity or interrelatedness of a culture for the writing of history was itself of the highest importance. But what of the process of change itself? The laws of the dynamics of history had, according to Hegel, a peculiar logic of their own. History, so far from being a simple succession of events, mechanically related, as the materialists had supposed, was a cataclysmic affair. Its internal dynamic was one of self-perpetuating conflict.

> " Spirit—consuming the envelope of its existence—does not merely pass into another envelope, nor rise rejuvenescent from the ashes of its previous form; it comes forth exalted, glorified, a purer spirit. It certainly makes war upon itself—consumes its own existence; but in this very destruction it works up that existence into a new form, and each successive phase becomes in its turn a material, working on which it exalts itself to a new grade." [2]

The principle of development in the perpetual becoming of the universe, manifested at every level of activity, physical and biological as well as social, is a dialectical one. The principle was arrived at by generalizing the principle of procedure observed in rational discussion as a means of arriving at the truth, best exemplified in the Socratic or dialectic method of the Platonic Dialogues. The propounding of a thesis evokes by its challenge a contradictory thesis, and out of the resultant conflict emerges a position which will command some measure of agreement in so far as it synthesizes the two contestant positions. On this view the truth of any statement can only be relative, since it will in its turn be subject to the self-perpetuating, dialectical process. But the process is a

---

[1] Cf. the discussion by I. Berlin, *Karl Marx*, 1939, Ch. III, " The Philosophy of the Spirit."

[2] Hegel, *op. cit.*, p. 73.

progressive one, for at each stage of the synthesizing process, the new position reached is higher than its predecessor. It approaches yet nearer to that final standard of absolute truth and perfection, towards which the eternal Spirit is leading us, by unfolding itself dialectically through our individual rational dialectic. Applied to history, the method enables us to see the laws of the development of the Idea at their highest level of expression. There is no need to give here Hegel's illustrations of the working of the dialectic in the historical realm. Suffice it to say that the progressive process is seen in the culmination of Germanic civilization which represents the highest degree of human freedom yet attained in the violent struggle to realize the eternal Idea.

> " The History of the World is the discipline of the uncontrolled natural will, bringing it into obedience to a Universal principle and conferring subjective freedom. The East knew and to the present day knows only that *One* is Free; the Greek and Roman world, that *some* are free; the German World knows that *All* are free." [1]

Thus although men do not consciously will what actually happens, do not make history rationally, since they do not perceive the full ramifications of their actions in the complex pattern of social relations, yet those actions are not fortuitous. They serve to fulfil the predetermined shape of human destiny, nothwithstanding the blindness of the instrumental agents to the inner logic of their acts. Possessed of the key to that logic, however, in the shape of the dialectic of the Spirit, we are enabled to become conscious of the laws which determine our fate, and thus give a rational explanation to an apparently irrational history. The present-day Hegelian, who does not look askance at an organic conception of the State, might well extend the parallel in the light of the Freudian principles of the Libido and the Id in individual psychology. Although the individual may be wholly unaware of the inner logic of his own mental life, and firmly convinced that his own rationalizations of his motives are the true ones, he is, it is claimed, none the less completely determined by the operation of these

---

[1] Hegel, *op. cit.*, p. 104.

principles at a profounder mental level. Again, as Freud argued in the case of the individual, Hegel contended that for society the first step towards genuine freedom is not to deny the evidence of determining factors, but to understand the laws of their operation, and thus find the release and fruitful application of our energies in submitting to and working to fulfil those laws. For Hegel true freedom was rooted in Necessity. Only through a knowledge of history's laws can we avoid being unwitting playthings of the gods, and emerge as rational creatures acting within the confines of those laws, and thus realizing the true freedom of obeying the will of God.

In this, there was, as we have seen, nothing remarkably new. What was new was the prestige the doctrine acquired and the influence it exerted in European historical thinking. But, aggressive and even arrogant as it was in its challenge, it did not effectively answer Hume's damaging analysis of the nature of our knowledge of both causation and moral law. By redefining the nature of causation itself as conceived by human beings, it provided no argument to convince the Humean sceptic that our rational powers are such as to enable us to perceive any necessary causal relations actually existing in the real world. The entire Hegelian philosophic edifice is raised on the epistemological assumption that the nature of Reality is ideal in content, and that human reason as a part of that reality, of the Ideal whole, is capable of direct, intuitive knowledge of the world in which it operates.

In few writers is the close affinity between their political theory and their philosophy of history more evident than in the thought of Hegel. The nation State, organically conceived, was held by Hegel to have an existence over and above the aggregate of the individual citizens who composed it; it was in truth no less than the instrument whereby we can most nearly realize the elements of the divine. For, although the divine spark exists in the individual, it is there but partially and imperfectly realized. Only in the collective wisdom of the group as revealed in the unfolding history of the nation State is the highest and most progressive realization of the Absolute to be found. From the divine tactic of history, it was but a short step to the subordination of the individual to the State, to the conviction that even the man, condemned to death by the just laws of the State, as he walks to the execution post, actually wills his own death and finds therein the consummation of his freedom. If he is not in fact conscious of doing so, that is because his reason is temporarily estranged on grounds not difficult to understand. The essence of Hegelian freedom lies in our willingness to recognize the State as the harbinger of the historical law and as the most complete manifestation of Spirit known to us, and in that spirit to carry out its decrees with good grace.

Although Hegel's philosophy of history exerted a crucial influence upon Marx's intellectual development, Hegelian assumptions concerning the nature of historical knowledge have since been developed (particularly in our own time) so as to constitute the core of a militant attempt to emancipate the historical disciplines from what is termed " the cloven hoof of naturalism." It is this view of the epistemology of history that I wish to discuss here, since if it be accepted as valid, the Marxist philosophy of history would have to be rejected *in toto* as grounded on wrongly conceived methods.

The controversy stated in crudely disjunctive terms as to whether history is a science or an art is a very old one. Already in the eighteenth century, people like Turgot and Priestley were at pains to explain why history could not be considered as a science. And ever since neither side in the dispute has lacked aggressive and uncompromising champions. "History," said Professor Bury, " is a science; no less, and no more." Spencer, Durkheim, Hobhouse, writing in the sociological tradition of Comte, sought to fashion out of the materials of history a science of human evolution, with the implication that the historical residue was fit for *mere* description and signifying nothing. On the other side of the barrier, the *historiens historisants* (to use an apt phrase of Professor Bloch), suspicious of positivistic arrogance, acutely conscious of the limitations of the historian's tools and of the pitfalls exposed by meticulous documentary analysis, tinged too perhaps by Cartesian scepticism as to the status of a necessarily highly selective discipline, insisted equally loudly that the historian's craft was essentially an art. Professor G. M.

Trevelyan, for example, is not content to defend the descriptive function of the historian who seeks to recreate in narrative form the life of the past as a valid activity in its own right, but roundly condemns in principle those who attempt to discover underlying uniformities on the scientific analogy.

> " For the study of mankind does not resemble the study of the physical properties of atoms, or the life-history of animals. If you find out about one atom, you have found out about all atoms, and what is true of the habits of one robin is roughly true of the habits of all robins. But the life history of one man, or even of many individual men, will not tell you the life history of other men. Moreover you cannot make a full scientific analysis of the life history of any one man. Men are too complicated, too spiritual, too various, for scientific analysis; . . ." [1]

Fifteen years earlier, he had stated even more categorically,

> " There is no utilitarian value in knowledge of the past, and there is no way of scientifically deducing causal laws about the action of human beings in the mass." [2]

And if we turn from the practising historians to the philosophers, we shall again find the Hegelian tradition well represented. Croce in Italy and Collingwood in Britain have both propounded the Hegelian thesis that all history is ultimately the life of the human mind. For Collingwood the crucial test enabling us to demarcate the material susceptible to scientific analysis from that which is not, lies in the distinction he makes between the " outside " and " inside " of human events. If Cæsar's crossing of the Rubicon be taken as the outside of an event, then the inside of that event (to which it is the historian's peculiar function to penetrate) is the thought in Cæsar's head, the mental response to his situation, which determined that his action should take the form it did and no other. By a historian reliving in his own mind a past which is not dead, but lives on in the mental life of the historian, the past is " incapsulated " into the present and thereby in a self-perpetuating process shapes the situation of the present. In

[1] G. M. Trevelyan, *History and the Reader*, 1945, p. 12.
[2] G. M. Trevelyan, *Clio, A Muse*, 1930, p. 147.

this way, and only in this way can mind be said to know itself. Mind is peculiar in that while it can never know directly the world of nature, which it attempts to organize and control on the basis of classified and experimentally controlled sense data, it is capable of direct, intuitive experience of the thought of another human being. Since there is no evidence that events in the physical world have an " inside " as well as an " outside," and since the scientist has no need of Berkeley's hypothesis that they are sustained by the mind of God, their lack of internality demonstrates that the difference between them as objects of human knowledge and events which result from thought processes is an ontological one. As Dilthey earlier expressed it,

> " Mankind, if apprehended only by perception and perceptual knowledge, would be for us a physical fact, and as such it would be accessible only to natural-scientific knowledge." [1]

And again,

> " The unit which is the element in the very complicated structure of society is given immediately to the intelligence— it is itself—while in the natural sciences it has to be inferred." [2]

If by a supreme effort of the historical imagination we are capable of reliving in our own minds the thoughts which caused the external historical events, then we have understood those events; we have knowledge of them, and our knowledge is as complete as it can be. To quote again from Collingwood,

> " If, by historical thinking, we already understand how and why Napoleon established his ascendancy in revolutionary France, nothing is added to our understanding of that process by the statement (however true) that similar things have happened elsewhere." [3]

If this view were to be accepted, then Marx, for example, would be condemned as a historian who attempted to use history for his own purpose by " pigeon holing " his data into

---

[1] H. A. Hodges, *Wilhelm Dilthey—An Introduction*, 1944, p. 142.
[2] *Ibid.*, p. 144.
[3] R. G. Collingwood, *The Idea of History*, 1946, p. 223.

synthetic categories, in order to give significance to an account, deprived of genuine meaning by false method.

The arguments of the metaphysical Idealists and anti-Naturalists may perhaps be summarized under two main headings.

(1) Whereas the material world is completely determined, thus enabling us to formulate causal laws of a universal kind, leading to remarkable precision of prediction, the world of mind, with which the historian is concerned, cannot by its nature be so explained because of the autonomy of the complex and non-rational human will. Unlike the robin or the atom, the human will is free and therefore in principle unpredictable.

(2) Whereas the natural sciences are essentially modes of generalization, whose material is susceptible to the formulation of laws, universally valid irrespective of time or place, historical studies are essentially individualizing processes, which treat of specific and unique events. Such events being unrepeatable preclude the clinical conditions for experimentation, a crucial tool of verification for the scientist, but beyond the reach of the historian. The historian is thereby restricted to the functions of description and narration.

The first point, contrasting the determinism of the one realm with the indeterminism of the other, although a prejudice with a strong hold upon the lay mind, does not appear to be shared by the scientists themselves in their own sphere. Even in physics, the most advanced of the sciences, it is not claimed that the more general laws will necessarily permit of 100 per cent. accuracy of prediction when applied to the real world.[1] That the laws themselves are capable of formulation with mathematical accuracy is due to the fact that they are not strictly speaking synthetic propositions, but are concerned with ideal entities. Professor Ernst Cassirer, discussing Galileo's methods in founding the science of dynamics, points out how starting from an assumption of an isolated body in uniform acceleration towards a given point, it is possible to deduce conceptually what will happen. If empirical observation then confirmed this, we may conclude that the conditions,

[1] Cf. the discussion by F. Kaufmann in Ch. XIII, " Physical Laws and Social Laws," of his *Methodology of the Social Sciences*, New York, 1944.

hypothetically established, are to be found in nature. But even if this confirmation were not forthcoming,

> ". . . our propositions would lose nothing of their validity, since in and for themselves they contain no assertions about existence, but only connect certain ideal consequences to certain ideal premises. . . . For him [Galileo] the law of inertia has throughout the character of a mathematical principle, and even if its consequences are applicable to relations of outer reality, they nevertheless in no way signify a direct copy of any empirically given fact. The conditions, of which it speaks, are actually never realized; . . ." [1]

Such laws, it would appear, so far from being rigid, viz. subject to invalidation by a single negative occurrence, are guides to the formulation of principles based on observation and experiment, but frequently of a less firm and less precise nature. To quote again from Cassirer, discussing in this instance the function of experiment as a means of analysis,

> ". . . however close we may come to all particular circumstances of the real process, nevertheless there is always the possibility that some coöperative factor in the total result has not been calculated, and will only be discovered with the further progress of experimental analysis. Each result established has thus only the relative value of a preliminary determination ; and as such only holds what is gained in order to use it as a starting-point for new determinations." [2]

And finally, since the notion that modern physics at least, if not the other natural sciences, is a discipline susceptible to a completely rigid determinism, dies hard in the minds of historians as of other laymen, it may be permissible to give one more authoritative statement on this issue. The following passage is taken from *The Logic of Modern Physics* of P. W. Bridgman, Professor of Mathematics and Natural Philosophy at Harvard.

> " Given a description of an isolated part of the physical universe in the most complete terms that have physical

---

[1] E. Cassirer, *Substance and Function; and Einstein's Theory of Relativity*, English Translation by W. C. and M. C. Swabey, Chicago, 1923, pp. 168–69.

[2] *Ibid.*, p. 254.

meaning, that is, down to the smallest elements of which our physical operations give us cognizance, then the future history of the system is determined within a certain penumbra of uncertainty, this penumbra growing broader as we penetrate to finer details of the structure of the system or as time goes on, until eventually all but certain very general properties of the original system, such as its total energy, are forever lost in the haze, and we have a system which was unpredictable." [1]

But, it may be said, even if it be conceded that we cannot predict with certainty in the physical world, the fact remains that whereas natural scientists do formulate laws which permit of reliable predictions given the fulfilment of specified conditions, students of the human disciplines cannot do so because they are confronted with an intrinsically different and incalculable phenomenon, the human will. In human affairs, the play of the contingent, the good fortune or the havoc wrought by " the magic hand of chance " are such as to render any attempt at reliable prediction mischievous as well as futile. The argument is a familiar one. In the eloquent words of Burke, " A common soldier, a child, a girl at the door of an inn, have changed the face of fortune, and almost of nature." [2] The difficulty with the statement that the will is free is that it is not easy to grasp clearly what is meant, still less to subject it to any kind of test. If the will is defined as a psychic source of individual behaviour that is itself without cause, then analytically it may be deduced that the will is " free." But such a statement, however true, would of course tell us nothing about the real world. On the other hand, we may be meant to infer that exhaustive investigation of the causes of human behaviour lead us back to an irreducible, ultimate entity, called " the will," beyond which we cannot go, and that this phenomenon appears to evince no stability or uniformity, but is rather random and arbitrary in its behaviour. If this statement were true, it would certainly not make the task of the naturalistic historian any easier, but neither would it cut the ground entirely from under his feet.

[1] P. W. Bridgman, *The Logic of Modern Physics*, New York, 1948, p. 210.
[2] Burke, *Letters on a Regicide Peace*, *Works*, 1826 edition, Vol. VIII, p. 80.

For if the group that is being studied shows no signs of a consistent trend in its willing activities, we would be obliged to conclude that the individual wills within the group effectively neutralized each other, and that in our quest for an explanation of the causal relations in this instance we should have to seek our evidence elsewhere. But if, on the other hand, the group in question is observed to exert its will in a given direction, then the evidence exists on which theories concerning the nature of the will itself may be formulated. We may not be able to establish a rigid law concerning the cause of social revolutions any more than a doctor can specify under what conditions any given patient will die. Medical diagnosis is not on that account to be despised as mere intelligent guess-work. No more should we refuse to consider the solid historical reasons which may be advanced to substantiate the hypothesis that any society that wishes to avoid revolution would do well to avoid a prolonged period of mercurial instability in its currency, for instance. The fact that precision and rigidity are not to be looked for in statements of what are trends rather than laws, indicates the complexity of human beings and the patience demanded of the student, not that the human will is of a different ontological order from the rest of nature.

But even though the actions of large numbers of men may not be beyond the reach of rational prediction in principle, it remains to consider the argument that from time to time isolated individuals arise who by their own genius, by their personal magnetism and influence over others succeed in decisively shaping the destinies of entire peoples. Although aphorisms that we tend to associate with a Carlyle or a Parkman to the effect that " the history of the world is but the biography of great men " are no longer fashionable, it is still worth raising the question whether the history of modern Europe would have pursued an essentially similar course, had a Napoleon or a Hitler been exposed at birth. Professor Sidney Hook in an interesting examination of such cases (*The Hero in History*, 1945) arrives at the distinction between " eventful " and " event making " men, that is, between men whom the necessities of the contemporary crisis demanded and who therefore played a role which would in any event have been comparably played by someone or other, and men whose decisive contribution was of a peculiarly individual and unique nature. After a fairly detailed analysis, he finds himself prepared to admit into the latter category at least one man, V. I. Lenin, without whom, he argues, the October Revolution would not have occurred. While not denying in principle the practicability or usefulness to the historian of examining hypotheticals contrary to fact, it is doubtful whether we may place much confidence in a judgment one way or the other concerning hypotheticals that raise issues so vast and complex as this one does. But again, as Professor Hook would himself agree, the possibility of formulating non-rigid laws in history does not stand or fall on this issue. Even if the causal efficacy of a Lenin were as far-reaching as Hook contends, the effect would be to increase the complexity and hence the difficulty of isolating the operative factors in an analysis of the cause of revolutions, not to exclude the task in principle.

When hard pressed, the anti-naturalist may concede that certain predictions can reliably be made concerning human activities, but then attempt to save his case by falling back upon an alleged distinction between the animal and the non-animal parts of human nature, with the latter of which only, the historian is concerned. It is argued by Collingwood, for instance, that

> ". . . so far as man's conduct is determined by what may be called his animal nature, his impulses and appetites, it is non-historical; the process of those activities is a natural process."[1]

To which the naturalist would no doubt retort that for him this is evidence of the cloven hoof of idealism, with its rigid separation of the mental and the physical. With this point of view in mind, it is interesting to take note of an article, entitled *Epidemiology and the Psychosomatic Affections*, by J. L. Halliday.[2] Although sub-titled " a study in social medicine," the paper could with equal justification have been called an

[1] Collingwood, *op. cit.*, p. 216.
[2] *The Lancet*, August 10th, 1946, p. 185.

essay in social history. The author contends that for a variety of reasons, which include such factors as changes in the theories and actual regimens of child nurture, reduction in the size of families, as well as increased insecurity in the social environment arising out of wars, unemployment, etc., there has in fact been a steadily rising incidence of personality disturbances, resulting in a manifold variety of psychosomatic affections, with obvious consequences of a complex nature throughout the whole field of social behaviour. This is an inquiry which presumably would qualify under Collingwood's definition as one primarily concerned with man's " animal nature," yet we could scarcely deny the vital relevance of any reliable findings which such an inquiry might reach to a social historian of the period.

The second of the basic anti-naturalist arguments, referred to above (p. 195), emphasizes the uniqueness of historical events and concludes that the historian's peculiar task is by an effort of the historical imagination to penetrate to the core of the individual and the particular. Because of the intrinsic nature of the raw material of his art, the historian has a means of direct knowledge denied to the natural scientist, namely, the direct understanding of one mind by another. We may thus attain as complete a knowledge as is possible of human causal relations, to which knowledge nothing is added by generalizations based on a knowledge of similar events elsewhere. This process of direct understanding may be interpreted in either of two ways. We may infer by analogy with our own introspection of our own egos that such self-knowledge may be generalized to explain similar behaviour on the part of others. Or, it may be held, the human mind includes among its attributes an innate faculty enabling it to feel its way into other people's minds by reason of a common bond of human sympathy, thus enabling it to have direct intuitive knowledge of psychical events other than its own. Either way, the contention is that the human psyche possesses a faculty of intuition which renders direct, immediate apprehension of the truth possible. The response to arguments, so radically rationalist in temper, must necessarily be of a historical and pragmatic kind. The *critical* rationalists of the seventeenth

century with their emphasis on the need for objective, experimental criteria of verification and the need to conceive every
synthetic proposition as a hypothesis subject in principle to
future elimination in the light of further evidence, launched
the modern scientific movement. The denial of ontological
validity, that we may know the inner essence of things as they
really are, independently of the limitations of the cogitative
apparatus of the inquiring agent, was for Galileo [1] a radical
step, but the principle gradually won general acceptance. It
is to-day an axiom of scientific method that every synthetic
proposition is in varying degree subject to possible invalidation
according to procedural techniques of objective or interpersonal status. It must, of course, be admitted that human
disciplines present a degree of complexity such as to render
the task of isolating the variable and the constant factors one
of very great difficulty. But in the light of scientific experience,
both in its successes and its struggles to win acceptance for its
methods, we should surely require weighty and convincing
evidence to justify departure in any field of inquiry from well-
tried methods and the adoption of verification of knowledge
by such a notoriously subjective procedure as intuition. Still
less are we entitled to conclude that the present limits to our
knowledge of human behaviour shut off from our gaze a realm
of intrinsic mystery, which is in principle unknowable, and
immune to the kind of penetration to which the rest of nature
has proved susceptible. The whole history of human inquiry
testifies to the unwisdom of making categorical assertions concerning the intrinsic nature of reality, which expose us to the
risk of future discoveries incompatible with such assertions,
however improbable a contingency we may consider that to be.

To deny that there is any ontological difference between
the realm of the physicist and the realm of the historian is not,
of course, to deny the very evident differences between their
centres of interest and their techniques in handling their very
different materials. He who sets out to write an account of
the elements of a science will necessarily have to rely mainly
upon generalizing and analytic techniques; while he who

---

[1] *Vide* E. A. Burtt, *The Metaphysical Foundations of Modern Physical Science*, 1949
edition, Ch. III, " Galileo," *passim*.

recounts the history of the development of that science will have recourse to descriptive, individualizing methods. But it is not the case that neither ever has recourse to the methods of the other. The historian sometimes essays induction even as the physicist sometimes describes his phenomena. It is true that the uniform repeatability of the natural scientist's materials enables him to experiment in a way largely denied to the historian. But even this distinction, important as it is in practice, requires some qualification. On the other hand, the experimental method is out of reach of the astronomer; while the historian's understanding is sometimes assisted by the raising of hypotheticals contrary to fact, a method which bears a structural resemblance to the experimental method, even if it can never be similarly conclusive. Although Professor Trevelyan's *If Napoleon Had Won The Battle of Waterloo* [1] is admittedly a playful, light-hearted piece, he did not at least reject the question out of hand as intrinsically absurd and unworthy of the historian's talents.

The importance for the historian of a nominalist method, and the need to understand the individual as the centre of historical explanation were strongly emphasized by the German historian and sociologist, Max Weber. Yet, at the same time, his outstanding contribution in the field of historical method consisted of his development of the " ideal type." The ideal type is not ideal in any sense of appraisal, but is artificially constructed by an eclectic fusion of elements which are separate in the world of experience. By such empirical distortion, he was able to increase his understanding of and to attempt generalizations of particular aspects of historical cultures. Historians were thus helped to a greater awareness of their methods, when in the interests of systematization and generalization, they employed such models as " the economic man," " the rational man," and other idealizations of personality types, as well as such idealizations of social structures as exemplified in such conceptions as " feudalism " or " capitalism." To those who do not look askance at

---

[1] G. M. Trevelyan, *Clio, A Muse and Other Essays*, 1930. The essay referred to was the prize-winning essay in a competition held by the *Westminster Gazette* in July, 1907. It is reprinted in the above-quoted volume, pp. 124–35.

analogies with the methods of the natural science, it is interesting to compare these developments with the function of " ideal " laws in the realm of physics, discussed above.

> " The efforts of the human intellect," wrote a great American scholar, Professor Morris Cohen, " may be viewed as a tension between two poles—one to do justice to the fullness of the concrete case before us, the other to grasp an underlying abstract universal principle that controls much more than the one case before us." [1]

If we go to the work of the great historians, we shall find no lack of evidence of the will to realize this dual purpose; and yet, the view persists that the methods implicit in these two admittedly distinct " efforts of the human intellect" are mutually incompatible, that history is a " science " or an " art." The truth is that in the study of human societies either of the past or our own age, events are vast in number and in their interactions much more complicated than physical events. For this reason, our generalizations are still mostly limited to a statement of tendencies, which will not bear rigid application to every individual circumstance. Because human character has so many facets, is so much a matter of light and shade, so various, so chameleon-like in its changes, so kaleidoscopic in its blending of strange undertones and qualities, the insights that we often associate with the great poet or novelist, if properly disciplined, are part of the qualities required of the great historian. Because our systematic knowledge of individuals and institutions, despite the very substantial advances made by historical science in the last century, is so relatively crude, there is and will long continue to be no substitute for the interpretations of the fallible judgment of gifted individuals. But that is not a good reason for giving up the attempt to obtain more exact knowledge of the kind which will enable us to exert a greater control over reality by the well-tried methods of science.

[1] Morris R. Cohen, *Reason and Nature: An Essay on the Meaning of Scientific Method*, London, 1931, p. 368.

CHAPTER X

Marxism

Our concern in this book, as was stated in the Introduction, has been primarily with the emergence of philosophy of history in the speculative sense, and our departure in the foregoing chapter into the realm of critical philosophy of history was necessitated by the implications which the Hegelian view of the status of historical knowledge have for the student of Marx. Although Hegel himself did not draw such a conclusion, Hegelian critical as opposed to speculative philosophy of history has been used to question the status of the mere attempt to induce general laws of a historical character. If such a view were accepted, then Marx's speculative philosophy of history would stand convicted in principle of false method, and further examination of the main structure of his thought would be of largely historic interest. It was the purpose of the preceding chapter to demonstrate that in our view Marxism cannot be impugned on such radically rationalistic grounds. From which it by no means follows, of course, that the content of Marx's view of history will necessarily stand up to scientific, historical criticism on the one hand and philosophical analysis on the other.

Approached analytically, it may be said that Marxist thought about history is at once a thesis concerning historical method and a doctrine about the direction of historical progression. In so far as Marx asserts the primacy of economic data in his approach to the problem of explanation of causal relations in history, his thesis directly concerns the historian; in so far as he holds that society is inevitably destined to achieve a classless social structure, he raises problems which are the predominant concern of the philosopher. Nevertheless, for the convenience of exposition, since method and doctrine are

so inextricably interwoven, there is much to be said in favour
of a historical approach to the development of Marx's historical thought as a whole, and that is the course that is proposed here.

The rapid growth of Marxism as a source of political influence can be explained on two grounds. In the first place,
the times were peculiarly ripe for it. The human waste and
misery left in the wake of the Industrial Revolution raised a
mounting volume of protest, not unreceptive to Marx's moral
denunciations. It is true that Marxism made more rapid
headway on the continent of Europe than in Britain. But
even in the land of his adoption, where the violence of Marx's
language, not to mention the crudity of his metaphors, constituted an additional deterrent to the absorption of ideas in
themselves highly inflammable, his indirect and leavening
influence was never negligible. In the second place, Marxism
as a doctrine constituted a most remarkable synthesis of many
and diverse currents of thought at that time influential. On
the one hand, there existed an uneasy alliance between the
determination to exemplify the highest standards of the British
empirical tradition in striving to achieve objective, scientific
status for historical and sociological disciplines, and a no
less strong insistence on the right or rather the obligation to
indict in the strongest possible terms moral error. For although
Marx exceeded even Bentham in his contempt for the assumptions of the Natural Law school, this did not prevent him
in his rabbinical moral fervour from drawing upon the susten-
ance of the Judeo-Christian tradition in which he had been
nurtured, despite, too, the virulence with which he assailed
that tradition. On the other hand, there was a less embar-
rassing confluence of ideas in the fusion of the jacobinical,
activist, revolutionary tradition, coming out of France and
perpetuated in the writings of the St. Simonians and the
Fourierists, with the thorough-going relativism of the German
Hegelian school of dialectical historicism. And it is this last
source of Marx's ideas that must constitute our starting point
in inquiring into the development of his ideas.

It was not so much Hegel's political philosophy which influenced the young Marx, as he pursued his legal and philo-

sophical studies in the University of Berlin in the late thirties of the last century. Rather was it the method, which he perceived to be implicit in the Hegelian philosophy of history, of investigating both historical and sociological phenomena, which impressed him so forcefully. The weakness in the dialectical method as propounded by Hegel appeared to Marx to lie in its idealism, and hence for him in its mysticism. His objections were twofold. In the first place, he saw clearly enough that Hegel's theory explained too much. Or rather, in so far as it offered an explanation, it was in terms of a metaphysic as unverifiable as any animistic belief. Any hypothesis whatever concerning the nature of historical change would be compatible with the thesis that the Real is the rational and represents the march of God in the world. On such criteria, no explanation is in principle excluded. An explanation of the process of development as a progressively dialectical one provides no explanation other than in terms of final cause of such crucial questions as to what sets the whole developmental process in motion, what provides the propulsion from the rear and maintains the driving force. In the second place, the theory had for Marx unfortunate social implications in so far as it postulated a passive and therefore reactionary role for the philosopher. Since the living are all engaged in the dialectical conflict, themselves interested agents of the forces contending for supremacy, they are compelled to take sides without any knowledge of the outcome of the conflict. Only when the dust has settled on the battle field, is the philosopher able to perceive which was the lost cause, which position was in fact relatively wrong.

" Philosophy," wrote Hegel in the Preface to the *Philosophy of Right*, " in any case always comes on the scene too late to give it [instruction as to what the world ought to be]. As the thought of the world, it appears only when actuality is already there cut and dried after its process of formation has been completed. . . . When philosophy paints its grey in grey, then has a shape of life grown old. By philosophy's grey in grey it cannot be rejuvenated but only understood. The owl of Minerva spreads its wings only with the falling of the dusk." [1]

[1] Hegel, *Philosophy of Right*, English Translation by T. M. Knox, 1942, pp. 12–13.

Marx, living in a time of social revolution opened up by the cataclysm of '89 in France, consumed as he was by a burning sense of injustice and hatred for the social evils of his time, was bound to reject such a view of the function of philosophy. As he wrote in the *Theses on Feuerbach* (xi) in 1845, " The philosophers have only *interpreted* the world in various ways; the point, however, is to change it."

The solution eventually arrived at by Marx retained the dialectical explanation of causality, but rejected the " Idea " as the motive force of the dynamics of the dialectic in favour of a materialist explanation.

> " For Hegel," wrote Marx, " the thought process (which he actually transforms into an independent subject, giving to it the name of ' idea ') is the demiurge of the real. . . . In my view, on the other hand, the ideal is nothing other than the material when it has been transposed and translated inside the human head." [1]

Before developing the capacity to think, man had first to come to terms with his material surroundings.

> " Men may be distinguished from animals by consciousness, religion or anything else. They begin to differentiate themselves from animals as soon as they begin to *produce* their means of subsistence, a step which is conditioned by their physical organization." [2]

Their lives and the circumstances which surround them are not the result of thinking about the problem of organizing themselves in relation to their environment. That is a later development after they have established some kind of existence.

> " It is not consciousness that determines life, but life that determines consciousness." [3]

When men first reach the stage of formulating their ideas, those ideas are necessarily rooted in the material conditions surrounding them. Thus already in the chrysallis stage of

---

[1] Marx, Preface to the second German edition of *Das Kapital*, Everyman edition of *Capital*, Vol. II, p. 873.

[2] Marx and Engels, *German Ideology, A Handbook of Marxism*, edited by E. Burns, 1936, p. 211.

[3] *Ibid.*, p. 213.

human society, man finds his freedom of thought and of action closely circumscribed by an environmental situation which is not of his own making.

In this initial relation between men and their physical environment is to be found the key to the entire fabric of society. For in bringing order out of material chaos, in organizing through the struggle to survive the available means of production, man unconsciously organizes his relations with his fellows as well as the means of production. His mode of getting a living exercises a direct influence upon his social relations. If land or water or animals are harnessed to men's purposes, regulations for their allocation and employment are required to determine both ownership and conditions of ownership. In short, the exchange of the earth's resources with the human metabolism necessitates some kind of property institution, the maintenance of which requires in its turn a juridical system. The property relations thus arising enjoin all kinds of social differentiæ characterising various groups within the society. Principally they distinguish men in their relation to power, according to whether they share in the exercise of power or whether they are subject to it. Men thus acquire group loyalties and common interests which they have a mutual incentive both to promote and defend against competing interests of other social groups. Their common interests dictate a set of common assumptions, governed in the last resort by a sense of the importance of acting in concert to hold what they have. For in a world of scarcity, the many must be excluded from the realm of privilege, and the privileged will have every incentive to elaborate a rationale which succeeds in reconciling the general interest with their narrow class interest. They may, indeed, rationalize their inner desires and needs to such effect that they succeed in deluding even themselves.

The element of crucial importance, then, in any society, essential to an understanding of the balance of forces within it, is the means whereby that society gains its livelihood, the technique and relations of production, in fact. Once we know the nature of the forces of production by which a society supports itself, we know also the limiting factors of the institutions,

social and political as well as economic, of the philosophy and
the law, of the whole culture of that society, or, to use Marx's
omnibus phrase, " the whole vast superstructure." It is true
that Engels in letters to Mehring, Starkenberg, and Bloch
after Marx's death considerably diluted this economic monism.[1]
And it may well be considered that the reduction of economic
phenomena from a position of exclusive importance to one of
mere primacy, seriously weakens the value of the theory as an
aid to historical and sociological inquiry. On the other hand,
in certain historical periods the primacy of economic relations
may be of such cardinal importance, as for example in Marx's
own day, that for practical purposes the theory may be used
with great effect as an instrument of analysis. Certainly, no
other contemporary historian was able to rival Marx, relying
on assumptions of economic monism, in the insight revealed
in his penetrating analyses of the political conflict in contemporary France. De Tocqueville's own masterly diagnosis
of the social malaise afflicting the *Ancien Régime* was based on
voluminous researches conducted more than half a century
after the events in question. Marx's brilliant dissection in

---

[1] *Vide* Engels' letter to Mehring, July 14th, 1893: " Only one point is lacking
which Marx and I did not sufficiently stress and in relation to which we are
equally to blame. We both placed and *had to place* the chief weight upon the
derivation of political, legal and other ideological notions, as well as the actions
which they led up to, from fundamental economic facts. In consequence we
neglected the formal side, i.e. the way in which these ideas arose, for the sake of
the content. . . . Because we denied that the different ideological spheres, which
play a part in history, have an independent historical development, we were
supposed therewith to have denied that they have any *historical efficacy* . . . an
historical factor, once it has been brought into the world by another—ultimately
economic fact—is able to re-act upon its surroundings and even affect its own
causes. . . ." (Quoted by S. Hook, *Towards the Understanding of Karl Marx*,
London, 1933, pp. 282–83.) A good example of a practical illustration of the
theory, when no more is claimed for it than this, is to be found in Marx, *Introduction
to the Critique of Political Economy*: " Is the view of nature and of social relations
which constitutes the basis of Greek phantasy and therefore of Greek art, possible
in an age of automatic machinery, railroads, locomotives, and electric telegraphs?
Where does Vulcan come in as against Roberts & Co.; Jupiter as against the
lightning rod; and Hermes as against the Credit Mobilier? All mythology
masters and dominates and shapes the forces of nature in and through the imagination; hence it disappears as soon as man gains real control over the forces of
nature. What becomes of the Goddess Fame side by side with Printing House
Square? . . ." (Marx, *A Contribution to the Critique of Political Economy*, English
Translation by N. I. Stone, 1904, p. 310.)

the series of articles, *The Class Struggles in France* (1848–50), *The Eighteenth Brumaire of Louis Bonaparte, the Civil War in France*, of the forces contending for mastery in the France of 1848 and 1870–71 has stood the test of time equally well, and was undertaken almost before the victims of those tragic uprisings had themselves been laid to rest. But it does not necessarily follow from this that in our present epoch, when a greater measure of control over economic relations has been achieved (partly, no doubt, due to the extent to which Marx's own insights have been absorbed into every-day assumptions), even a person of Marx's extraordinary talents would be able to employ his analytic methods with comparable effect. But whatever view we may take on this vexed question of the degree of importance to be attached to economic phenomena, at the least the importance of Marx's salutary influence in stressing (if almost certainly exaggerating) their significance cannot be gainsaid in an age when economic studies still tended to be neglected by historians.

In the charge, on the other hand, that Marx's economic determinism betrayed a failure on his part to cherish anything other than merely " materialist " values, there is no substance whatever. " Bread and circus " values were as repellent to Marx as to any man, but no less repellent were " spiritual " values which evinced no awareness of the social price paid by the many to create the conditions out of which those values emerged. Marx's point was that so long as men do not understand the laws of history that determine their conditions; so long as social groups exploit one another in the class war which characterizes the " pre-history " stage of man's development, then for so long will man be condemned to wrestle with the forces of nature for a bare subsistence. For so long will his efforts be rewarded by scarcity instead of the abundance and leisure, now confined to the few, which are essential means to gracious and dignified living. To speak of the virtues of the higher life of cultural pursuits to people who were compelled to work sometimes an eighteen-hour day for a bare subsistence suggested to Marx a certain want of proportion.

Marx's personal character was, it is true, marred by the urge to dominate of one denied the conventional outlets of

success and power, by the harshness and egocentricity of the
Ishmaelite, and (in the closing stages) by the embittered dis-
trust and near misanthropy of the déraciné expatriate. He
was quarrelsome, intolerant of differences of opinion, and
though wholly free from self-pity and the morbid compensation
of martyrdom, querulous and irritable under the combined
burdens of domestic sorrow, grinding poverty and insecurity.
Proud, defiant, without reverence, inflexible in his resolve
neither to yield nor to be broken, he looms larger than life-
size, a rugged, near-Biblical figure of truly Promethean proportions. It is very easy to caricature him as a scarce-human
monster, launching his thunderbolts and poisoned shafts
against a society he despised, giving no quarter and expecting
as little as he got in return. Such a picture neglects one simple
truth. A creative genius, possessed of the indefatigable
thoroughness and patience of the scholar, he yet had the
practical energy and imagination to organize a great political
movement. The rewards of the world could have been his
and his family's in full measure. In fact, he deliberately
renounced that for which men in every generation hunger in
the shape of wealth, power, acclaim, honour, in order to recall
men to a sense of their responsibilities for the outrages which
were daily permitted to pass unnoticed in the factory, the field,
the mine and the home; in order to make the comfortable
and the indifferent less comfortable and less indifferent, and
the hopeless less resigned and less submissive. Such men are
exceedingly rare, and after they are gone the world generally
deems it wise to laud their example as faithfully as it eschews
their practice. We are still too near to Marx, too intimately
affected by him and the things done in his name for that process yet to have happened in his case. The harsh outlines
have not been softened by time, nor is there much disposition
to appreciate the extent to which Marx's character defects
were the price he paid for his isolation, his determination not
to be corrupted by the " bourgeois " values surrounding him.
Trollope, it may be noted, used a similar theme in one of his
most convincing and moving studies of human character, but
the conflict of the parson of Hogglestock with diocesan
opinion in *The Last Chronicle of Barset* is, of course, confined to

the personal sphere, since it was no more open to the Rev. Mr. Crawley than to Trollope himself to call in question the basic economic premises on which the fabric of Barsetshire society rested.

We have now seen in what consisted Marx's substitution of a materialist for an idealist explanation of the determining factor in the social process. The Hegelian explanation had referred everything back to a super-sensible Idea, which existing in no individual mind could provide no better authentication than Hegel's own *ex cathedra* statement that the Idea existed in the mind of God. In its place, Marx provided an explanation which in principle, it was claimed, was verifiable in terms of empirical, economic conditions.

The other element in Hegel's system of dialectical Idealism to which, as we have said, Marx took exception, was the view taken of the philosopher's function. For Hegel the philosopher was essentially a spectator, confined to the passive role of interpreting the world. It was Marx's intent to change it. In Marx's epistemology the knowing process is never confined to a mere observation of the external world. Rather is it a stage in the process whereby man acts upon his environment. Once we have learnt something about a given situation, the mere fact of our new knowledge in itself acts upon the situation and modifies the precise nature of our relations with it. The kind of " knowledge " that has no such effect, Marx would have rejected as spurious, as outside the terms of his definition of the knowing process. Although Marx does not himself make the distinction in such terms, he would in all probability have agreed with the distinction that has been drawn between *knowing that* and *knowing how*.[1] We may, for instance, read a good deal of psychology and get a sound grasp of the intellectual argument which advances the evidence for certain propositions, and yet, unless what we read strikes a genuine chord within our own personal experience of the world of people, our understanding, our " knowledge " in the formal sense may be confined to a series of verbal responses that we are accustomed to make when the subject in question is under discussion. And such reponses lacking genuine internality, cannot be said

[1] *Vide* Gilbert Ryle, *The Concept of Mind*, 1949, pp. 27–32.

to be inwardly meaningful. The distinction can perhaps be more simply illustrated by considering the stages in learning any new accomplishment. After formal instruction, we may know *that* we have to keep our eye on the ball and follow through, pedal and steer in this way or that, mix and bake eggs, flour, milk and butter, without knowing *how* to golf, cycle, or make a soufflé. The moment we know *how* we have learnt to give new meaning to our former recipe or text-book knowledge. It has become genuine as distinct from formal knowledge, meaningful, that is to say, in terms of the life situation to which it applies.

Knowledge in this sense, then, inevitably reacts upon the material environment, which thus modified in its turn reacts upon the agent, changing him in the process. It is in this ceaseless reciprocity of interaction between the living agents and the material world in which they have their being, that the perpetual becoming of the real world consists. In this process lies the explanation of the dynamics of social development, and the relative nature of all our knowledge of social problems. That knowledge is " true " which enables us to adjust most successfully to the problems inherent in the particular historical situation in which we happen to find ourselves. The solutions of one epoch are not directly applicable to those of another, because by the mere passage of time, the dialectic has moved on and synthesized afresh, changing in the process both the objective situation and the human beings involved in it. Strictly speaking, objective truth and disinterested thought are alike unattainable in principle. We are, all of us, part and parcel of our changing external conditions, intrinsically bound up with them, and our thought is conditioned by the problems they set. Marx erected this to the status of a sociological principle.

> " . . . mankind always sets itself only such problems as it can solve; for when we look closer we will always find that the problem itself only arises when the material conditions for its solution are already present or at least in process of coming into being." [1]

[1] Marx, Preface to *The Critique of Political Economy*, *A Handbook of Marxism*, pp. 372–73.

In so far as Marx here implies that a solution exists to every problem which men have to face, we may well consider him unduly optimistic since history is not lacking in examples of societies so far gone in the process of degeneration and cultural disintegration as to leave no means of recovery. On the other hand, he was probably right in believing that those whose ideas are not realistically related to contemporary conditions are naïve utopians, who pay the price of being ineffectual in the contemporary conflict.

So far as society is concerned, the interaction of man and his environment is expressed in the continuous development of the material forces of production. Changes in the technique of production as a result of human ingenuity and invention, as for example the discovery of fire or the wheel (to instance primitive advances of a revolutionary kind) or the supplanting of coal-fired power production by nuclear power (to cite a probable future development), changes in the conditions of nature itself such as soil erosion or altered river courses or harbour siltage, change of climate, changes in the social relations of men themselves all interact upon one another to transform society. The most notable feature of the modern era has been the remarkable acceleration in the pace of development of the instruments of production. But to understand the repercussions of this silent revolution in the allied field of social relations, it is necessary to discuss the other basic idea in Marx's philosophy of history, namely, his concept of class. Whereas, according to Hegel, the dialectical conflict of the elements of the eternal Idea expressed itself in history in the guise of a conflict of nation states, the agents of dialectical conflict in history, according to Marx, are the social classes.

Although Marx may be said to have underestimated as much as Hegel exaggerated the role of the nation and the strength of men's allegiance to it, his view of the relation between the individual and the group has Hegelian affinities. Substituting the class for the nation state as the significant instrument of historical progress, his conviction regarding the primacy of class relations assumed the organic unity of classes which made them in a sense more real than the individuals composing them. Men might delude themselves that they functioned and held beliefs as autonomous individuals, but in truth their ideas as well as their emotions were largely shaped by the particular social class to which they belonged by virtue of their birth, employment, cultural heritage, social and financial interests. This view of the significance of the class in the social structure is important and obviously not altogether wide of the mark, but the issue is not nearly so simple as Marx seemed to imagine. It would be unwise to dogmatize either way in a matter complex, difficult to investigate, and about which our knowledge is still very limited. It is, for instance, fairly clear that the role of class in evoking men's loyalties varies considerably according to the society and the historical period. It played a more decisive role in the France of 1940 than it did in Britain at the same time, when both countries were compelled to summon up the last reserves of national loyalties under the threat of extreme peril. It is also highly probable that Marx's observations on the primacy of class relations were truer then than they are now, when for many reasons the former acerbity of class relations has been considerably reduced. But whatever view we take, it is imperative to recognize the importance of this view in the elaboration of Marx's philosophy of history.

As the material forces of production develop they come into conflict with the existing social and property relations, now at variance with the new economic conditions. Thus anachronistic in relation to the changed needs, the outmoded social relations of the older epoch are ripe for a transformation which is inevitable. The change from the slave economy of the ancient world to the feudal economy of the mediæval world, and from that in its turn to the capitalist economy of the modern world necessarily involved a concomitant change in the entire cultures of those living, organic societies. But, Marx believed, that change cannot take place until the old system has exhausted its potentialities for further growth and has begun to show definite signs of contraction and decay in the form of inefficiency and incapacity to meet existent demand. At that point the social revolution will inevitably occur as a parallel to the economic revolution which has silently taken place already, thus restoring anew the requisite equilibrium and social stability.

It is at this stage that Marx's class concept becomes all-important in the function of interpretation. Since each social system builds up as an integral part of it an elaborate network of property relations and social privileges, the dominant class of the period has a firmly entrenched interest in maintaining the existing order intact. They can, accordingly, be relied upon to fight a vigorous but necessarily futile rear-guard action to protect their class interests against the onslaught of the class, marked out by history's dialectic to supersede them. Although Marx hinted that this class conflict need not invariably culminate in the dispossession of the " reactionary " class by bloody revolution (instancing the unusual capacity of the English for tolerant compromise [1]), he believed that the weight of the evidence suggested that the dialectical conflict can normally resolve itself only through violence, since no class is anxious voluntarily to abdicate power. He thus took a cataclysmic view of history. And he himself laboured tirelessly to promote the revolution which on his economic analysis contemporary capitalist society was ready to undergo. For by its internal contradictions bourgeois capitalism was destined to be superseded by the dictatorship of the new class created by the capitalist mode of production, namely, the proletariat.

His own classic enunciation of this principle of social revolution is expressed in a famous passage from the Preface to *The Critique of Political Economy*.

" At a certain stage of their development the material productive forces of society come into contradiction with the existing productive relationships, or what is but a legal expression for these, with the property relationships within which they had moved before. From forms of development

[1] *Vide* Engels, Preface to the first English translation of *Capital* (1886), where reference is made to Marx's life-long study of English economic history, which led him " to the conclusion that, at least in Europe, England is the only country where the inevitable social revolution might be effected entirely by peaceful and legal means." It is important to note, however, the qualifying sentence immediately following: " He certainly never forgot to add that he hardly expected the English ruling classes to submit, without a ' pro-slavery rebellion,' to this peaceful and legal revolution." (*Capital*, Everyman edition, Vol. II, p. 887.)

of the productive forces these relationships are transformed into their fetters. Then an epoch of social revolution opens. With the change in the economic foundation the whole vast superstructure is more or less rapidly transformed. In considering such revolutions it is necessary always to distinguish between the material revolution in the economic conditions of production, . . . and the . . . ideological forms wherein men become conscious of this conflict and fight it out." [1]

Thus the task of the philosopher or social scientist is not to conduct a post-mortem on the conflict after it is settled and a new synthesis is empirically evident; it is one of active participation on the side of those forces to which, his analytic methods have revealed, victory must go. Equipped with his knowledge of the dialectic and the significance of the social class as an instrument of that dialectic, he is not deceived by the rationalizations of the warring ideologies. He becomes aware of the authentic psychological and social factors at work influencing what the actors in the struggle naïvely believe to be their autonomous and dispassionate convictions. With no illusions as to the finality or absolute nature of his own view of the truth, he directs his energies to giving added impetus to and smoothing the way for the forces which are bound to win, to acting as " a midwife to Necessity." For there is no alternative course open to an intelligent man, since to range oneself with the predestined lost cause would be tantamount to banging one's head against a brick wall.

With Marx's economic analysis of the society in which he lived, with, for example, his labour theory of value and his theory of surplus value, we are not here concerned. On this he based his prediction that capitalist society was scheduled to succumb to the proletarian dictatorship, in its turn destined to usher in the classless society wherein the State as an instrument of class rule would wither away, leaving the way free to a completely communist society. But it is quite possible to reject parts or indeed all of this application of the Marxian theory of history to contemporary conditions, without necessarily rejecting the method. It may be argued, for instance, that the sustained rise in the workers' standard of living in the

---

[1] Marx, Preface to *The Critique of Political Economy, op. cit.*, p. 372.

closing decades of the nineteenth century falsified Marx's prediction that the exploitation and expropriation of the poor by the rich would under capitalism's internal contradictions be intensified by the passage of time. Or again, we may argue with Professor Burnham that all the evidence goes to show that the capitalist phase of society is destined to be superseded not by socialism or the classless society but by the managerial society, which will enforce the rule of a technocracy. But this is to quarrel with (to use a favourite term of Marx) the superstructure only. The foundation of the whole compact edifice of Marxist thought, on which it must stand or fall, is the philosophy of history underlying it. Marx's political theory, with its insistence on the relativism of all theories of the State, and its analysis of the bourgeois theories as so much ideological camouflage for a State which was simply the agency of domination over the subordinate class, is directly derivative from his belief in dialectical materialism as the key to history. And it is that key alone which will enable us to escape from the mercy of forces we do not understand to that freedom in which by an understanding of Necessity we may adjust our aims and methods to the sphere of the practicable.

We are now in a position to pass in review the nature of Marx's attempt to meet the intellectual challenge of his time, and to elicit in the brief recapitulation the crucial elements to be weighed in the balance in assessing its claims to validity. Impressed by Hegel's attempt to formulate the principles of a non-Aristotelian logic with which to penetrate to the reason beneath the apparently meaningless welter of historical events, yet no less impressed with the methods and achievements of the British scientific empiricists, Marx strove to make Hegelianism palatable to the empiricist by rejecting the idealist explanation of history's dynamic. In this way he hoped to steer a course which would avoid the shoals of Natural Law on the one hand and the shallows of Humean scepticism on the other. For the liberals and humanitarians, with their appeals to innate and eternal rights of men, to the principles of justice, freedom, equality, of the universal brotherhood of men, Marx had an undisguised contempt. When such men appealed to the authority of internal conviction or moral

intuition authenticated by the greatest and best men of all
times, and apparent as the still small voice of conscience to
even degenerate men, Marx remained an inveterate sceptic.
For him, eternal truth when analysed turned out to be wish-
fulfilments, testifying to the infinite ingenuity with which men
strive to endow their own personal and class desires with
spurious authority.

Marx thought it possible to bridge the gap between fact and
value by demonstrating that the rightness or wrongness of
given values was an empirically verifiable question within
the context of the problems of the time.   And this relative
validity was the only kind of validity which they possessed.
The question we have to decide is how far dialectical materialism as a philosophy of history succeeded in demonstrating that
the validity of the ends which men seek in society may be
established on a degree of certainty similar to that accorded
to laws in the physical world.   In short, was Marx successful
in his effort to turn Hegel right side up? [1]   Was he more successful than Hegel in demonstrating his belief that human
history is as much as the physical world governed by inexorable
laws?   Of course, even if we succeed in proving that there are
laws which determine the direction of social development, we
are under no logical compulsion to adjust our values to conform to history's inevitabilities.   The knowledge that ours is
a lost cause does not oblige us to surrender to the forces of
triumphant darkness.   Progress is a term meaningful only in
the context of human values.   Tragic though it would be to
discover that there are evolutionary laws at odds with our conception of progress, the knowledge that our ideals are doomed
need not prevent us from cherishing them.   Such reasoning
was as absurd to Marx as to Hegel.   It was not open to Marx
as it was to Hegel to refute this argument by claiming that the
laws of history were themselves the highest expression of a
reason, higher than that of human beings, and that to claim
validity for other incompatible values was accordingly to

---

[1] In the Preface to the Second Edition of *Capital* (1873), Marx wrote, " In
Hegel's writings, dialectic stands on its head.   You must turn it right way up
again if you want to discover the rational kernel that is hidden away within the
wrappings of mystification."   (Everyman edition, Vol. II, p. 873.)

stand convicted of irrationality and cosmic impiety. Marx did argue, however, that we are not entitled to differentiate judgments of fact from judgments of value. All our judgments are made in and profoundly conditioned by living social situations. Our beliefs as to what ought to be are closely related to and constantly modified by our knowledge of what is. Ethical judgments, purporting to be true or false, must refer to empirical phenomena, and their criteria of validity must ultimately be grounded upon empirical observations. Our beliefs on the *is* issues and on the *ought* issues influence each other in a mutually reciprocal relation. Over long periods, even our long-term ends are adjusted in the light of changing conditions and increased knowledge, while the adjusted ends are gradually reflected in our own circumstances. The central question still remains, viz., is Marx's philosophy of history a valid one? Is it susceptible of empirical verification?

The sociologist of knowledge, applying Marx's own technique of analysing the social factors underlying the genesis of a belief, might relate Marx's historical determinism to the rapidity and apparently random nature of the social and economic changes of his time. The momentum of the Industrial Revolution swept men along in its wake regardless of their own desires. In an age of individualism, the individual saw in the economic revolution striking evidence of his own comparative impotence. While the *laissez-faire* economists sought an explanation in terms of iron laws of nature, Marx found the key to intelligibility of the apparent chaos in the iron laws of history. At a time when the interplay of the free activities of countless individuals resulted in a state of affairs foreseen by no one, a predisposition to seek a deterministic explanation of the totality of events is not surprising. The clearest indication that Marx was consciously motivated by this kind of reasoning is to be found in a passage from Engels, whose thought is, of course, inseparable from that of his collaborator.

" For here, also, on the whole, [in history] in spite of the consciously desired aims of all individuals, accident apparently reigns on the surface. That which is willed happens but rarely; in the majority of instances the numerous desired ends cross and conflict with one another, or these ends themselves are from the outset incapable of realization or the means of attaining them are insufficient. Thus the conflict of innumerable individual wills and individual actions in the domain of history produces a state of affairs entirely analogous to that in the realm of unconscious nature. The ends of the actions are intended, but the results which actually follow from these actions are not intended; or when they do seem to correspond to the end intended, they ultimately have consequences quite other than those intended." [1]

This belief, as we have seen, Marx and Engels shared with many previous thinkers, but to none was it more vital than to Marx. In view of our evident inability to learn the nature of each individual will in history, it is essential to maintain that there are are extra-conative factors at work determining the outcome of the interaction of myriads of individual wills, if we are to claim the power of prediction on the basis of comparatively rigid laws. A more detailed criticism of this view will be postponed to the following chapter (Cf. pp. 233–238 below). But so far as the alleged scientific status of the laws themselves is concerned, on the evidence so far adduced, it would seem impossible to accord them any higher status than that attaching to any metaphysical intuition. In principle, it is true, the law should be capable of empirical verification, but in fact neither Marx nor any of his disciples seems to have found it possible to state the conditions under which the hypothesis that there are such laws at work would be abandoned. If the empirical facts of historical development falsify our predictions, there is a great temptation to fall back on the time factor and explain our misjudgment by arguing that we have been premature in our expectations and must claim an extension of time to give history a further opportunity of vindicating our rendering of its laws.

The assertion that there are such laws is in fact no scientific hypothesis but a metaphysical intuition. It does not, of course, follow that we are compelled to revert to a complete indeterminism in all humanistic disciplines, and go to the other

[1] Engels, *Ludwig Feuerbao'i*, edited by C. P. Dutt, Martin Lawrence, London, n.d., p. 58.

extreme of asserting that the upshot of the interaction of human wills in society is completely a matter of chance, that it was possible, in other words, for everything that has happened to have happened otherwise than it did. We may well discover, for example, by studying the history of capitalist society and comparing it with that of other societies grounds for supposing it to be in a state of incipient collapse. But such a social-economic diagnosis might itself give rise to the birth of a capitalist economist who might prescribe a remedy providing for the patient at the least a fresh lease of life. This does not, of course, purport to be an accurate description of what has in fact happened. But certainly Marx's inability to foresee a Keynes represents a major handicap in attempting to predict the certain outcome of capitalist contradictions of the late nineteenth century.

It will be recalled that in opening this discussion, mention was made of the Christian tradition, with its emphasis on justice, as one of the formative influences on Marx. This element in his make-up, it is important to note, for in spite of his consistent attempts to sustain the attitude of the implacable social scientist, who excluded the emotions from the laboratory, Marx's own hatred of injustice, shaped out of the tradition of which he was himself a living part, frequently got the better of his naturalism. The fire and fury with which he assailed the odious borgeoisie is difficult to reconcile with his analysis of the Necessity of History, through the operation of whose laws the bourgeoisie are compelled to play their allotted role in the dialectical conflict by fighting to defend their own interests. Readily though we may sympathize with the dilemma arising out of the determination to be scientific and at the same time actively to engage as a social reformer, it is interesting to note this dualism in Marx's practice. It illustrates vividly the difficulty for even such a thoroughgoing monist as Marx on the *is* and the *ought* issue in avoiding an appeal to what were in fact normative principles.

The truth is that underlying Marxist political thought is the characteristic belief of the European Enlightenment in the inevitability of progress. This assumption is so deep-seated that it is very rarely questioned, and constitutes as effective a

spur and guide to action as the belief in the proximate end of
the world, the Day of Judgment and the life to come in the
Middle Ages. Marx's belief in the pre-history stage of man's
development ultimately destined to give way to the stage of
history proper, when man will at last realize his true freedom
in a classless society, has affinities which link it with previous
non-secular as well as secular eschatologies. These markedly
" progressive " assumptions are in evidence in a great deal
that Marx wrote, of which the following is a characteristic
example, taken from the Preface to *The Critique of Political
Economy*.

> " In broad outline, the Asiatic, the ancient, the feudal and
> the modern bourgeois modes of production can be indicated
> as progressive epochs in the economic system of society.
> Bourgeois productive relationships are the last antagonistic
> form of the social process of production—antagonistic in the
> sense not of individual antagonism, but of an antagonism
> arising out of the conditions of the social life of individuals;
> but the productive forces developing within the womb of
> bourgeois society at the same time create the material con-
> ditions for the solution of this antagonism. With this social
> system, therefore, the pre-history of human society comes
> to a close. . . ." [1]

Marx, as we have seen, has only been one of many to pro-
pound the conviction that there is a determinate order of
human progress, the laws of which can be learnt by examining
the historical process in its totality. But as a systematic
philosophy of history and as a method of investigating history,
Marxism is unique both in the extent of the influence it has
exerted and in the high degree of consistency and systematic
application it has achieved in many fields of knowledge. By
the side of Marxist philosophy of history, such others as have
followed it like those of Comte, Spencer, Spengler and Toynbee,
to mention the more outstanding, will not stand serious comparison. It is no exaggeration to say that to-day those who
permit their course of political action to be shaped and motivated by the ingrained assumption that " history is on their
side " or that " history proves them right " are to be numbered

---

[1] Marx, *op. cit.*, *A Handbook of Marxism*, p. 373.

in millions. To be able to fortify our doubts by the conviction that destiny is with us is an undeniable source of strength. It is the exceptional, not the average man who feels any attraction for lost causes in a world where the rewards of those who are shrewd enough to get on the band waggon in time, tend to be matched only by the severity of the penalties which attach to those who do not. To invoke the laws of history and the authority of science is to equip oneself with high credentials, whose force as an instrument of political propaganda is very considerable.

It is, perhaps, significant that Marxist philosophy has reaped its richest harvest in Russia. As Professor Berdyaev writes in a different context,

> " Messianic consciousness is more characteristic of the Russians than of any other people except the Jews. It runs all through Russian history right down to its communist period." [1]

For Russians, whose interests had been diverted into more secular channels by the extent of their sufferings at the hands of the Tsarist oligarchy, the appeal of Marxism is not difficult to understand. As a tool of political and economic analysis, its value was obvious enough, but in addition it was peculiarly suited (particularly in the corrupt forms it sometimes assumed in the hands of its more fanatical devotees) to appeal to a secularized Messianic consciousness. For many people in all lands, Marxism has stimulated an apocalyptic vision of a secular life to come in which the proletarian harbingers of destiny will finally redress all the ills which throughout recorded history have afflicted men in their misery, and in so doing will inherit the earth. The vision is one of dignity and nobility, but in its perfectionist assumptions and in its impatience, it is apt to be tinged with aggressively intolerant qualities. Men do not as a rule experience undue difficulty in persuading themselves that they speak with a higher authority than they do in fact possess. Few among us, it is true, could be found to emulate the Cambridge Vice-Chancellor who, when it was first proposed to run excursion trains to that city, wrote to the offend-

---

[1] N. Berdyaev, *The Russian Idea*, 1947, p. 8.

ing authority " that such a proceeding would be as displeasing
to Almighty God as it is to the Vice-Chancellor of the University of Cambridge." [1]   But intolerance does not often wear
a guise of such a crass or amusing nature.   And it is the
peculiar danger of philosophies of history which lay claim to
certain foreknowledge of the direction of humanity's course
that they tend to foster the spirit of intolerance.   If we believe
that we have inside information to the effect that our opponents
are wasting their efforts in an attempt to achieve the impossible,
the temptation to restrain their freedom for their own good is
a considerable one.

[1] Quoted by C. R. Fay, *Great Britain from Adam Smith to the Present Day*, 1944
edition, p. 201.

CHAPTER XI

Conclusion

THE faith of the Age of Reason has been a positive and enduring one because, however close its affinities with the Cartesian repudiation of the errant past, its roots in the ancient traditions of European civilization were deeper than it was itself prepared to recognize. Progress consisted in the march towards liberty and equality, but those ideals, at once humanitarian and humanistic in temper, had always been implicit in the Græco-Christian tradition. The humanitarianism of the *philosophes* was demonstrated in many ways. They waged unremitting warfare upon the evils of legal torture and upon the institution of human slavery, and in both they were successful. They came to recognize the " exploitation " involved in wage labour under an untrammelled market economy; they brought within the pale of the contemporary social conscience the claims of those whose weakness had left them without formal social protection, the claims of children, of lunatics, of criminals and eventually, even of prisoners of war. The *Illumination* was a movement quickened by that human compassion that Pater once defined as " humanity's standing force of self-pity." At the same time, in its sensitivity to the *peculiarly* human qualities in all men, it was a worthy heir to the classical, humanist culture of the Renaissance. While the eighteenth century believed that the proper study of mankind was man, it recognized as a corollary to this the importance of establishing social and political conditions in which free inquiry could be pursued without impediment. If society was to apply to its social problems the methods so successfully demonstrated in the physical sciences, then it must learn to tolerate free speculation, however unorthodox or seemingly dangerous the implications might be. Since each individual's experience of the world was necessarily unique, it was a vital interest of society that each individual should be guaranteed in his right to contribute the peculiar features of that experience to the common pool. For every human problem was in principle amenable to, if not soluble by the free play of the intelligence investigating the objective material and exchanging ideas with others in the pursuit of a common inquiry. Uninhibited discussion was a sovereign specific, if not a sovereign remedy.

The keynote of the discussion in the eighteenth century was the equality that should prevail among men everywhere by virtue of their common humanity. The Voltaireans themselves, were, it is true, very far from being democrats, in our understanding of the term, but they were none the less militant in their rejection of privilege. Implicit in their egalitarian aspirations was the conviction made explicit by Rousseau, that the appropriate education alone was wanting to the masses to enable them to assume the responsibilities of government. Only in this way could the tension between the claims of liberty and order within society be resolved without sacrificing the claims of either. If, for Rousseau, liberty meant the capacity to do that which was right, the more negative view of Bentham which was content to interpret liberty as immunity from the compulsion of others, was the more representative libertarian conception of the eighteenth century. If in the past most people had enjoyed this immunity only in the narrowest of personal spheres, the reason lay not in any inherent deficiency of human nature, but in the monoply of the sources of enlightenment by ruling élites. These " sinister interests " were defined by Condorcet as the interests of clerics and courtiers, and by Marx in terms which arraigned the bourgeoisie as the guilty party. Both again shared the assumption that once these oppressive forces had been eliminated, the fundamental harmony of human interests would finally emerge. The past was the Age of Unreason, essentially because the potentialities of the many had been sacrificed, and as a result a gulf had been created between government and governed so wide as to exclude the vast majority from any participation in the direction of affairs.

Bravely as they were proclaimed, neither liberty nor equality were ever adequately defined in their actual social context in the eigthteenth century, and the underlying confusion rapidly became apparent when applied to the dynamic society of the nineteenth century. The vital distinction between liberty and licence was recognized, but there was no clear idea as to where the line should be drawn in restricting the individual's freedom of action in accordance with this distinction. Specific civil liberties were insisted upon, for example, the personal right to freedom of movement and marriage; the economic right to own property, to the choice of employment and freedom of contract; the intellectual right to freedom of speech, of association, of education and religious worship. Experience was to demonstrate, however, that these liberties included in practice other liberties that lay within the existing definitions but which, under the impetus of the Industrial Revolution, raised chronic social and political problems. Freedom of contract too often meant in fact the right to sell personal labour at a price determined by an unimpeded law of supply and demand conjoined with a corresponding right of the employer to hire labour at rates below the minimum subsistence level. The right to free speech could be extended to include the liberty of the Press to disregard the principles of fair and accurate reporting in the interests of profit and power. Freedom of association often included in practice the right of powerful pressure groups to short-circuit the democratic process by applying improper pressure at the focal point of administrative power.

The principle of equality was no less vague in its general connotation. Civil equality, equality before the law, raised no problems, and was properly recognized as resting on the ground of the common possession by all men of the capacity for moral understanding. But it is less sure that justice demands absolute equality in the strictly material sense which Utopians like Mercier and Babeuf were apt to attach to it. Just as for Godwin, progress in knowledge consisted of the continuous abstraction of amounts of truth from a fixed quantum of existent truth, so egalitarians tended to identify moral progress with the advance towards a society in which no man possessed more than his neighbour. Both Morelly and Mercier seemed to be aware of what this implied in terms of liberty, if we are to judge by the meticulous detail with which they proposed to regulate the social conditions of their ideal communities. Nor is it at all clear that in the event of a conflict between the claims of liberty and the claims of equality, those of liberty would not be sacrificed. In the case of Rousseau, for example, the traditional institutional bulwarks of freedom assumed a diminished importance once the principle of the sovereignty of the people had been established. The enlightened nature of that popular consent that constituted the General Will, from which by definition the citizen could not wish to be protected, was easily assumed. In Marx's case, such principles as the separation of powers, habeas corpus, or freedom of the press, were in their contemporary expression no more than elaborate smoke screens behind which lurked the reality of the oppression of the toiling masses by the ruling bourgeoisie.

This lack of precision, sometimes amounting to confusion in the content of the fundamental values of the Enlightenment is the less surprising when we consider how very unsure they were of the foundations on which they grounded the status of those beliefs. The attack on metaphysics did not generally preclude a belief in Natural Law, sometimes supported as in Voltaire by a vaguely defined deism. Having rejected the doctrines of authority, of divine right or special Revelation, the commonest appeal made by the *philosophes* was to rationally self-evident natural rights. Even in an explicitly utilitarian writer like Helvetius, it is evident that there is an unshakable conviction in a universal Law of Nature, discernible by right reason in men of every time and place. And yet, this was, as we have seen, precisely the period when the doctrine of Natural Right was destined to sustain the most trenchant of all assaults upon its validity. For those who stood in the eighteenth century rationalist tradition, the doctrine of Natural Law never recovered from the shock administered to it by Hume's mordant analysis of the role of reason in morals and politics. The difficulty with Hume's analysis is that, while it proved an effective polemic against the alleged capacity of reason to intuit moral truths, the argument concluded, under the impetus of its own logic, by reducing the role of reason to the status of a mere handmaiden of the passions. Logically impeccable, the doctrine owed its persuasiveness to its relentless and salutary insistence on the principle that significant propositions should be empirically verifiable by interpersonal techniques. We have witnesses in our own time a powerful restatement of the thesis by the school of linguistic analysts who similarly confine the term " reasoning " to the strictly deductive function, with the consequent extrusion of reason from the field of value judgments.

Within the main stream of the Enlightenment tradition, two schools of thought appeared, which, while rejecting the Natural Law doctrine, were nevertheless not prepared to accept Hume's self-denying ordinance in the matter of reason's function. Both the Utilitarians and the Marxists sought in their different ways to give a rational, non-subjective validity to their value systems. In the outcome, however, these attempts suffer alike from the fact that they rob the moral relationship of all content of obligation. " Nature," wrote Bentham, " has placed mankind under the governance of two sovereign masters, *pain* and *pleasure*. It is for them alone to point out what we ought to do, as well as to determine what we shall do." [1] As Kant pointed out, the identification of duty and interest in this way rendered the very concept of duty meaningless. And while the younger Mill became painfully conscious of this dilemma, his discovery that the end of happiness cannot be realized by its direct pursuit, true though it is, is no more than an evasion of the issue. The explanation that moral behaviour consists in the pursuit not of self-interest but of " enlightened " or " benevolent " self-interest, does nothing to advance the inquiry as to the true source of moral obligation, since it leaves unexplained the grounds of " enlightenment " in Mill's sense. The attempt fails ultimately because it seeks to reduce ethics to a branch of psychology.

The case is even worse with the Marxian version of the status of obligation. Even if we were to grant the empirical validity of the progressive, dialectical law of historical development; if we granted that within the limits set by history the values

---

[1] Bentham, *An Introduction to the Principles of Morals and Legislation*, edited by Wilfrid Harrison, 1948, p. 125.

of the proletariat as the " progressive " class were in some sense more valid than bourgeois values, the dilemma would still remain. It is impossible to escape the illogicality of condemning the individual bourgeois for behaviour which, it has been asserted, is historically determined. If such a man, lacking through no fault of his own the " insight " afforded by dialectical materialism, acts in opposition to the forces directing the course of history, we are no more justified in charging him with a dereliction of duty than we would be so justified in the case of Bentham's hypothetical individual, bound by the laws of psychological hedonism. This is to reduce ethics to the category of historical or sociological law.

It has been necessary to stress the unsatisfactory nature of the attempts to establish a rational basis for moral and political appraisals, since awareness of the difficulties involved in the enterprise has been one of the profoundest motivations of the beliefs in necessary historical progress. In the nineteenth century, it is true, there were solid social and economic reasons why a belief in unilinear progress should have appeared especially plausible. European ascendancy in almost every aspect of the world's life had finally been established. The benevolent despotisms of the eighteenth century were rapidly giving way to liberal, democratic institutions throughout the West. As the foundations of the ancient and imperial House of Habsburg began to crumble, the principle of national self-determination, epitomized in the Italian Risorgimento, was translated from aspiration to political actuality. Censorship of the Press and denial of freedom of speech which were commonplaces in the Europe of Metternich were fast becoming execrated anachronisms. Slavery and legal torture were abolished. Despite Marx's dire predictions, the standard of life of the masses was beginning to rise as a result of the increase in the volume of production and the expansion of world trade occasioned by the Industrial Revolution. In spite of the reduction in infant mortality and the extension of the average expectation of life occasioned by the advances of modern medical science, Malthusian fears seemed finally to have been laid to rest by the spectacle of an expanding population paralleled by a rising standard of life. At the same time, the revolution in technology was transforming the physical background of the citizen and in the process reducing some of the routine drudgery of the struggle to live. If the career was not yet open to the talents, steps were made in that direction in the shape of universal, compulsory education. The long freedom from wars of Napoleonic dimensions gave rise to confidence in the possibilities of enduring peace, which even the Crimean fiasco and the wars of 1864–70, short and restricted in their aims as they were, did little to impair. Of overwhelming importance, too, for the nineteenth-century belief in progress was the psychological impact of the discovery of the incalculable age of our planet and of man's own genesis by evolution from primitive forms of life in a very remote past.

In these circumstances, it is no matter for surprise that the nineteenth century should have been exuberantly confident. But the prevailing belief in progress went beyond the conviction that history provides evidence of specific progressive developments when appraised in the light of present human purposes. Most apostles of progress in the nineteenth as in the eighteenth century assuredly believed that purposive, progressive direction was inherent in the events themselves, and accordingly, the temptation to find in the idea of progress a validation of their own cherished values more trustworthy than other attempts at a rational validation was a very real one. It is this motive which, if not always conscious, has led to a twofold error by those whose belief in progress has so often found expression in such phrases as " history is on our side " or in the thesis that the logic of history, by its own immanent laws, will fulfil its destiny. In the first place, history with its immense wealth of material recording the long history of human achievement and frustration, offers a rich opportunity to those with a genius for systematic organization calculated to reveal order beneath the surface confusion of events. History may thus be made to appear significant to an audience ever ready to embrace any evidence which might suggest that there exists some purpose larger than man's, some " destiny that shapes our ends, rough-hew them how we will," in obedience to which men can find increased security. But although large-scale history may be made to exhibit some kind of order, it is not possible to attribute that order to the fulfilment of the known purpose of individuals or groups of individuals. It appears to bear no relation to any conscious willing on the part of any specific body of human beings. And if the order exhibited by (or read into) history is not consciously controlled by human agency, the conclusion would appear to follow that the order in question must conceal the operation of " natural " historical laws. And secondly, arising out of this belief in historical law, is the tendency to deduce criteria of appraisal from the law of historical development. If it is held that the direction of social development is prescribed in accordance with historical necessity regardless of human will, it is difficult to distinguish between the desirable and the necessary. If what will happen, will happen, it is futile to urge its desirability or undesirability. It is no accident that a thorough-going determinism is often accompanied by the value criteria implicit in the idea of progress as a means of softening the harshness of a doctrine calculated to arouse the resistance of the libertarian. It is comforting to know that history's iron necessity at least ensures progress.

The first argument, emphasizing the gap between the direction of development and the conscious human will, concludes that the purpose at work is extra-human. This teleological type of explanation is familiar and tends to be readily acceptable in periods of unusually rapid social change. At the time of the Industrial Revolution or in a period like our own when the economic pressure towards world unity exceeds the political ability to realize it, there is a heightened sense of inadequacy on the part of human beings to direct and control their fate. The strength that stems from the sense of conscious control gives way to a sense of being in the grip of forces that can at most be guided within narrow limits. Only in the light of some such analysis does it become possible to understand the vogue of such philosophies of history as Spengler's in the German *Götterdämmerung* of 1919 or of Professor Toynbee's in the English-speaking world of the nuclear age. The point is well made by Heine,

Zu fragmentarisch ist Welt und Leben.
Ich will mich zum deutschen Professor begeben,

Der wiss das Leben zusammensetzen,
Und er macht ein verständlich System daraus.
Mit seinen Nachtmutzen und Schlafrockfetzen
Stopft er die Lücken des Weltenbaus." [1]

Teleological determinism of this kind did, no doubt, receive added impetus from Darwin's formulation of the biological laws of evolution, although he himself refrained from drawing this kind of conclusion. Perhaps the most notorious example of such distortion of evolutionary theory applied to history is the thesis advanced by Benjamin Kidd in his *Social Evolution* (1894). The law of natural selection is interpreted by Kidd to indicate the necessity of institutional religion as the only means of reconciling to their sufferings those individuals whose relative unfitness requires their elimination in the struggle for survival. But many less eccentric figures than Benjamin Kidd have been misled by evolutionary theory to suppose that the Darwinian hypothesis somehow strengthens the belief that hidden purposes are at work beneath the surface flux of historical events. As a corrective to this kind of confusion, it is pertinent to quote from one of the foremost contemporary biologists on this point. Professor Julian Huxley in his volume on *Evolution* writes,

" The purpose manifested in evolution, whether in adaptation, specialization, or biological progress, is only an apparent purpose. It is just as much a product of blind forces as is the falling of a stone to earth or the ebb and flow of the tides. It is we who have read purpose into evolution, as earlier men projected will and emotion into inorganic phenomena like storm or earthquake. If we wish to work towards a purpose for the future of man, we must formulate that purpose ourselves. Purposes in life are made, not found." [2]

[1] Heine, *Die Heimkehr*, 58.

> Too fragmentary is the world and life,
> I will betake myself to the German Professor,
> Who knows how to organize life,
> And to make an intelligible system therefrom;
> With night-cap and tattered gown
> He stops up the holes of the cosmic systems.

[2] Julian S. Huxley, *Evolution*, 1942, p. 576.

This particular error does, of course, precede the evolutionary discoveries, and unites in its advocacy a curiously ill-assorted company. We have had occasion to examine its espousal by Bossuet, Turgot, Kant and Hegel, as well as Marx and Engels. It is clearly enunciated by Engels in the specific context of progress in his *Ludwig Feuerbach,*

> " The great basic thought that the world is not to be comprehended as a complex of ready-made *things*, but as a complex of *processes*, . . . in which, in spite of all seeming accidents and of all temporary retrogression, *a progressive development asserts itself in the end*—this great fundamental thought has, especially since the time of Hegel, so thoroughly permeated ordinary consciousness that in this generality it is scarcely ever contradicted." [1]   (The last italics are mine.)

There is, admittedly, some confusion on this issue among Marxists, since there is an intelligible desire on the part of such political activists as Marxists to escape the consequences of a thorough-going determinism. (Witness such statements as Engels' and Lenin's to the effect that " People make their own history.") One of the most lucid and persuasive of all statements of the view that the course of human activity is directed by extra-human willing agencies is to be found in the writings of Bernard Bosanquet. In a paper, entitled *The Meaning of Teleology*, delivered in April, 1906, he wrote,

> " The large-scale patterns of history and civilization are not to be found as purposes within any single finite consciousness ; the definite continuity and correlation of particular intelligent activities, on which the teleological character of human life ultimately depends—the ' ways of Providence '—are a fact on the whole of the same order as the development of the solar system or the appearance of life upon the surface of the earth. It is impossible to attribute to finite consciousness the whole development which springs from the linked action of separate and successive finite consciousnesses in view of the environment." [2]

He then proceeds to give an apt and striking illustration of his thesis in the form of a comparison in principle between the

[1] Engels, *Ludwig Feuerbach*, edited by C. P. Dutt, p. 54.
[2] *Proceedings of The British Academy*, 1905–1906, p. 243.

role played by a leader of a Greek colony to Ionia during the
Dark Ages and the function of a coral insect in the Pacific.
The Greek colonist could no more have been aware that his
labours were paving the way for Christianity than can the
coral insect know that its activities are designed to build a
coral reef. " Nothing," concludes Bosanquet, " is properly
due to mind, which never was a plan before a mind." [1]

This plausible conclusion stems ultimately from a twofold
error. There appears, on the one hand, a reluctance to recognize that social processes are as complex as they in fact are;
and, on the other hand, there seems to be a sharper distinction
between purposeful and random action than the facts warrant.
What appears on the surface as the march of destiny or the
divine tactic of history is in fact the outcome of the activities
of legions of individuals who by their separate efforts contribute to the development of the social entity to which they be-
long. The fact that they bring about consequences coincident
neither with their desires nor their expectations is attributable
in part to the parochial outlook of the individuals in question,
to the extent to which their intelligence is overruled by the
claims of prejudice, self-interest, and localism of class or
national character. For the rest, the explanation lies with the
exceeding complexity of the relations between individuals
and groups one with another, so that the chain of cause and
effect in human activity has so many ramifications as to present the intelligence in its quest to unravel them with its greatest single challenge. The truth of the matter is that only a
small minority of men even attempt consciously to regulate
their actions and their views by a consistently intelligent
adjustment of the relation of means to ends. The majority
are the prisoners to greater or less degree of traditionally
accepted local *mores* and the stress of powerful emotional
tensions of a largely unconscious character. The consequences
of the actions of such individuals may well be a source of
frequent surprise and disappointment to them, but even in
these cases the willing activity of the agents is not a random
one nor are the consequences fortuitous. Most individuals
have a fairly well defined personality or character structure

[1] *Proceedings of The British Academy*, 1905–1906, p. 244.

which provides a discernible underlying consistency to their actions if observed continuously over a long enough period. When things go wrong, a reluctance to look for painful defects in ourselves or in our society together with a corresponding readiness to explain what has happened in terms of the irony of fate or plain bad luck, is understandable enough. It is the only seemingly rational way of absolving ourselves from further responsibility in the matter. Nevertheless, even though the full explanation of the chain of cause and effect may not always lie within reach, there is no need to look for an explanation beyond the field of data supplied by individual character, social relations, and the observed consequences of social action, unless, of course, physical environmental phenomena are also involved. To posit the need for an additional factor in the shape of chance or Providence or the dialectic is an obscure way of expressing the limitations of our existing knowledge; it does not add to that knowledge.

In the case of relations between nation-states, the difficulties of unravelling the chain of cause and effect are naturally much greater still. Understanding of the relations between large groups presents greater obstacles even than the grasp of relations between the individuals who compose those groups. So that the temptation is even greater, although no less pardonable, to resort in the writing of international relations or world history to destiny or immanent law or the will of God for a satisfactory explanation. But no more than in the case of the individual are we entitled to shelve our responsibility in that way. The correct explanation, although it may be beyond the reach of our limited tools of inquiry and comprehension, must lie ultimately somewhere in the character and inner structure of all existing nations or sovereign societies. As in the case of individuals, so in the affairs of nations, where the consequences of actions are other than those anticipated, the remedy lies not in seeking for inherent laws in the development of the unwanted events, but in closer study of the structure of groups, social and national, and of the complex nature of the interaction of human actions one upon another. So long as individuals and nations continue to have their actions governed in large part by prejudice and conceptions of narrow self-interest, so long, of course, will their attempts to promote the general good suffer frustration. And in this situation, the relation between means and ends is necessarily complicated, since the willing process itself is only imperfectly understood. If we were to suppose a world of individuals governed by reason, co-operating with one another in ever expanding groups until the whole world were embraced, it is at least probable that world history would then appear to be the outcome of conscious and rational willing on the part of the agents of that history. In that case, the need to invoke Providence or dialectical law or destiny to provide an emotionally satisfying explanation would presumably be weakened to the extent that human beings had obtained insight into the sources of their willing activities and control over the relation between means and ends. On the other hand, assuming a basic psychophysical structure common to all men and a sufficiently similar physical and social background to the races of mankind, it would then be theoretically possible to discover by normal induction certain uniformities in the processes of social change throughout the world. But such a degree of unity and common purpose is utopian in conception when measured against the actual conditions now prevailing. In the words of Professor Ginsberg,

"... the trends of sociological facts, ... so far as I can see, do not point with any certainty to a unitary principle which would enable us to pass from the partial and relatively external processes of unification, which have been occurring amidst much violence and conflict, to a deeper form of organic connections binding into a unity the whole of mankind." [1]

Closely allied to this type of error in theories of historical progress is the attempt to identify fact and value in the shape of necessary historical law. The view of Julian Huxley, whom we have already had occasion to quote, to the effect that the term " evolution " should be used in a value-free or ethically neutral sense, would doubtless meet with general agreement among the majority of present-day biologists. The biologist, that is to say, confines himself to recording certain empirical

[1] Morris Ginsberg, *Reason and Unreason in Society*, 1947, p. 290.

facts. While certain types of organisms adjust to and survive in their environment, they yet do not go on to develop further, and may be said to have reached an evolutionary cul-de-sac. Other types, on the other hand, said to be dominant, are observed to be extremely complex and potentially capable of differentiation into innumerable different stocks. But the classification of such types as " dominant " is not done by reference to a value judgment. The definition is reached by normal induction on the basis of the observed fact that certain organisms share a common attribute such as independence of environmental conditions. No judgment is assumed as to the intrinsic value of the quality of being able to control or exist independently of the environment. But when, for instance, Herbert Spencer, on the analogy of evolutionary law in biology, formulated a law purporting to demonstrate how all human societies are as part of a cosmic, evolutionary process scheduled to pass from a military to a contractual type of society, he did not hesitate to term such a law progressive. " Progress, therefore, is not an accident," he wrote, " but a necessity. Instead of civilization being artificial, it is a part of nature." [1] Spencer, like so many others, was thus led to hail the laws of biological evolution as means of giving scientific validity to his own cherished ethical beliefs. There were exceptions, of course. Witness T. H. Huxley in the Romanes Lecture of 1893,

> " Let us understand, once for all, that the ethical progress of society depends, not on imitating the cosmic process, still less in running away from it, but in combating it." [2]

Those who attempt to identify value with the fact of evolutionary law or of historical law are compelled to smuggle the value judgment into the description of empirical phenomena. If, for instance, the evolutionary process, whereby types with greater capacity for differentiation or less vulnerability to environment dominate other types, is termed a progressive one, such a statement depends for its validity upon an undisclosed premise. It can be demonstrated only if we can prove

[1] H. Spencer, *Social Statics*, 1851, p. 65.
[2] T. H. Huxley, *Evolution and Ethics and Other Essays*, 1906, p. 83.

that capacity for differentiation or invulnerability to environment, as the case may be, is in itself a good. Such a judgment
cannot be demonstrated from a law of development, although
in practice our actual behaviour may be modified as a result
of our awareness of such a law. The temptation to fall into
this error is a very real one, particularly for those who find it
difficult to reconcile themselves to the state of things as they
are. The reformer, with a more than usually developed
sensitivity to the notion of obligation, naturally feels himself
under a burden to provide a rationally unimpeachable certificate of authenticity for the criteria in the light of which the
status quo is measured and found wanting. It is understandable that support should be looked for in the history of morals,
but whatever consistency of development we might find
therein cannot of itself obligate us to conform to that pattern
of development.

The difficulty with the teleological theory of progress which
prevailed in the eighteenth and nineteenth centuries consists
in the fact that its validity depends upon the suppressed
premise that the end product of the chain of development, be
it liberty or the moral will or social justice or the happiness of
man, is an entity of intrinsic, absolute value. Again and again
we have noticed that progressivists have unconsciously arro-
gated to the present a kind of divine right, which is arbitrarily
denied to all other periods of time. This belief is implicit in
the claim, asserted most nakedly in the historical writing of
the Chevalier de Chastellux, to measure all past human
endeavour in the light of present values and purposes. The
fact that present values are not necessarily those adopted by
bygone ages and that we have no means of knowing how they
may accord with or conflict with those of future generations,
is entirely overlooked. And in the same way that the relativity
of *time* has been left out of account, the conditioning factors of
place have been inadequately recognized. There has been,
for instance, right down to the present a strong inclination on
the part of European historians to assume that the development of their own civilization represents the main line of the
historical " permanent way " and that Europeans are in the
vanguard of history. Philosophers of history have repeatedly

committed the error of universalizing the achievements of particular societies at specific stages of their development without questioning the degree of permanence, let alone the universal validity of those achievements. The error of ignoring geographical relativity is even less pardonable than the view that overlooks historical relativism, since while we can never transcend our own position in time, the corrective to over-subjective judgments of cultures other than our own lies in intensified sociological investigation. There can be no better safeguard against the facile assumption that the improvements we note in our own culture are the fruits of an evolutionary law embracing all human life.

What we reject, then, is the supposition that a final or definitive history of the past, revealing the existence of " real " historical progress possessed of ontological status, is a legiti-mate object of human knowledge. We are ourselves set in-escapably in the midst of the stream of history, and when we study the past, it is misleading to say that we are attempting to reconstruct what actually happened, " *wie es eigentlich gewesen.*" Our knowledge of the past is itself subject to varia-tions in contemporary standards of what the historical evi-dence obliges us to believe. Our knowledge of the " facts " of history has, for example, recently been modified by new techniques developed by archæologists and psychologists. And this relativity is, of course, even more apparent as soon as we begin to construct an intelligible narrative by selecting and interpreting the events of the past. It is a truism to say that every generation must write its history anew. For our assumptions regarding method and our canons of evaluation we cannot ourselves transcend. And accordingly, our criteria for measuring progress are unavoidably based on present human values.

But this is far from meaning that the idea of progress has no validity or is unworthy to sustain the motives of men who seek to serve an idea greater than themselves. Because our judg-ments cannot claim absolute validity, it by no means follows that they are arbitrary. If we reject a universal law of progress, we do not thereby deny the fruitfulness of comparative studies of human achievement in different periods and different societies. Because we recognize that our judgments are conditioned by strictly contemporary methods and modes of appraisal, we do not thereby deny that their status is governed by recognized modes of authentication. This has been admirably expressed by the late Professor Karl Mannheim.

> "Just as the fact that every measurement in space hinges upon the nature of light does not mean that our measurements are arbitrary, but merely that they are only valid in relation to the nature of light, so in the same way not relativism in the sense of arbitrariness but *relationism* applies to our discussions. Relationism does not signify that there are no criteria of rightness and wrongness in a discussion. It does insist, however, that it lies in the nature of certain assertions that they cannot be formulated absolutely, but only in terms of the perspective of a given situation." [1]

Even if the historian or sociologist decides to eliminate all value judgments from his work, to pursue a policy of *Wertfreiheit*, as Max Weber, for instance, insisted he must, his angle of vision or perspective cannot but be affected by social and psychological factors of an extreme complexity. Merely to recognize that our angle of vision is affected by our membership of the capitalist or proletarian class, of the conservative or liberal tradition, of our American or German birth is at once to achieve some degree of emancipation from subjective bias. Scientific objectivity, difficult though it is to attain in the field of the humanities, demands that *Fachgenossen*, coworkers within a given discipline throughout the world should strive to reach a set of agreed rules of procedure and a common interpretation of standard conditions, in the light of which obviously one-sided perspectives would be discernible, if not actually measurable. The degree of objectivity attained will depend upon the depth of knowledge available of the distorting subjective factors.

It may be objected that on the relativist's own assumptions, there can be no possibility of making comparisons between the achievements of different societies at different points in time, since what is regarded as moral achievement by one age may not be so regarded by the different standards of another age.

---

[1] K. Mannheim, *Ideology and Utopia*, 1946, p. 254.

And if such comparisons are ruled out, the notion of progress can have no meaning. It is true that, apart from the factor of the availability of evidence, the period of time over which we may seek to make such comparisons will depend upon the degree of relationism attaching to the specific phenomena under examination. Now the idea of progress has always carried with it a strongly ethical flavour; and while explanations of the status of moral judgments vary enormously with variations in time and place, there is remarkable stability as to what constitutes the core of moral behaviour. If things like women's fashions at one extreme merit a maximum rating for historical instability, it is difficult to withstand the conviction that so long as man is recognizably historical man he will continue to value the moral qualities of kindliness, compassion, courage and generosity in preference to their opposites. This fundamental point is well made by Hobhouse in his *Morals in Evolution*,

> " If, . . . there is ethical progress . . ., it is to be found, not in the development of new instincts or impulses of mankind or in the disappearance of instincts that are old and bad, but rather in the rationalization of the moral code which, as society advances, becomes more clearly thought out and more consistently and comprehensively applied.' [1]

Implicit in the foregoing argument and indeed, in the critical standpoint from which this book has been written, is the assumption that a rational ethic is in principle attainable, that it is not excluded on logical grounds. Without some such assumption it is difficult to see what enduring validity the concept of progress can have. But before we attempt to make explicit the grounds for a belief in a rational ethic, it is necessary to distinguish such a contention from the assertion that a universal moral code acceptable to rational men everywhere is in principle attainable. Men cannot, even if they would, escape the controlling influences of tradition and immemorial custom; the most rationalistic of thinkers must yield something to the claims of prescription. Moreover, our needs and wants vary through geographical as well as historical factors; our

---

[1] L. T. Hobhouse, *Morals in Evolution*, 1951 ed., p. 30.

very understanding of them depends in some degree on the extent of our psychological knowledge. It would, to cite an obvious example, be unreasonable to expect a Muslim and Christian, however emancipated from theological dogma, to agree upon the desirability of any *a priori* code of matrimonial ethics. No system of rights and duties can profitably be divorced from the historical social context in which it is set. Even within a given national culture, grounds for major differences of opinion must unavoidably occur both from the diversity of individual experience and from the limits to our knowledge at any time of cause and effect in social processes. The very fact that the proper limits to social action in promoting the well-being of the individual has for so long constituted the central problem of political theorists is evidence of the appalling difficulty of the problem. Although the capacity to distinguish between the respective spheres of law and morals represents in itself a major achievement, we are still uncertain as to what constitutes a proper principle of demarcation or even where precisely to draw the line in any given case. And finally, moral actions can never be divorced from the total character structure of the responsible agent, since it is perfectly possible for a man to act consistently according to an advanced moral code, and yet not come within the definition of a good man. When Alice Vavasor in Trollope's *Can You Forgive Her?* broke her engagement to John Grey, her father enquires solicitously,

"He has not made himself disagreeable, has he?"
"Not in the least. He never does anything wrong. He may defy man or woman to find fault with him."
"So that is it, is it? He is just a shade too good."[1]

And, although Alice is subsequently shown to be mistaken in her assessment of Mr. Grey, our sympathies are at once enlisted on Alice's behalf. The mental and "spiritual" life of human beings is characterized by a profundity and richness, by a degree of elusiveness that compels us to admit that when we have analysed and classified to the utmost of our resources, there is still a great deal left to be explained. And the in-

[1] Trollope, *Can You Forgive Her?*, 1864, Vol. I, p. 90.

tangibles that then confront us oblige us in our judgments to fall back on a sense of this world's wisdom. For we have reached a realm where at any rate as yet rules and codes cannot be of much help to us.

Nevertheless, when all this has been conceded, we contend that the minimal constituents of the moral relationship are susceptible of definition; and that there exists a sufficiently common human experience of this relationship to substantiate the view that ethics is an autonomous discipline with its own rational justification. To establish a human relationship, no more need be posited than two human beings, possessed of the power of communication. But if the parties to that relationship could impart only information concerning their own appetites and wants, in the event of a conflict of desires, since neither party could establish anything in the nature of a " claim " upon the other, the only arbitration possible would be the resort to force. The faculty of communication, in fact, suffices to establish a relationship of authority and subjection, based on the law of the stronger; it does not suffice for the birth of the idea of " obligation," without which a *moral* relationship is impossible. " To yield to force is an act of necessity, not of will," wrote Rousseau, " at the most, an act of prudence. In what sense can it be a duty? " [1] Such a relationship may validate the principle of conformity but not the principle of agreement. Agreement or consent assumes the opportunity for dissent; it is the result of an act of will; and an act of will presupposes a consideration of the respective merits of the alternatives. Without reasoning, therefore, actions cannot result from the activity of the will, only from the dictates of appetite or from the necessity of bowing to the appetites of another. Among animals, possessed only of the faculty of communication, the only law is the law whereby the weaker submits to the impulses of the stronger.

But in contrast to other animals, men are not confined simply to communication; they are possessed of the capacity for *rational* communication. And it is this capacity that enables men to pass beyond the animal relationship to the distinctively human relationship, the moral one. Able to reason, men may

---

[1] Rousseau, *The Social Contract* (Everyman, 1947 reprint), p. 6.

enter into mutual relations, the basis of which is mutual consent. And once the process of obtaining agreement based upon rational argument is embarked upon, the principle of equity is unavoidably introduced. If one party finds that the arguments advanced against him take into account only the desires of the other party and consistently ignore his own, he will, as a matter of experience, find no cogency in those arguments. They will fail in their persuasive intent; and if circumstances do not permit a deadlock, it will be broken only by the submission of the weaker party. In short, the attempt at a moral relationship will have broken down. To have succeeded, each should have recognized his own fallibility, have conceded (in Bishop Butler's phrase) " the doubtfulness things are involved in." Each should have been ready to follow the argument to its logical conclusion. Each should have sought to understand the other's point of view, to gain sympathetic insight into the working of his mind, and into the factors underlying his assumptions. " The free mind," wrote Gide, " has the superiority of not wanting to be alone in having the right to speak." [1] A complete moral relationship assumes mutual observance of the canons of courtesy and good manners, mutual trust and respect for the other's good faith and integrity. It involves acknowledgement of the principle of equality implicit in the knowledge that neither party can escape the responsibility of making decisions worthy of a man confronted with the challenge of living among his fellows.

It is, in short, contended that the principle of reciprocity is already implicit in the process of reasoning itself, since reasoning embraces the effort to understand as well as pure ratiocination. If the attributes of a rational creature may be taken to include the attempt to establish relations with fellow creatures on the basis of agreement, rationality will be seen to entail reciprocity as a condition of its effective functioning. Appeal is being made only to the fact that each party is a man, and as such is potentially capable of behaving as a rational being. And such a principle is a public one in that it involves no more than that which is common to everyone's experience of

[1] *The Journals of André Gide*, Vol. IV: 1939–1949, London, 1951, p. 172.

the human situation. While genius is required to express elemental truths in imperishable language, no man need be a Donne to learn from life itself that " no man is an *Iland* intire of it selfe; every man is a peece of the *Continent*, a part of the *maine*." [1] Such a view of ethics is internally consistent in that it appeals to no principle that would confine the moral relationship to any particular group of men, and thus be self-defeating. It is a reciprocal principle in that it appeals to the particular quality that distinguishes the human. If, on the other hand, ethics is viewed as a branch of theology, if the willingness to understand is restricted by a prior assumption that all value problems must be subject to an absolute test in the form of the will of God, for example, a common basis for agreement must depend upon the coincidence of the private experiences of the parties to the relationship. As soon as appeal goes beyond the evident fact that two men are attempting to reach a mutual understanding, the mutuality and reciprocity of the relationship are broken in principle. And this for the reason that appeal, having ceased to be public, has proceeded further to include private experience. Once the Muslim and the Christian invoke their respective deities, each has retired into the internality of his private experience, against which the other cannot possibly appeal.

It will, of course, be objected that this analysis, whatever its descriptive validity, does not solve the problem presented by Hume's " ultimate why," since it leaves unanswered the question as to why anyone should recognize the claims of moral behaviour. Having settled what our course of conduct ought to be in any given situation, why should we do what is right? This ultimate question by its nature is not susceptible of a direct answer, it is true. But we may profitably inquire whether this question is similar in logical form to those which have led up to it. We may, in fact, ask whether or not it is a valid question in the sense of being significant. We may ask if there is any conceivable kind of evidence which would enable us to set about answering it. The questions preceding the ultimate " why " may have reflected the questioner's uncertainty as to the moral consistency of the proposed course

[1] Donne, *Complete Poetry and Selected Prose*, Nonesuch Press, 1942, p. 538.

in the light of all its possible repercussions. They may have been genuine requests for information, for a correct moral decision requires as extensive a chain of consequential reasoning as possible in order to be consistent with the principle of universal applicability. But beyond that point, further questioning compels us to speculate concerning the motives behind the question. We may point out that if it is wished to explain the cause of a physical event, the chain of causal sequence will similarly run on endlessly. But when every available avenue of inquiry has been exhausted, the inquiring agent will eventually be compelled by the situation which gave rise to his initial questions to act in that situation. He may then choose to act in defiance of the rational explanation, if he so wishes, and the consequences will be upon his own head. But his choice is irrelevant to the rationality of the explanation he has chosen to defy. Of course, a man is free to ignore the claims of the moral argument, to put himself beyond the bounds of the moral relationship, and to take the consequences of so doing; but this fact in no wise detracts from the rationality of that moral relationship.

Finally, we may find that the ultimate question is masquerading under false logical colours, and is in fact a statement concerning the questioner's emotional condition. The visitor to India, after the first shock of the spectacle of so much human suffering, may well ask for an explanation, and he will be entitled to a full historical and economic account of the conditions of that country. But if after listening to it, he says, " But why must men suffer so? " we may recognize in this a cry of anguish, of indignation or of despair; we may feel that it does credit to the visitor's sensitivity or simply reflects a certain embarrassment on his part. But we would not suppose that we had been asked a genuine question, requiring an examination of further evidence. Similarly, if I ask " Why should I behave in a manner that befits a man? " or " Why should I eschew evil? " it may be that I am expressing a sense of wonder or reverence or even astonishment at finding myself alive in a universe where I have been endowed with the capacity and the responsibility for moral choice. And in that case, no answer would be called for or possible, since the question is one in form only and not in content.[1]

In conclusion, if the case for a rationally grounded ethic be acceptable, and if such a minimal ethic be deemed to be comparatively stable, a meaningful conception of progress is possible. While we reject any doctrine of inevitable progress, we do not repudiate the attempt to direct the immediate goals of human endeavour in accordance with the best attainable historical knowledge of man's capacities and of the conditions which restrict the free play of those capacities. And it does not seem to us that that record is a discouraging one. Of course, there is a darker side to the picture. " Men," observed Benda bitterly, " are not going to revise their values for wars which last only fifty months and kill only two million men in each nation." [2] The fact that we can now do infinitely better than Benda could have foreseen, deprives his argument of little of its force. It is true, as Freud has demonstrated, that the irrational forces motivating human behaviour are much more deep-seated than many of us had supposed. If the Freudians have succeeded in awakening us to the magnitude of the task of expanding the role of intelligence in human affairs, they have also provided us with instruments of diagnosis and therapy exceeding in efficiency those available to our predecessors. If the forces of war are more terrible than in the past, the revulsion against war is more widespread and more intense than ever before. If the forces of racial intolerance and persecution are still with us, this fact needs to be measured against a new sense of dignity and equality which characterizes the Asian and Negro mental revolutions of our time. If the class war has not been eliminated, there is some evidence to suggest that the institutions and policies of welfare-conscious governments have gone some of the way in achieving a more equitable distribution of national income. If we have witnessed the nihilistic revolt of Nazism against every civilized

[1] Cf. the discussion of " ' limiting ' questions " in S. E. Toulmin, *The Place of Reason in Ethics*, Cambridge, 1950, Ch. 14, " Reason and Faith," and the discussion in Guido Calogero, *Faith, Doubt and Freedom* (*The Listener*, Vol. XLIX, pp. 131–33 and pp. 179–82).

[2] J. Benda, *La Trahison des Clercs*, 1927, p. 237.

value, we have also seen its overthrow by an unprecedented display of democratic solidarity.

It is a truism of our present situation that the problem which overshadows all others is the problem of ensuring stable and cordial relations between nations. The major evil in the world is the threat of war, with its attendant diversions of human productive energies into destructive channels, and the concomitant atmosphere of universally engendered fear. It may be true to say that we have nothing to fear but fear itself, but fear is a dreadful thing to have to fear. It is often argued that the division of the world into two mutually suspicious camps springs directly from a difference lying at the very roots of the criteria of moral appraisal. Together with the argument that since values like tastes are not in principle disputable, it behoved each of the contending parties to accept this logic in the resolution to agree to disagree, this was the central thesis of an earlier work of Mr. T. D. Weldon, *States and Morals*. It seems to the present writer that there is less truth in this belief than in the opposite assertion, namely, that the so-called iron curtain that divides the world is founded not so much on incompatibility in fundamental value systems, as on inability to agree as to what constitute facts. It is harder for men to agree as to what *is* than for them to agree as to what *ought* to be, when the *is* in question involves a degree of abstraction and induction so large as to put it beyond the capacity of any single individual to obtain verification from his own limited experience of reality.

The communist nations of the world hold to the belief that any economic system which is predominantly capitalistic in structure, which depends for its stability primarily upon its appeal to the motive of private profit, is doomed by the inherent logic of those institutions to eventual collapse amidst widespread human suffering. The democratic, capitalist nations, on the other hand, are similarly convinced that the denial of political liberty as a condition of the effective functioning of a society's institutions, constitutes so violent a breach of the fundamental and legitimate aspirations of men *qua* men as to make such a system a menace to its neighbours in the present, and in the long run an invitation to violent revolt from below. Each of these statements is a statement of fact, not of value, but in each case the facts are exceedingly difficult to verify in the present limited state of political and economic knowledge. The long and short of it is that men disagree about what is happening in the world and the reasons for what is happening. The precarious foundations of the beliefs on these issues, the inadequacy of our knowledge, so far from adding to the caution and moderation with which the beliefs are expressed, engender on the contrary a more rigid, compulsive and dogmatic attitude in the disputants on both sides. Men tend to be relentless and unyielding in direct proportion to the extent that they are half aware that they might be mistaken. The greater the doubt, the greater the certainty of affirmation.

That doubt exists on both sides that fundamental premises are not wholly impregnable, that each is aware that there may be more than a grain of truth in their opponents' arguments, is as impossible to deny as is the likelihood that either contestant will publicly admit that this is the case. On the one hand, exist the baleful and frightening memories of the economic collapse of 1929; on the other, there is the evidence of the workers' rising in East Germany and the revolt in the Vorkuta Labour Camp. At the same time, in all public affirmations of policy as well as in the periodic attempts at mutual negotiation, the West insists as relentlessly on the antithesis of the " free world " and slave labour as the East inveighs against the " aggression " inherent in a capitalism whose equilibrium may only be purchased by " imperialism." The strength of the emotions engendered by fear and uncertainty on both sides distorts judgment and puts almost beyond reach the minimal conditions without which objective investigation of difficult, possibly intractable problems is impossible. The situation is fraught with danger arising from mutual inner uncertainty and doubt. This doubt might be all to the good, if it were brought to the surface, but fear is powerful enough to secure its constant repression. And as yet no Freud has arisen to explain the nature of national myths and rationalizations as convincingly as Freud was able to do for the individual.

Greater national self-awareness with corresponding diminution in national self-righteousness would not, of course, dissolve the problem.   This would be to underestimate the gravity of the problem of power in human affairs, and to assume too easily the universal good intentions of men.   The problem itself is a very real one and is bound to remain so. For intelligence can do no more than clear the way for clinical conditions for objective research and diagnosis.   In the last resort the problem of peace is a challenge to the human will. Lasting peace is scarcely more likely to be achieved between nations than it is between social classes so long as there exists the present gross inequality in the distribution of the world's wealth.   Although there is some discussion of the need to help the backward areas of the world, if only to counteract the danger of communism breeding in those areas, the suspicion is too frequently justified that the motivation springs from requirements of security rather than from any consideration for human wellbeing as such.   Although the accomplishment of this end is in large part a technical, economic problem, the willingness to undertake it with resolution, on a large scale, if necessary without flinching material sacrifices that may be involved, is a moral and political problem.   For those who believe that the term " progress " has genuine meaning and a strong ethical connotation, it is suggested that this problem is the one which demands the most urgent, practical attention of our generation.   What are the prospects of fulfilment when so much is being asked? the sceptic might enquire.   To that, there can be no conclusive answer.   But it is not unreasonable to affirm that historical justification is not altogether lacking for adhering to the belief that human beings are oftentimes capable both of mastering their fears and their avidity for power by their intelligence, and of adjusting their behaviour to changing and more exacting conditions.

Bibliography

FOR the primary sources consulted, *vide* the footnotes throughout. The volumes asterisked in the following short list of recommended secondary sources contain particularly useful bibliographical suggestions for the student of the idea of progress.

BAILLIE, J.	*The Belief in Progress*, 1950.
BECKER, C. L.	*The Heavenly City of the Eighteenth-Century Philosophers*, 1932.
BROAD, C. D.	*The Mind and its Place in Nature*, 1925.
BURY, J. B.	** The Idea of Progress*, 1924.
COHEN, M. R.	*Reason and Nature*, 1931.
COLLINGWOOD, R. G.	*The Idea of History*, 1946.
DAWSON, H. C.	*Progress and Religion*, 1929.
DELVAILLE, J.	*Histoire de l'idée de progrès jusqu'à la fin du 18ème siècle.* 1910.
DEWEY, J.	*The Quest for Certainty*, 1930.
FLINT, R.	*History of the Philosophy of History*, 1893.
FRANKEL, C.	** The Faith of Reason*, 1948.
FREUD, S.	*Civilization and its Discontents*, 1930.
GINSBERG, M.	** The Idea of Progress : A Revaluation*, 1953.
HAZARD, P.	** La Pensée Européenne au XVIIIème siècle*, 1946.
HOBHOUSE, L. T.	*Morals in Evolution*, 1906. *Seventh edition*, 1951.
LÉVY-BRUHL, L.	*History of Modern Philosophy in France*, 1899.
LICHTENBERGER, A.	*Le Socialisme Français au XVIIIème siècle*, 1895.
MANDELBAUM, M.	*The Problem of Historical Knowledge*, 1938.
MARTIN, K.	*French Liberal Thought in the Eighteenth Century*, 1929.
MOULIN, L.	*Socialism of the West* (English translation), 1948.
POPPER, K. R.	*The Open Society and its Enemies*, 1945.
SABINE, G. H.	*A History of Political Theory*, 1941.
STEPHEN, L.	*English Thought in the Eighteenth Century*, 1876.
WALSH, W. H.	*An Introduction to Philosophy of History*, 1951.

Acknowledgements

for Copyright Material

THE author and publishers gratefully acknowledge the permission of the following to use extracts from copyright books: Messrs. George Allen and Unwin Ltd. for *German History: Some New German Views* (ed. H. Kohn) and Julian Huxley's *Evolution*; Messrs. G. Bell & Sons Ltd. for H. Butterfield's *The Whig Interpretation of History*; Messrs. Geoffrey Bles Ltd. for Nicolas Berdyaev's *The Russian Idea*; Cambridge University Press for C. E. Vaughan's *The Political Writings of Rousseau*, G. M. Trevelyan's *History and the Reader*, and *The Philosophical Works of Descartes*, translated by E. S. Haldane and G. R. T. Ross; Messrs. Cassell & Co. Ltd. for Fyodor Dostoevsky's *The Diary of a Writer*; Messrs. Chapman and Hall Ltd. for L. T. Hobhouse's *Morals in Evolution*; Messrs. J. M. Dent & Sons Ltd. for the Everyman Library edition of Pascal's *Pensées* and Rousseau's *Social Contract*; Messrs. Gerald Duckworth & Co. Ltd. for Chekhov's *The Three Sisters* (from *Six Famous Plays*); Messrs. Longmans Green & Co. Ltd. for G. M. Trevelyan's *Clio: A Muse*, and C. R. Fay's *Great Britain from Adam Smith to the Present Day*; Messrs. Macmillan & Co. Ltd. for Laurence Binyon's translation of *Paradiso*, and J. B. Bury's *Idea of Progress*; The Macmillan Company, New York, for P. W. Bridgman's *The Logic of Modern Physics*; Manchester University Press for Marc Bloch's *The Historian's Craft*; Messrs. Methuen & Co. Ltd. for H. D. F. Kitto's *Greek Tragedy*; Messrs. Burns Oates and Washbourne Ltd. for Father Copleston's *History of Philosophy*, Volume III; Oxford University Press for Isaiah Berlin's *Karl Marx*, Arnold Toynbee's *A Study of History*, G. M. Young's *Victorian England: Portrait of an Age*, and *The Essays of Montaigne*, translated by E. J. Trechmann; The Clarendon Press for R. G. Collingwood's *The Idea of History*, T. M. Knox's translation of Hegel's *Philosophy of Right*, and C. R. Morris's *Locke, Berkeley, Hume*; Messrs. A. D. Peters for Arthur Koestler's *Arrow in the Blue*; Messrs. Routledge and Kegan Paul Ltd. for H. A. Hodges' *Wilhelm Dilthey*, Karl Mannheim's *Ideology and Utopia*, and M. R. Cohen's *Reason and Nature*; Messrs. Secker and Warburg Ltd. for *The Journals of André Gide*, Volume IV; and Yale University Press for David Riesman's *The Lonely Crowd*.

Index

255